Slave Revolts

Recent Titles in
Greenwood Guides to Historic Events, 1500–1900

Slave Revolts

JOHANNES POSTMA

Greenwood Guides to Historic Events, 1500–1900
Linda S. Frey and Marsha L. Frey, Series Editors

GREENWOOD PRESS
Westport, Connecticut • London

Library of Congress Cataloging-in-Publication Data

Postma, Johannes.
   Slave revolts / Johannes Postma.
      p. cm.—(Greenwood guides to historic events 1500–1900, ISSN 1538-442X)
   Includes bibliographical references and index.
   ISBN 978-0-313-33854-0 (alk. paper)
      1. Slavery—History. 2. Slave insurrections—History. 3. Slave trade—
History. I. Title.
HT871.P67 2008
306.3′6209—dc22   2007048632

British Library Cataloguing in Publication Data is available.

Library of Congress Catalog Card Number: 2007048632
ISBN: 978-0-313-33854-0
ISSN: 1538-442X

First published in 2008

Greenwood Press, 88 Post Road West, Westport, CT 06881
An imprint of Greenwood Publishing Group, Inc.
www.greenwood.com

Printed in the United States of America

The paper used in this book complies with the
Permanent Paper Standard issued by the National
Information Standards Organization (Z39.48–1984).

10   9   8   7   6   5   4   3   2   1

CONTENTS

Photographs follow page 90.

SERIES FOREWORD

American statesman Adlai Stevenson stated, "We can chart our future clearly and wisely only when we know the path which has led to the present." This series, Greenwood Guides to Historic Events, 1500–1900, is designed to illuminate that path by focusing on events from 1500 to 1900 that have shaped the world. The years 1500 to 1900 include what historians call the early modern period (1500 to 1789, the onset of the French Revolution) and part of the modern period (1789 to 1900).

In 1500, an acceleration of key trends marked the beginnings of an interdependent world and the posing of seminal questions that changed the nature and terms of intellectual debate. The series closes with 1900, the inauguration of the twentieth century. This period witnessed profound economic, social, political, cultural, religious, and military changes. An industrial and technological revolution transformed the modes of production, marked the transition from a rural to an urban economy, and ultimately raised the standard of living. Social classes and distinctions shifted. The emergence of the territorial and later the national state altered man's relations with and view of political authority. The shattering of the religious unity of the Roman Catholic world in Europe marked the rise of a new pluralism. Military revolutions changed the nature of warfare. The books in this series emphasize the complexity and diversity of the human tapestry and include political, economic, social, intellectual, military, and cultural topics. Some of the authors focus on events in U.S. history such as the Salem witchcraft trials, the American Revolution, the abolitionist movement, and the Civil War. Others analyze European topics, such as the Reformation and Counter-Reformation and the French Revolution. Still others bridge cultures and continents by examining the voyages of discovery, the Atlantic slave trade, and the Age of Imperialism. Some focus on intellectual questions that have shaped the modern world, such as Charles Darwin's *Origin of Species*, or on turning points such as the Age of Romanticism. Others examine defining economic, religious, or legal events or issues such as the building of the railroads, the Second Great Awakening, and abolitionism. Heroes (e.g., Meriwether Lewis and William Clark), scientists (e.g., Darwin), military leaders (e.g., Napoleon Bonaparte), poets (e.g., Lord Byron) stride across the pages. Many of these events were seminal in that they marked profound changes or turning points. The Scientific Revolution, for example, changed the way individuals viewed themselves and their world.

The authors, acknowledged experts in their fields, synthesize key events, set developments within the larger historical context, and, most important, present well-balanced, well-written accounts that integrate the most recent scholarship in the field.

The topics were chosen by an advisory board composed of historians, high school history teachers, and school librarians to support the curriculum and meet student research needs. The volumes are designed to serve as resources for student research and to provide clearly written interpretations of topics central to the secondary school and lower-level undergraduate history curriculum. Each author outlines a basic chronology to guide the reader through often-confusing events and presents a historical overview to set those events within a narrative framework. Three to five topical chapters underscore critical aspects of the event. In the final chapter the author examines the impact and consequences of the event. Biographical sketches furnish background on the lives and contributions of the players who strut across the stage. Ten to fifteen primary documents, ranging from letters to diary entries, song lyrics, proclamations, and posters, cast light on the event, provide material for student essays, and stimulate critical engagement with the sources. Introductions identify the authors of the documents and the main issues. In some cases a glossary of selected terms is provided as a guide to the reader. Each work contains an annotated bibliography of recommended books, articles, CD-ROMs, Internet sites, videos, and films that set the materials within the historical debate.

Reading these works can lead to a more sophisticated understanding of the events and debates that have shaped the modern world and can stimulate a more active engagement with the issues that still affect us. It has been a particularly enriching experience to work closely with such dedicated professionals. We have come to know and value even more highly the authors in this series and our editors at Greenwood, particularly Kevin Ohe and Michael Hermann. In many cases they have become more than colleagues; they have become friends. To them and to future historians we dedicate this series.

Linda S. Frey
University of Montana

Marsha L. Frey
Kansas State University

PREFACE

Scholarly interest in the history of slavery was considerably stimulated by the post–Second World War civil rights movement and the dismantling of European colonial empires, but slave rebellions received only sporadic attention until quite recently. This lack of interest may be due in part to the perception that slave rebels were violent criminals. In contrast, those rebels who used violence to fight against dictatorial rule or for freedom from foreign domination were usually acclaimed patriots and freedom fighters. In recent years, however, the historical spotlight on rebel slaves has shown that they were also fighting for liberty and against oppression.

After devoting four decades to the study of the Atlantic slave trade, particularly Dutch involvement in it, I expanded my interest in shipboard rebellions and then to slave revolts in general. The result is *Slave Revolts*, a global overview of four centuries (1500–1900) of struggle against bondage and exploitation. While the book focuses on slave revolts, it includes rebellions by peasants who were exploited by systems of servitude similar to slavery. The slave and peasant revolts covered in this text are only the most consequential and largest of the thousands that took place during these four centuries.

Slave Revolts is intended for high school seniors and junior college students, but it might also appeal to the general public. The book is divided into three interrelated units: seven chapters of text, seventeen biographical essays of notable individuals, and fourteen primary documents. An introductory chapter examines slavery and rebellion from ancient times until about 1500 CE. Chapters 2 to 5 examine revolts in different regions of the world during the years 1500–1900. The last three chapters are thematic, focusing on marronage, leadership, and the legacy of slave revolts for our day. The notes and annotated bibliography direct readers to sources for further study.

ACKNOWLEDGMENTS

Because I have been retired from teaching for the past few years and am far removed from former colleagues, writing this book has been a fairly solitary process. I am fortunate to reside in the vicinity of the University of Massachusetts, Amherst College, Smith College, and Mount Holyoke College, all of which have excellent libraries with very friendly and helpful librarians, for which I am very grateful.

I owe special thanks to Professors Herbert Klein at Columbia and Stanford Universities, and to Wim Klooster at Clark University, for reading the manuscript and offering helpful suggestions and encouragement for the project. I also want to thank the editors of the Greenwood Guides to Historic Events, 1500–1900, Marsha L. Frey and Linda S. Frey, for their encouragement and constructive editorial advice. Mariah Gumpert, editor of the series at Greenwood Press, has also been very helpful with advice and support in the production process. I also wish to thank Randy Baldini and his team at Cadmus Communications for editing the manuscript. Above all, I want to thank my wife, Joelle Million, for her encouragement and support in the entire process of researching and writing this book, and for editing the manuscript and making it more readable.

Credit is due also to several authors and publishers who generously permitted republication of primary documents or illustrations: Richard Price and Sally Price, Robert E. Conrad, the National Library of Jamaica, Widener Library at Harvard University, the John Carter Brown Library at Brown University, and Oxford University Press.

CHRONOLOGY OF EVENTS

1521	First recorded African slave rebellion in Americas, at Spanish colony of Santo Domingo, on Caribbean island of Hispaniola.
1524–1526	Peasants' War in Germany.
1525	Peasant uprising in Austria.
1526	First recorded slave rebellion in North America, in Spanish colony in present-day Georgia.
1527	African and Arawak slaves revolt in Spanish Caribbean colony of Puerto Rico.
1537	Slave conspiracies in Mexico City, New Spain.
1548	Slave rebellion in gold mines of Colombia, South America.
1594–1597	Peasant uprisings in Austria.
ca. 1605	Escaped slaves establish Brazilian *quilombo* Palmares.
1606–1607	Ivan Bolotnikov leads peasant rebellion in Russia.
1612	Slave conspiracy in Mexico City, New Spain.
1626	Peasant uprising in Austria.
1627–1646	Peasant war in China contributes to fall of Ming Dynasty.
1644	Sakura Sōgorō leads peasant protest in Japan.
1646–1648	Peasant rebellions in Brandenburg (eastern Germany).
1670–1671	Stenka Razin leads peasant uprising in Russia.
1675	Slave conspiracy in British Caribbean colony of Barbados.

1678	Opposition faction rejects treaty signed by Brazilian maroon king Ganga Zumba.
1679–1680	Peasant rebellion in Bohemia (Czech Republic).
1684; 1688	Slave rebellions in Korea.
ca. 1685	Escaped slaves establish maroon communities in Suriname, on northern coast of South America.
1692; 1701	Slave conspiracies in British Caribbean colony of Barbados.
1693	King of Spain offers freedom to slaves fleeing to Florida from British colonies.
1694	Brazilian colonial forces destroy Palmares *quilombo*.
1695; 1719	Slave rebellion and conspiracies in Bahia, Brazil.
1702	Slaves rebel against new slave codes in Barbados.
1716	First slave rebellion at Dutch Caribbean colony of Curaçao.
1719	Slave conspiracy in Minas Gerais, Brazil.
1730	Slave rebellion aboard American ship *Little George*, resulting in the freedom of many enslaved Africans.
1732	Combined Indian and slave conspiracy in French New Orleans.
1733	Rebelling slaves take control of Danish Caribbean colony of St. John.
1736	Slave conspiracy in French Caribbean colony of Antigua.
1737	Peasant rebellion in Hungary.
1739	Stono (or Cato) Rebellion near Charleston, South Carolina.
	Jamaica's Leeward and Windward Maroons negotiate treaties granting them freedom and autonomy.
1753; 1755	Peasant rebellions in Hungary.
1756	Slave conspiracy at Minas Gerais, Brazil.
1760	Suriname's Saramaka maroons sign treaty granting them freedom and autonomy.
1760–1761	Tacky Revolt in Jamaica.

1762	Suriname's Djuka maroons sign treaty granting them freedom and autonomy.
1763–1764	Kofi and Accra lead slave rebellion in Dutch colony of Berbice, on northern coast of South America.
1763–1764; 1784	Peasant rebellions in Hungary.
1773–1774	Emelian Pugachev leads serf and peasant rebellion in Russia.
1774	Slave rebellion at French Caribbean colony of Tobago.
ca. 1775	Yanga establishes Mexican maroon community Cofre de Perote.
1775; 1780	Peasant uprisings in Bohemia (Czech Republic).
1776	Hannover Conspiracy in Jamaica.
1785–1796	Mandingo Rebellion in present-day Guinea, West Africa.
1791	Farcel leads slave rebellion in British Dominica.
1791–1804	Slave rebellion in French colony Saint-Domingue on Hispaniola.
1793	Peasant rebellion in Silesia (Poland).
	Slave rebellion in French Caribbean colony of Guadeloupe.
1794	France abolishes slavery in French colonies.
1795	Tula leads slave rebellion in Dutch Caribbean colony of Curaçao.
	Pointe Coupee Conspiracy in Louisiana.
1795–1796	Jamaica's Second Maroon War; Trelawny Maroons deported to Nova Scotia.
	Fédon leads slave rebellion in French Caribbean colony of Grenada.
1797	Slave rebellion aboard British ship *Thomas*.
1798; 1811	Peasant rebellions in Silesia (Poland).
1800	Gabriel's Conspiracy in Richmond, Virginia.
1802	French Emperor Napoleon reinstates slavery in the colonies.

1804	Saint-Domingue Rebellion results in establishment of Haiti as independent republic.
1807	Slave conspiracy in Bahia, Brazil.
1808	Yanga negotiates treaty granting his Mexican maroons freedom and autonomy.
1809	Slave rebellion in Bahia, Brazil.
1811	Charles Deslondes leads slave rebellion in Louisiana.
	Slave rebellion on French island colony of Réunion in Indian Ocean.
1812	Slave rebellion in Venezuela.
	Aponte Rebellion in Cuba.
1814	Slave rebellion in Bahia, Brazil.
1816	Boxley Conspiracy near Richmond, Virginia.
	Bussa leads slave rebellion in British Caribbean colony of Barbados.
1817	First Seminole War.
1822	Denmark Vesey Conspiracy in Charleston, South Carolina.
1823	Jack Gladstone leads slave rebellion in Demerara.
1825	Galant Rebellion at Bokkeveld, South Africa.
1831	Nat Turner's Rebellion in Southampton County, Virginia.
1831–1832	Samuel Sharpe leads Christmas Revolt (Baptist War) in Jamaica.
1834–1838	Slavery abolished throughout British Empire.
1835	Malê Rebellion at Salvador, Bahia in Brazil.
1835–1842	Second Seminole War results in deportation of Black Seminoles to Oklahoma.
1838	Bilali establishes maroon community Laminyah, West Africa.
1839	Slave rebellion aboard *Amistad*.
1840	Britain abolished slavery in India.
1841	Successful rebellion aboard American ship *Creole* traveling to New Orleans.

1842	Russia abolishes slavery.
1843	Slave rebellions in Venezuela and Colombia.
1848	France abolishes slavery in all its colonies.
	Slave demonstration at Saint Croix leads to abolition of slavery throughout Danish West Indies.
1859	John Brown's raid at Harpers Ferry, (West) Virginia.
1860s	Maroon town Yalwa established in Nigeria, West Africa.
1861	Russia abolishes serfdom.
1863	The Netherlands abolishes slavery in its colonies.
1865	United States abolishes slavery.
1886	Cuba abolishes slavery.
1888	Brazil abolishes slavery.

CHAPTER 1

Slavery and Slave Rebellions before 1500

Slavery has existed from the beginning of recorded history and has been an accepted institution in most societies around the globe. As slavery scholar Orlando Patterson states in the recently published *Chronology of World Slavery:*

> [S]lavery was a worldwide institution. It has existed in some form in every region of the world, at all levels of sociopolitical development, and among all major ethnic groups. All peoples had ancestors who at some time suffered the ultimate inhumanity, the social death that was slavery. And nearly all peoples can count slaveholders among their ancestors.[1]

Not until a few centuries ago was the legitimacy of slavery seriously challenged, and although it is now illegal in most countries, it is still far from being entirely eradicated.

Enslaved and otherwise bonded people inevitably resented their status and used every conceivable means to improve or escape their condition. In desperation and against overwhelming odds, many rebelled against their masters, even when their efforts might result in brutal punishment or death. Most often they acted as individuals, but occasionally they rebelled en masse. Such revolts are the focus of this book.

Because slave uprisings were rarely successful and officials usually did not find them worthy of recording, relatively little documentation about slave revolts survives. Because scholars have only recently begun to delve into this scarce record, historical literature devoted specifically to the subject is still quite limited. This book provides a summary of what is known about slave rebellions on a global scale.

Slavery Defined

Throughout recorded history, human societies have generally been stratified into hierarchical layers of privilege and power. In most societies, small minorities wielded control over the majority of the people, who were poor and often powerless. With few exceptions, the least powerful members of society were slaves, who were regarded as property by those who claimed to own them.

Defining slavery is no easy task because there were so many variations in the practice, particularly when viewed from a worldwide perspective. In the United States we tend to think of slavery as it was practiced here until the nineteenth century. This extreme variation of slavery, called *chattel slavery*, was practiced in other parts of the world as well, but there were also many milder forms, some of which gave enslaved persons opportunities for upward social mobility. Generally, however, institutions of slavery have been based on certain ideas held in common:

> that slaves were property; that they were outsiders who were alien by origin or who had been denied their heritage through judicial or other sanctions; that coercion could be used at will; that their labor power was at the complete disposal of a master; that they did not have the right to their own sexuality and, by extension, to their own reproductive capacities; and that the slave status was inherited unless provision was made to ameliorate that status.[2]

In nearly every time and place where slavery has existed, slaves were considered property. Roman law defined slavery as "an institution of the common law of peoples by which a person is put into the ownership of somebody else, contrary to the natural order." Military commanders, it explained, had the right to own and sell their captives instead of killing them.[3] People were enslaved through a variety of other means besides being taken prisoners in war. They could be condemned to slavery for crime or indebtedness or by being kidnapped, abandoned, or orphaned. Sometimes destitute people sold themselves or their children into slavery. But by far the most common way of becoming a slave was to inherit the status from parents, usually from the mother.

The lives of slaves varied depending on the role assigned to them, the work they had to perform, and the position and attitude of their masters. They were usually forced to perform menial tasks, but some—particularly in Asia and Africa or in the Roman and

Byzantine empires—rose to managerial positions. Many slaves were employed in large-scale enterprises such as agriculture, construction, mining, or the military. Others worked as skilled craftsmen or domestic servants, and some were forced to work as sexual slaves. Soldiers and concubines had the best opportunities for advancement, but regardless of the position, most slaves were severely exploited.

Serfdom

Societies have developed a variety of forms of bondage and servitude in addition to slavery: serfdom, tenancy, peonage, indenture, debt-bondage, and pawnship. Some of these were more flexible and open to upward mobility than slavery, and therefore less vulnerable to mass rebellion. Serfdom, one of the more common types of bondage found around the world, has generally been considered a milder alternative to slavery. In the European context, serfs were bound to the land and had specified labor obligations, but as a rule they also had certain rights, such as the use of a plot of land and the right to marry. Nevertheless, because some forms of serfdom have been quite similar to and just as harsh as slavery, this book also examines some serf and peasant revolts.

An interesting conjunction of slavery and serfdom is the history of the words themselves. *Servus* (plural, *servi*) was the word for a male slave in the Roman Empire and is the origin of the words *serf* and *serfdom*, as well as of our modern-day words *service* and *servant*. By the early twelfth century, however, as the word *serf* had come to mean a dependent peasant, a new word was coined for actual slaves, derived from the name of the ethnic group from which the largest number of slaves was taken in the medieval times—the Slavs. This word has cognates in all Western languages: *slave* in English, *esclave* in French, *esclavo* in Spanish, *escravo* in Portuguese, *schiavo* in Italian, and *Sklave* in German.[4]

Why Slaves Rebelled

Although slavery is usually considered the opposite of freedom, this is a fairly new perspective, popularized through revolutionary slogans of freedom and equality at the end of the eighteenth century. Before that, freedom was generally seen as a privilege for the elite, while the lives of the vast majority of people were severely restricted, by either law or tradition, and labor obligations were nearly always coerced in one form or another.

Where treatment of slaves was relatively benign, and law or tradition assured protection and some measure of freedom, desperate people sometimes became slaves voluntarily to gain security, which was more important to them than freedom. But when slavery was too oppressive, some slaves were willing to risk death to escape an unbearable existence.

Individuals rebelled against their enslavement by running away, shunning or sabotaging work, or poisoning or killing their masters. Sometimes groups of slaves and serfs staged mass revolts despite their lack of organizing skills and weapons, and despite the fact that such uprisings rarely succeeded and usually ended in the rebels' brutal deaths. Motivations varied, but many group rebellions were responses to harsh treatment or withdrawal of privileges.

Slavery scholar Eugene Genovese has outlined the following preconditions for massive slave revolts in the Americas, and most of these apply to other times and places as well: (1) large slave-holding units, (2) slaves heavily outnumbering slaveholders, (3) high master absenteeism, (4) economic distress and famine, (5) war or conflict within or with other countries, (6) foreign-born slaves outnumbering native-born, (7) emergence of autonomous slave leadership, and (8) a geographic terrain conducive to escape.[5] Other conditions conducive to slave revolts include the presence of a large number of slaves of the same ethnicity in a group, extreme brutality by slaveholders, and the emergence of religious or ideological motivation.

Slave and Serf Rebellions in Europe

It has been said that "Civilization bred warfare, and warfare created the institution of slavery."[6] Although slavery emerged after sedentary societies replaced hunter-gatherer communities, and states and empires were established that allowed class distinction and specialization to develop, it became entrenched as an institution when large multiethnic empires developed in the ancient Near East about six thousand years ago. The warfare that accompanied state and imperial expansion produced many captives who, as Roman law recognized, were enslaved rather than killed, and transported to other parts of the empire to fill jobs vacated by conscripted soldiers.

Ancient Greece

Even before Alexander the Great created his Hellenistic Empire during the fourth century BCE, slavery had become an important institution in the Greek city-states. Although the Greeks initially practiced slavery on a small scale, colonial expansion throughout the Mediterranean region and raids among neighbors from 700–500 BCE increased their slave population significantly. Foreign-born slaves were also purchased from pirates, and local people could be enslaved through debt bondage or criminal conviction. By 500 BCE, Athens had become a true *slave society*, that is, a society in which slaves comprised 30 percent or more of the total population.[7]

Initially, Athenian slaves were mostly outsiders, or *barbarians*, as the Greeks called them. Although they occupied the bottom of the social scale, performing a variety of menial tasks, some worked as skilled craftsmen or held teaching or supervisory positions. Most worked alongside free persons and were usually part of the master's household. Athenian slaves were provided opportunities for advancement and the possibility of emancipation, which may explain why Athens experienced no large-scale revolts.

Conditions in the city-state of Sparta, a frequent adversary of Athens, were quite different. In a string of wars during the eighth century BCE, the Spartans conquered their neighboring Messenians and subjected them to servitude. Whereas few Athenian slaves worked the land, in Sparta all agricultural work was done by slaves. Forced to perform menial labor while the Spartans served as soldiers and rulers, the Messenians rebelled several times but were unable to throw off the Spartan yoke. Finally in 370 BCE, they were freed when another rival state, Thebes, defeated Sparta.

Ancient Rome

Through constant warfare over the last five hundred centuries BCE, Rome built an empire across the Mediterranean region and took large numbers of captives as slaves. During the seven years from 58–51 BCE, Julius Caesar took a million slaves from Gaul (France) alone. This massive influx of slaves gradually replaced the agricultural peasant class, which was increasingly conscripted into the military and forced to sell their land to the elite, whom booty, plunder, and tributes made increasingly wealthy. These affluent Romans established large estates worked by slave gangs, similar to the plantations later established in the New World. Long before Augustus Caesar officially established the Roman Empire in 27 BCE, Rome had become a slave society with an economy based on slave labor. In addition to agricultural workers and herders, slaves worked as household servants and craftsmen, as miners, on such public works projects as roads and aqueducts, and as gladiators, forced to fight each other to the death for the entertainment of the urban public.

Captives sometimes staged collective rebellions. In 290 BCE and again in 130 BCE, major slave revolts occurred on the island of Chios, locale of one of the Mediterranean region's most active slave markets, but both were quickly quelled. In 198 BCE, a group of Carthaginian prisoners of war collaborated with Carthaginian slaves to take over the town of Setia, but a Roman military force of two thousand crushed the rebellion and executed some five hundred rebels.

The second century BCE saw many Roman slave uprisings, all brutally suppressed. In 196 BCE a revolt in the province of Etruria (Tuscany) was suppressed before it was fully set in motion, and several of its leaders were crucified, a cruel method of execution borrowed from the Carthaginians. In 185 BCE more than seven thousand rebelling cattle herders in southern Italy were quickly subdued. In 176 BCE, thousands of slaves were killed after a rebellion on the island of Sardinia. A 132–129 BCE revolt inspired by the Stoic philosopher Gaius Blossius in Rome's province of Asia Minor (Turkey) was also quashed.

Slaves assigned to the empire's mines, who worked under extremely harsh conditions and suffered high mortality rates, managed to rebel despite being carefully guarded. An uprising at the Greek silver mines of Mount Laurium in 134 BCE, and another at the gold mines in Spain in the year 50 BCE, were both brutally suppressed.

These were minor rebellions compared with three uprisings so vast that they came to be called *slave wars.* As many as twenty thousand slaves are estimated to have lost their lives in the first of these rebellions, which took place on the island of Sicily. It actually started as two separate uprisings around 139 BCE, one led by a slave magician and religious leader named Eunus and the other by a herdsman named Cleon. After supporters proclaimed Eunus king, the men joined forces and Eunus appointed Cleon his chief military leader. With tens of thousands of followers, they captured several towns, killing masters who had treated slaves cruelly and sparing those who had shown kindness. But after a long siege, Roman forces retook the final rebel stronghold of Enna and crucified the captured rebels. Eunus, protected by a thousand bodyguards, managed to escape, but when his position became futile he allowed himself to be captured. His soldiers beheaded each other rather than surrender to certain torture, but Eunus subsequently died in prison—a surprising fate for a rebel leader.

The second slave war (104–99 BCE) also took place on Sicily and, like the earlier one, was a confluence of separate rebellions. It began with an uprising in the town of Halicyae, where a slave named Varius persuaded thirty fellow slaves to kill their masters. They were subsequently joined by two hundred additional slaves, but an informant within their ranks allowed the island's governor to quickly organize a militia and put down the rebellion. Almost immediately another eighty slaves rose up, and within weeks their force had swelled to over two thousand. Led by a capable domestic slave named Salvius, whom they made king, this army won decisive victories over Roman forces. Meanwhile, a rebellion in western Sicily produced another army of tens of thousands under the leadership of Athenion. The two armies merged under Salvius but were defeated by a Roman army during the second year of the war. Salvius appears to have been killed in this battle, for the rebels regrouped under Athenion and, after inflicting several defeats on the Romans, gained control over extensive territory. Additional Roman troops under a new commander broke the back of the rebellion in 101 BCE. Within a year, Athenion was killed and nearly a thousand remaining rebels were forced to surrender. The captives were taken to Rome and scheduled to fight wild beasts in an arena but killed each other instead, with the lone survivor committing suicide.

The third slave war is well remembered in literature and film as the Spartacan Revolt after its leader, Spartacus, the gladiator who, with an army of escaped slaves that numbered in the tens of thousands, held off Roman forces for two years. In the summer of 73 BCE, Spartacus and seventy fellow gladiators escaped from their training camp in the city of Capua and fled to nearby Mount Vesuvius, where they were reinforced by scores of fugitive slaves. From this stronghold the rebels plundered the region, although it is said that Spartacus tried to restrain them. Thousands of slaves escaped and joined Spartacus and co-leader Crixus, who organized huge armies that became a serious threat to Rome. For more than two years, Spartacus directed the rebels from southern to northern Italy, defeating several Roman legions. However, the Romans defeated a rebel army under Crixus, who was killed in battle. Spartacus moved his forces to northern Italy, but instead of crossing the Alps, he led them once again to southern Italy. Pursued by ten Roman legions, the rebels continued southward toward the sea, perhaps with the intent of crossing over to Sicily. In 71 BCE, Spartacus and his army were trapped at the Bruttium Peninsula and decisively defeated. Spartacus was killed in battle, but six thousand followers were captured and, as a warning to other slaves, allegedly crucified along the Appian Way between Capua and Rome.

After the Roman Republic officially became the Roman Empire in 27 BCE, the rate of territorial expansion slowed and the acquisition of new slaves declined. No longer considered outsiders, second and subsequent generations of slaves assimilated into Roman society and had better opportunities for advancement. Many were emancipated and became Roman citizens, and some eventually gained prominent positions such as governors of provinces or advisors to the emperor. In 285 CE a former slave even became Pope Calixtus I. Stoics and Christians encouraged better treatment of slaves, but neither sought to end slavery. As the possibilities of meliorating their condition improved, slaves no longer resorted to mass rebellions during the imperial era.

Medieval Europe

As the population of the western Roman Empire declined during the second and third centuries CE, estate owners increasingly abandoned gang slave labor and gave their slaves tenant status, providing them with a plot of land in return for labor service. An imperial decree in the third century limited the movement of free peasants in order to facilitate tax collection, which furthered the merging of rural labor into a single peasant class. Unable to maintain its borders against barbarian invaders, Roman authority collapsed in the west, and many townspeople fled to rural areas in search of security under the protection of landed nobility. Invasions by Vikings from the north, Magyars (Hungarians) from the east, and Saracens (Muslims) from the south during the ninth and tenth centuries increased instability. As a result of these various forces, central authority gave way to a social system in which nobles wielded power over the amalgamated peasant population of their domain, giving rise to serfdom.

Despite the shift toward serfdom, slavery persisted for several centuries in Europe. It did not disappear in England until after the Norman invasion in 1066. It thrived on the Iberian Peninsula under Visigoth kings and Spanish Moors until at least the eleventh century. Not until the twelfth century did serfdom displace slavery in most of France and other parts of northwestern Europe. Slavery continued in Scandinavia and Iceland until after 1335, when the king of Sweden decreed that children born to slave parents would henceforth be free. In Russia, in many towns in western Europe, and especially in the Mediterranean region, slaves could be found well after 1500.

Even though social and economic conditions varied greatly from one place to another in ethnically diverse Europe, serfdom and a self-sufficient rural economy became the norm. Serfs were often not much better off than slaves, however, particularly in times of natural disaster and famine, and they were often treated harshly by their social superiors. There is truth to the image of the downtrodden serf that permeates medieval literature, and some scholars warn against dismissing its historical significance. In many respects, the status and condition of Russian serfs were similar to those of slaves in the Americas.[8]

Given the condition of serfs, it is not surprising that they rebelled. Occasionally, slaves, serfs, and free peasants collaborated against their oppressors. During the years 250–286 and 435–454, slaves and free peasants joined forces in the so-called Wars of the Bacaudae in Gaul (France), but brutal repression reinstated subservience. Again in Gaul, serfs killed several overlords during the ninety years 643–733. Peasant revolts occurred in Asturias, in northwestern Spain, in 770, and in Normandy in 996. Around the year 1000, great famines produced significant peasant unrest in western Europe. In 1038, the French aristocracy crushed a major peasant revolt and punished some rebels by chopping off their hands.

Serfdom did not remain the dominant system of agricultural labor in Europe. Gradually, peasants' labor obligations transformed into burdensome monetary obligations. But economic expansion and population growth from the eleventh century through the thirteenth allowed many serfs to develop new agricultural lands in marshes and forests. And as commerce and the money economy expanded, many landowners forced serfs from their manors and replaced them with wage laborers. Then in the fourteenth century, natural disasters and bad harvests, followed by a devastating pandemic known as the Black Death (1348–1350) that killed up to a third of the European population, hastened the demise of serfdom by creating a labor shortage and enabling survivors to leave their estates and find employment elsewhere.

Despite these changes, the vast majority of Europe's peasantry remained impoverished and exploited by their superiors. The late Middle Ages saw a wave of popular disturbances and peasant revolts throughout Europe, including a string of rebellions in Flanders (Belgium) in 1323–1328, the Jacquerie Revolt in France in 1358, the Remaça Revolt in Catalonia (Spain) in 1380, and the "Great Peasant Revolt" in England in 1381. There were so many rebellions during 1378–1382 that the period has been referred to as the "years of revolution." In nearly all cases, nobles suppressed the revolts with unrestrained brutality.

Although serfdom was gradually replaced by wage labor, especially in northwestern Europe, the system survived in eastern Europe until the nineteenth century (see Chapter 2).

Slavery and Slave Revolts in the Middle East and Africa

The Byzantine and Ottoman Empires

Slavery was practiced in western Asia and northern Africa long before the Roman Empire expanded into those areas. While the West fell prey to Germanic invasions, the Byzantine Empire (330–1453) survived as a successor state to Rome in the East, encompassing much of the region of southeastern Europe, the Middle East, and northeastern Africa. As in the West, serfdom became the norm in rural Byzantium, but slavery continued as a primarily urban phenomenon, with slaves working as domestics and craftsmen. Many castrated slaves, or *eunuchs*, served in important administrative and managerial positions. For centuries, Byzantium's capital of Constantinople (now Istanbul) maintained a large slave market through which tens of thousands of enslaved Europeans were transferred to the Islamic world. No large slave revolts seem to have occurred in the Byzantine Empire.

Invading Ottoman Turks gradually conquered Byzantine territory and, after capturing Constantinople in 1453, established a powerful Islamic state centered in Asia Minor (now Turkey), known as the Ottoman Empire (1300–1922). Expanding over the Middle East and North Africa, the Turks continued slavery as practiced by their predecessors but also made great use of slave soldiers, known as *Janissaries*. A privileged class of slaves, which arose from those who served as administrators and the offspring of slave women and slave soldiers, Janissaries produced many Ottoman leaders. While some Ottoman slaves were undoubtedly severely exploited, slaves were a relatively small percentage of the population and sufficient opportunities for amelioration existed to make slave revolts rare in the Ottoman Empire.

The Islamic World

Founded by the prophet Mohammed in 632, the religion of Islam spread rapidly from Arabia throughout the Middle East and

North Africa. By the end of the first millennium it had spread to parts of sub-Saharan Africa and Spain, as well as to parts of southern and southeastern Asia. Commerce played a prominent role in the spread of Islam, and Muslim merchants were also active in the slave trade, transporting enslaved Africans across the Red Sea, the Indian Ocean, and the Sahara Desert to the Islamic heartland.

Like the Christian Bible, the Koran justified slavery, but it also advocated humane treatment of slaves. While it condoned the enslavement of non-Muslims, particularly pagans, it decreed that Muslims, by definition, were free persons. Whereas ethnic origin had often been the primary difference between slave and free persons in Europe, religion was the dividing line in the Islamic world, and slaves could assimilate more easily into a culture where religion was the defining criterion.

Islamic societies used slave labor in a variety of occupations but not predominantly in agriculture. Male slaves were commonly employed as soldiers; female slaves, as household servants and concubines. Female slaves were in such high demand that slave caravans to Islamic regions usually included more women than men. The prominent fourteenth-century Muslim traveler Ibn Battuta noted a trans-Saharan caravan of six hundred enslaved women. Eunuchs, or castrated male slaves, were often employed as overseers of the harems. The children of privileged slaves, such as concubines and soldiers, were usually considered free persons.

Although slave revolts were rare in Islamic societies, there were some. African slaves revolted in Medina, Arabia, in 765 CE, but little is known about the uprising. In 1260, on the instigation of a Muslim cleric, a group of Cairo slaves serving as stable boys staged a revolt, but they were quickly suppressed and crucified.

A massive slave war in southeastern Iraq that lasted for fourteen years was known as the Zanj (or Zendj) Revolt because the rebelling slaves originated from East Africa, once known as the Zanj. Rulers of the vast Abbasid Empire (762–1258) had brought thousands of enslaved male Zanj to the marshes of the Tigris and Euphrates rivers to clear the land of salt and make it suitable for cultivation. Living in huge camps and working under abominable conditions, they had rebelled in previous years but had always been defeated. When they revolted again in 869, they were led by Alî bin Muhammad, a charismatic Muslim who emancipated those who joined the revolt and led his armies to repeated victories. Over a period of ten years, the rebels captured several towns, established their own capital, and at times threatened the imperial capital of Baghdad. However, imperial armies defeated the rebels in 879, killing Alî bin Muhammad in battle, capturing and beheading several other leaders, and pressing surrendering soldiers into their own service.

Because slaves were outsiders with no family or clan loyalties, Muslims generally trusted them as soldiers, and Islamic societies made great use of them. Some military slaves gained prominence and power, and in some instances they revolted and established themselves as a ruling class. In 1522, for example, the Mamluk military slaves in Egypt overthrew Turkish rule and controlled the country for nearly three centuries.

Sub-Saharan Africa

Before the intrusion of Islamic and European influences on Africa, slavery and other types of dependencies were a common feature of most African societies. Traditional African slavery has often been portrayed as a type of serfdom, but there were also cases of severe exploitation, depending on the local economy and the position of the masters. Without family roots in the community, slaves were treated as outsiders, but domestic slaves (those not destined for export) and their children were gradually assimilated into the community and rarely sold. Employed in all sorts of labor services, slaves were also used in marriage arrangements, in sacrificial functions, and as financial pawns. Until the African diaspora assumed large proportions after 1600, chattel slavery rarely played a major role in African economies.

With all its variations, African slavery was essentially an open system that provided opportunities for advancement. This is illustrated by the unusual case of a slave named Sakura, who belonged to the royal family in thirteenth-century Mali, West Africa, and managed to rise to commander of the army and eventually usurped the throne of the legitimate but incompetent emperor. He turned out to be a very capable ruler.[9]

While enslaved Africans were involved in revolts elsewhere, only after the Atlantic slave trade affected slavery in Africa did slave revolts become more prevalent there (see Chapter 3).

Slave and Peasant Rebellion in Asia

Chattel slavery existed in most Asian societies before the modern era, and many other social institutions confined the vast majority of Asian people in servile dependency. Nevertheless, only in eastern Asia were slaves concentrated enough and destitute peasants desperate enough to rise in mass rebellions.

India

The Indian Subcontinent is well known for its caste system, which divided society into hereditary social groups with designated status and labor obligations, and prohibited intermarriage between castes. The system was rife with exploitation, particularly for the lowest caste, the so-called *untouchables*, who were often treated worse than slaves.[10] India's various forms of servitude also included chattel slavery, in which people could be enslaved through capture, indebtedness, and birth, and could be bought and sold. The ancient Hindu text of *Mahabharata* recognized both the reality and injustice of slavery: "Men acquire [other] men as slaves, and by beating and otherwise subjugating them make them work day and night. These people are not ignorant of the pain that is caused by beating and chains."[11]

Indian slaves worked primarily as domestic servants but also in a variety of other occupations and functions, including agriculture, crafts, and concubinage. Slavery provided more flexibility than the caste system, and slaves often had opportunities to improve their lot. There is little evidence of slave revolts in India, probably because chattel slavery was never so concentrated that it became a central feature of the economy. When Islam spread to India during the Middle Ages, it introduced new forms of slavery, including extensive use of concubines, eunuchs, and military slaves. One rare instance of slave revolt in India was a 1486 rebellion of African soldiers against the sultan of Bengal, in today's Bangladesh. The soldiers ousted the ruler and replaced him with their own leader, but their victory was short-lived. The rebels were defeated, and those who survived were exiled to another region of the Indian Subcontinent.

Southeast Asia

Various forms of servitude including chattel slavery flourished in Southeast Asia. Like most traditional cultures, these societies were hierarchical in nature with a variety of status and power levels. As in Africa, slaves and their offspring could gradually improve their status and be assimilated into the community. Poverty, indebtedness, and pawnship were common causes of enslavement, but many slaves were war captives. Raiding less-developed societies also produced captives for the slave markets.[12] Not widely used in agricultural production, the slaves of Southeast Asia were primarily household servants and used for status enhancement purposes. There is little evidence of slave rebellions before European imperialism impacted the region in modern times (see Chapter 3).

China

The Chinese Empire knew slavery throughout its long history but never developed a slave-based economy as the Roman Empire did. The vast majority of China's population was poor peasants who often lived on the verge of starvation. Rarely needed for agricultural labor, slaves were used primarily as domestics, craftsmen, and concubines.

During the Han Dynasty (206 BCE–220 CE), large numbers of war captives and condemned prisoners were used on public projects, often in gang labor. Their brutal treatment resulted in a series of brief rebellions within an eight-year period. In 22 BCE, 180 public slaves escaped and, after stealing weapons and freeing others, killed several of their managers before being overpowered by the government's army. Four years later, another sixty shackled slaves escaped, attracted a numerous following, and created an army that gained control over a sizable region. It took an army of thirty thousand soldiers to defeat them. In 14 BCE, a large rebel army led by a slave named Su Ling invaded several provinces before being subdued.[13]

While no other slave revolts seem to have occurred in China, slaves may have been involved in a major peasant revolt in 17 CE called the Red Eyebrow Rebellion. The rebels were instrumental in ousting an ineffective Han emperor and installing a government official named Wang Mang, who implemented several reforms including the abolition of slavery. However, with the suppression of another revolt a few years later, Wang was forced from power and assassinated, and slavery was reestablished.

Eunuch slaves gained considerable power in the imperial bureaucracy during the final years of the Han Dynasty, and in the years of anarchy (184–204) they practically controlled the government. Several centuries later, in 1416, the eunuch Zheng (Cheng Ho) attained the rank of admiral and commanded a Chinese fleet to East Africa. Obviously, such slaves lived in comfort, but they generally remained subject to their masters' will.

Instead of slave revolts, Chinese history was peppered by peasant uprisings. The vast majority of China's population was impoverished peasants, either tenants or desperately poor small-holders exploited by overlords and the governmental elite, the Mandarins. Their situation was similar to that of European serfs, but they were also heavily taxed by the imperial government. Natural disasters such as floods and famines frequently drove them to rebel, but their uprisings were usually limited in scope and rarely mentioned by historians unless they brought about drastic changes.

Mongols invaded China in the thirteenth century and established the oppressive Song (Sung) Dynasty (960–1279), which enslaved not only prisoners of war but also free peasants. Peasant rebellions helped terminate Mongol rule and establish the Ming Dynasty (1368–1644), whose first emperor, T'Ai Tsu (1368–1398), abolished slavery. While this formal action did not abolish slavery entirely, it did reduce the number of slaves to a very small percentage of China's population.

Japan and Korea

Although Japan had a small number of slaves and outcast groups, the vast majority of Japanese people were peasants who periodically rose in rebellion. Korea, on the other hand, had a substantial slave population, called the *nobi*, which was the lowest strata in its four-class system. Although the number of slaves fluctuated with repeated foreign invasions and natural disasters that allowed slaves to escape their bondage, during the fourteenth century, private and state slaves may have constituted more than 30 percent of the population, making Korea a true slave society. Peasants, one step up in the hierarchy, were often not much better off than slaves and could easily be reduced to slave status. Slave escapes and rebellions were not uncommon in Korea but had little effect. The Man-jok Revolt in 1170–1173 killed government officials and destroyed official records before being suppressed by government troops. Another slave rebellion, in 1200, was easily quashed.[14]

Pre-Columbian America

A worldwide phenomenon, slavery also existed in pre-Columbian America. Like most traditional empires, the Aztec Empire of the Mexica people, which flourished for two centuries before it was brought down by Spanish conquistadors, had a social hierarchy with slaves at the bottom. The Aztecs frequently enslaved captives, and they often received slaves as tribute from subjected peoples. After visiting an Aztec market, one of Cortes's soldiers recorded that among the many kinds of merchandise being sold were as many men and women as the number of Africans recently brought by the Portuguese. "Some were tied to long poles with collars around their necks, so they could not escape. And others were left free."[15] The Aztecs used women as sexual slaves and both adults and children as religious sacrifices. Slaves were always a minority of the Aztec population, however, as most agricultural work was apparently performed by servile peasants. Slave revolts were rare, but subject people rebelled by assisting the Spanish invaders conquer the empire in 1521.

The Inca Empire in South America, which flourished for more than a century before Spanish invaders killed its ruler in 1532, was a multiethnic empire ruled by a king and noble class. Conquered peoples had to pay tribute, and the vast majority of subjects was strictly regimented in various public works. The result was a highly structured and efficient society that exacted heavy work obligations but also provided benefits such as public roads and safety. Chattel slavery does not appear to have existed among the Inca, nor was internal rebellion a common occurrence. Sporadic Inca resistance to Spanish rule, on the other hand, continued until the late eighteenth century.

Conclusions

Chattel slavery and other forms of bondage were omnipresent before 1500. While many victims of these systems saw their place in society as an unalterable fate, others rebelled and sought to improve their lot. Individual action, such as escape, was a form of rebellion, but as oppression and exploitation became unbearable, slaves, serfs, and peasants occasionally resorted to group uprisings. Rarely did such insurgencies produce improvements for the oppressed. Instead, they usually resulted in brutal punishments or death for those who challenged the hierarchical structure of authority.

Much of the historical record of premodern slave revolts has been lost or was never documented. The following chapters examine slave and peasant revolts for the 1500–1900 period, for which the historical record is better preserved.

Notes

1. Orlando Patterson, "Foreword," in *Chronology of World Slavery*, ed. Junius P. Rodriguez (Santa Barbara, CA: ABC-CLIO, 1999), ix. See also Jennifer Marquis, "Theories of Slavery," in *Chronology of World Slavery*, 4–5.

2. Paul Lovejoy, *Transformations in Slavery: A History of Slavery in Africa*, 2d ed. (New York: Cambridge University Press, 2000), 1.

3. Quotation from the *Digest* of Roman law, in Thomas Wiedemann, *Greek and Roman Slavery* (London: Croom, Helm, Ltd., 1981), 15.

4. William D. Phillips, Jr., *Slavery from Roman Times to the Early Transatlantic Trade* (Minneapolis: University of Minnesota Press, 1985), 57.

5. Eugene Genovese, *From Rebellion to Revolution* (Baton Rouge: Louisiana State University Press, 1979), 11–12.

6. *Chronology of World Slavery,* 2.

7. Keith Hopkins, *Conquerors and Slaves: Sociological Studies in Roman History,* vol. 1 (London: Cambridge University Press, 1978), 101. Hopkins considers Athens, Roman Italy, Brazil, the southern United States, and Cuba to have been slave societies because at their peak 30–35 percent of their populations were slaves.

8. Michel Mollat and Philippe Wolff, *The Popular Revolutions of the Late Middle Ages,* trans. A. L. Lytton-Sells (London: Allen and Unwin), 334; Werner Rösener, *The Peasantry of Europe,* trans. Thomas M. Barber (Oxford: Blackwell, 1993).

9. Suzanne Miers and Igor Kopytoff, eds., *Slavery in Africa* (Madison: University of Wisconsin Press, 1977), 48, 51, 53, 55.

10. Dev Raj Chanana, *Slavery in Ancient India* (New Delhi: People's Publishing House, 1960), 3–5.

11. Uma Chakravarti, "Of Dasas and Karmakaras: Servile Labor in Ancient India," in *Chains of Servitude: Bondage and Slavery in India,* ed. Utsa Patnaik and Manjara Dingwaney (New Delhi: Sangham Books, 1985), 65.

12. Anthony Reid, "Introduction," in *Slavery, Bondage, and Dependency in South East Asia* (New York: St. Martin's Press, 1983), 1–14.

13. C. Martin Wilbur, *Slavery in China during the Former Han Dynasty, 206 BC–AD 25* (New York: Russell & Russell, 1943), 11–12, 40–41, 63, 86, 224–226.

14. Bok-Rae Kim, "Korean Nobi Resistance under the Chosun Dynasty, 1392–1910," *Slavery and Abolition* 25 (August 2004): 48–62.

15. Quoted in Nigel Davies, *The Ancient Kingdoms of Mexico: A Magnificent Re-creation of Their Art and Life* (New York: Penguin Books, 1983), 198–199.

SLAVE AND PEASANT REVOLTS IN EUROPE AND THE MEDITERRANEAN WORLD, 1500–1900

By 1500, slavery and serfdom had virtually disappeared from western Europe, but peasants, subject to heavy taxation by the landed nobility that kept them destitute, frequently rebelled to protect eroding rights and gain political influence. In the eastern and southern parts of Europe, slavery persisted well into the modern era. In Russia, slaveholders were legally barred from manumitting their slaves until 1805, and public slaves could be branded until 1863.[1] Slavery flourished in European towns around the Mediterranean Sea until the seventeenth century as well as in the Ottoman Empire until the middle of the nineteenth century.

European discovery of ocean routes to the Far East and new lands in the Western Hemisphere in the fifteenth century resulted in vast slave-based trading networks that reached across the Atlantic and Indian oceans. So while slavery declined in most parts of Europe, European slavery survived not only in Russia and the Mediterranean world, but also at overseas trading stations and plantations as well as on slave ships plying the seas.

European Peasant Revolts

The peasant revolts that became such frequent occurrences during the two centuries after the Black Death continued unabated into the modern era, with hundreds of protests and rebellions occurring throughout Europe. Scandinavian and Austrian peasants rebelled during the fifteenth and sixteenth centuries. French peasants staged a series of local and regional rebellions in 1548 and 1594, several between 1620 and 1680, and another in 1707. In Bavaria, revolts occurred in 1633–1634 and in 1705. The generally submissive peasants of Italy staged a massive revolt in 1647–1648. Swiss peasants rebelled frequently, most notably between 1725 and 1745. But after so many costly rebellions, peasants and overlords in western Europe gradually began settling conflicts by means of negotiation.

While most peasant revolts were local or regional uprisings aimed at protecting traditional rights, revolts that took place in western Germany and Russia were so massive and radical in their aims that they were called peasant wars.

The Peasants' War in Germany

Spread across a wide geographical area with almost complete peasant backing, Germany's 1524–1526 Peasants' War was the largest and perhaps most well organized peasant movement in the history of modern Europe.[2] As German princes expanded their powers at the expense of the peasants during the early sixteenth century, the Protestant Reformation emboldened many peasants to resist the growing oppression. Unwilling to lose gains made during the previous centuries and fearful that traditional serfdom might be reinstated, they organized resistance groups in 1524 and launched local revolts against land-owning authorities. Among the grievances and objectives their leaders enumerated, known as the Twelve Articles, was an appeal for greater involvement in the political process. But the princes and bishops refused to negotiate and set their professional armies against the rebels.

As the revolt spread, a combined force of some three hundred thousand peasants and urban workers captured a number of towns, with brutal acts perpetrated by both sides. Peasant leaders, including the radical preacher Thomas Münzer (ca. 1489–1525), hoped that Martin Luther, leader of the Protestant movement, would support them, but in a pamphlet entitled *Against the Robbing and Murderous Peasants' Hordes*, Luther scathingly condemned the revolt and admonished the princes to crush it in a "blood bath."[3] By the spring of 1526, the military forces had suppressed the rebellion.

An estimated one hundred thousand peasants were killed in the fighting and the brutal repression that followed. Many were executed outright, but others had limbs removed and eyes gouged or were otherwise tortured. In some regions, peasants were able to negotiate concessions, but most lost many traditional privileges, and the outcome of the revolt set a pattern for the German power structure for centuries to come.

Peasant Wars in Russia

When the wilderness east of Germany's Elbe River was cleared for agriculture during the Middle Ages, labor was scarce and peasants enjoyed considerable freedom. But gradually over three centuries, the landed nobility and state governments of Bohemia, Russia, Hungary, Prussia, and other Polish and German states imposed restrictions that increasingly bound peasants to the land and gave landowners control over them, turning virtually all peasants into serfs.

Serfdom became particularly repressive in the expanding Russian Empire. Until the sixteenth century, most Russian peasants had enjoyed considerably more freedom than slaves, who were about one-tenth of the population throughout most of the seventeenth century. But in the eastern steppe regions, some peasants were driven into voluntary slavery to avoid crippling taxes, starvation, or military service. As peasants became increasingly bound to the land of either the nobility, state, or church, who had the power to sell, trade, or even gamble them away, they became an oppressed class that was closer to American chattel slavery than to traditional serfdom. By 1795, peasants and slaves together constituted about 90 percent of the Russian population.[4]

Russian serfs rebelled against their slave-like condition in many ways, both individually and through collaborative group action. While historians have identified 2,700 local rebellions during the period of 1801–1860 alone, four earlier insurrections were so massive that they became known as peasant wars. Led by Cossacks, a people who lived on the southern and eastern frontiers and possessed military expertise and expert horsemanship, the wars were also called Cossack Wars.[5]

The first of these massive uprisings occurred in 1606–1607 and was led by Ivan Bolotnikov (15??–1608), a fugitive serf who had taken refuge with the Cossacks and was subsequently captured by Ottoman Turks, but escaped and found his way back to Russia. Taking advantage of political turmoil caused by a succession struggle and Polish invasion, Bolotnikov claimed he was the rightful heir to the tsarist throne and, in 1606, launched a rebellion against the government. With a following that included nobles, Cossacks, and vast numbers of serfs attracted by his call for the abolition of serfdom, he took control of large areas of southern Russia. Although his army surrounded the capital of Moscow, it failed to overthrow the government. In the spring of 1607, after about fifteen months of fighting, Bolotnikov's army was defeated and he was executed.[6]

Stepan "Stenka" Razin (1630–1671), leader of the second peasant war, came from a well-to-do Cossack family but had developed strong sympathies for the poor. In an attempt to overthrow the government, he led an army of seven thousand Cossacks up the Volga River in 1670, killing many landed nobles and promising freedom to serfs. Many serfs and urban poor, enraged by rising taxes used to finance wars with Poland and Sweden, joined the revolt, and several towns in southeastern Russia enthusiastically welcomed the rebel troops. Nevertheless, a government cavalry forced a retreat and defeated the rebels in 1671. Captured and cruelly tortured before being executed, Razin became a folk hero whose story is still told in song and legend.[7]

Thirty-five years later, another Cossack, named Kondraty Bulavin (16??–1709), led a rebellion against Tsar Peter I, who ruled Russia 1682–1725. Both Cossacks, who feared the encroachment of Peter's police state into their territory, and serfs, who saw Peter's reforms as an assault on their orthodox religion and traditional way of living, opposed his attempts to "Westernize" Russia and build a centralized modern state. Large numbers of serfs abandoned their estates, either leaving the country entirely or fleeing to the rural frontiers inhabited by the Cossacks, but Peter authorized bounty hunters to capture and return the runaways. In October 1707, a band of Cossacks led by Bulavin shot a prince who was heading a group of bounty hunters, and the incident triggered a general uprising aimed at dethroning the "evil" tsar. However, the rebels' lack of cohesiveness and poor organization permitted the professional army to contain the uprising. The shooting death of Bulavin in July 1709, perhaps at the hand of one of his followers, brought the shortest and least successful of the Russian peasant wars to an end.

Russia's last and most violent peasant revolt (1773–1774) was led by Emelian Ivanovich Pugachev (1740–1775), a Cossack from the Don River area who had abandoned his military post and been imprisoned for desertion. Apparently Pugachev bore some resemblance to Tsar Peter III, who had been ousted and killed on orders of his wife, Catherine, who then became ruler of Russia (1762–1796). Backed by religious traditionalists, Pugachev claimed he was the deposed tsar and was ready to reclaim his rightful position. In October 1773, he led a group of Cossacks against the government, and expecting freedom, large numbers of peasants flocked to his aid. The rebel armies captured forts along the Volga River and in the Ural mountain region, killing opponents and destroying numerous estate mansions. In August 1774, a government army finally defeated the insurgents at Tsaritsyn (now Volgograd), killing or capturing approximately ten thousand rebels. Pugachev's position rapidly deteriorated, and within a month he was betrayed by his own followers and turned over to government forces. He was carted off to Moscow in a metal cage and publicly executed in January 1775. While Cossack rebels were invited into government service, peasants were punished for their part in the revolt. The government tightened control over those who worked on state lands and gave the nobility complete control over the serfs on their lands.

Slave Rebellion in Southern Europe and the Mediterranean Region

Slavery also persisted in countries surrounding the Mediterranean Sea, particularly in the urban centers of Portugal, Spain, and Italy, and in the Ottoman Empire, which stretched from Greece through the Near and Middle East and along the northern coast of Africa.

Enslaved people sold at markets in such southern European towns as Venice, Genoa, Lisbon, and Seville had primarily been from the Slavic regions of eastern Europe until the Ottomans blocked the entrance to the Black Sea during the mid-fifteenth century. Thereafter, these markets looked to Africa and the Iberian Peninsula (now Spain). During the sixteenth century, some Moriscos, descendants of the Moors (Muslims) who had once ruled the area, were enslaved and exported.[8] In southern Europe, slaves were employed primarily in urban areas as domestic servants, craftsmen, and concubines. With greatly improved conditions and more opportunity for manumission, they rarely banded together to rebel.

The Slavic region of eastern Europe, although closed to European slave trade, continued to be a primary source of slaves for the Ottoman Empire and wider Muslim world. Crimean Tartars frequently raided the region and sent an estimated three million Slavs, primarily Ukranians, to Ottoman slave markets well into the nineteenth century. Little is known about slave resistance in Ottoman areas around the Mediterranean, except for the Barbary states, from which many enslaved Europeans escaped.

Revolts by Galley Slaves

One form of servitude practiced throughout the Mediterranean region, by southern Europeans and Ottomans alike, was galley slavery.

Most navies of Mediterranean powers had galleys, shallow-bottomed warships propelled by teams of enslaved oarsmen. Many European galley slaves were convicts whose enslavement saved them from execution. Others were purchased from Muslim slave traders, and after 1685, some were French Huguenots (Protestants) condemned to galley slavery because they refused to convert to Catholicism. Galley slaves of the Ottoman Empire were often European Christians who refused to convert to Islam.

Galley slavery was gang labor in the extreme, enforced by the whip. The oarsmen were chained to their stations and so well guarded that revolt was extremely difficult. However, sometimes in the heat of battle galley slaves allowed themselves to be captured by the enemy in hopes of being liberated. In a 1571 naval battle between Spain and the Ottoman Empire, many Christian galley slaves turned against their Ottoman masters and helped the Spanish win the battle. As a result, some fifteen thousand slaves gained their freedom and returned to Europe.

Most records of galley slave revolts involve European crews and passengers taken by Barbary pirates. The Barbary states of Tunis, Tripoli, and Algiers, along the North African shore, were technically part of the Ottoman Empire but acted independently from the sixteenth to the early nineteenth centuries. At their peak, they and the port of Salé in neighboring Morocco had hundreds of pirate ships, called *corsairs*, operating in the Mediterranean Sea and Atlantic Ocean. In addition to taking ship crews and passengers, Barbary pirates also raided Mediterranean islands and the mainland of southern Europe, especially the Italian Peninsula, but also the Atlantic coastlines of Spain, France, and even southern England.[9] Some of the captives from European ships ended up as galley slaves on the corsairs, and some rebelled or tried to escape. One successful revolt by European galley slaves was led by an English captain who, with his crew, was taken captive in the Atlantic in 1621. Installed as a pilot on a corsair because of his knowledge and experience, Captain John Rawlins led a successful mutiny and then, with his Barbary masters now taken prisoner, sailed the ship to Plymouth, England.[10]

Slave Rebellions on the Barbary Coast

While many Barbary captives ended up as galley slaves, most were taken to prisons in the pirates' home ports. Because a primary reason for taking captives was to ransom them, the pirates targeted ships from countries willing to pay for their release. So many western Europeans were held for ransom that churches regularly took up collections for their redemption. Many European ships carried so-called Turkish passes purchased from the Barbary states to insure against capture by pirates, and several countries paid tribute to prevent capture or insure the release of captured sailors. It has been suggested that nearly a million slaves—mostly from southern and western Europe but also America—passed through the Barbary prisons. However, the prisons probably housed no more than fifty thousand captives at any one time because they were ransomed or sold as quickly as possible. The vast majority of Barbary captives were not ransomed, but became slaves and either died in enslavement or converted to Islam and were assimilated into North African society.

With the Sahara Desert to the south and the Mediterranean Sea to the north, escape was almost impossible for Barbary slaves. Although many tried, few succeeded. One of the few successful attempts took place in 1532, when twelve thousand captives gained their freedom only because their revolt coincided with a Spanish military incursion that captured Tunis. Six years later, another Spanish fleet tried to take Algiers but failed, with the result that many of the would-be liberators were themselves captured and enslaved. In 1579, an English captive named John Fox escaped with a dozen other slaves by killing their guards and stealing a galley. After twenty-eight days at sea, five survivors reached safety at the island of Crete. In 1672, seventy-four Barbary slaves managed to reach the Spanish coast safely (see Primary Document 1), and about the same time, another forty-six escaped to Majorca.[11]

The corsair activities of the Barbary states weakened during the eighteenth century. During the early nineteenth century, several countries, including the United States, sent warships against them, but not until 1830 did a French invasion neutralize the coastline and halt the piracy.

Slave Revolts on European Slave Ships

With the establishment of ocean routes to the Far East and the discovery of North and South America, European capitalists established various commercial ventures in Asia, Africa, and the New World. After mining and plantation agriculture created an unprecedented demand for slave labor in the Americas in the sixteenth and seventeenth centuries, several European nations entered the business of transporting enslaved Africans across the Atlantic (see Chapter 4). Although nearly equaled by the trans-Saharan slave trade of 650–1900, the Atlantic slave trade became the largest forced migration in human history, with approximately eleven million Africans taken to South America, the Caribbean region, and North America between 1520 and 1865. European traders also transported several thousand Africans and Asians to their various enterprises in the Indian Ocean littorals. Without the threat of shipboard rebellion, the volume of the Atlantic trade at least might have been considerably higher.[12]

Shipboard Revolts in the Atlantic Slave Trade

Data collected about the Atlantic slave trade suggest that about one in ten voyages experienced some form of collaborative slave insurrection, some more than one. While enslaved Africans rarely succeeded in taking control of a ship and even less frequently managed to return to their homeland, shipboard revolts resulted in considerable loss of life among both the slaves and the crew. The threat of slave revolt was great enough to induce traders to invest in such costly preventive measures as shackles, firearms, cannons, and additional crew to guard the slaves. The greatest expense came from having larger crews—usually 50 percent larger than on other ships of the same size.

Few reports of shipboard rebellions date from before 1700. Most of the five hundred rebellions identified in the Atlantic trade come from the last half of the eighteenth century, especially during the years of peak traffic between 1751 and 1775. Three out of four of these rebellions occurred during the loading process off the African coast, a process that generally took twice as long as the actual voyage and gave captives a longer time frame in which to rebel. Because there were fewer witnesses to revolts at sea, during what was called the Middle Passage, and in American coastal waters, records for revolts there are scarce.

Data on shipboard revolts suggest that rebellion occurred more frequently on ships with a larger than normal percentage of female slaves aboard. While the vast majority of slaves taken across the Atlantic were men, and men led the revolts and suffered higher casualties, women seem to have played an essential supporting role. Female slaves were rarely shackled while on board and were housed separately from men and closer to officer quarters, where they were closer to weapons and keys. As they were sometimes sexually abused by crew members, women also had access to information that was essential to planning a revolt.[13]

Rebelling slaves succeeded in taking control of a ship, at least temporarily, in thirty-two known cases, most of these occurring while still in sight of the African coast. In 1730, captives on the

American slave ship *Little George* escaped, reached shore at Sierra Leone, received support from the local population, and apparently regained their freedom (see Primary Document 2). But generally, the proximity of other European ships that could offer assistance, and the unwillingness of local Africans to assist escapees made chances of a successful rebellion along the African coast very slim. In 1769, enslaved Africans on the French ship *Guadeloupe* rebelled while off the Niger Delta coast, gaining control of the front deck after killing some of the crew. But they were subdued by cannon fire that killed about twenty of their number. Similarly, a British slaver ended a revolt on the Dutch ship *Neptunis* in 1785. With the ship anchored off the coast and its captain ashore, African captives had killed most of the crew when the British slaver opened fire. A cannon hit the *Neptunis's* powder chamber, however, and the resulting explosion killed nearly everyone on board. Local Africans rescued eight surviving rebels from the sea and delivered them to the ship's captain.[14]

The British ship *Marlborough* experienced an insurrection soon after leaving the African coast in 1752 with twenty-eight slaves from the Gold Coast and four hundred from the Niger Delta port of Bonny. The rebels killed the captain and all but eight of the crew, who were forced to sail the ship back to the Bonny coast. During the night, about 370 Africans disembarked in small boats, but a hundred drowned in the process. The Gold Coast Africans, who had led the revolt, then had the crew sail the ship to their homeland, but before they could disembark, another British slaver attacked. While the Africans successfully defended themselves against recapture, the *Marlborough* drifted out to sea to an unrecorded fate.

Enslaved Africans were identified only by a number or brand mark, but one off-shore revolt, in 1769, resulted in records that identify the African name of its leader—Essjerrie Ettin (see Biographies). The Dutch ship *Guineese Vriendschap* had completed loading 358 slaves and was ready to begin its voyage across the Atlantic when some of the slaves overpowered the crew, cut the anchor, and set the ship adrift. But a Dutch warship in the vicinity sent two boatloads of soldiers to recapture the ship. Ten suspected leaders were taken to the Dutch West India Company's headquarters at Elmina, the largest trading post on the West African coast. After authorities questioned three of the slaves individually, Ettin was determined to have been the leader and appears to have been the only rebel condemned to death.[15]

A revolt during the Middle Passage occurred on the British slaver *Thomas* in 1797, which had left Loango with 375 enslaved Africans on board. With weapons smuggled by the women, the

Africans seized control of the ship, killing the captain and all of the crew except for twelve who escaped in the stern boat and a few who were spared to help navigate the ship. After sailing aimlessly for six weeks and running out of water, they encountered a small American merchant ship from which they somehow managed to get barrels of rum. The thirsty Africans quickly became intoxicated, enabling the *Thomas's* remaining five crew members to kill the rebel leader and escape to the American ship. An alerted British ship subsequently recaptured the *Thomas* and the Africans on board.[16]

The *Baskenburg* is an example of those few ships that experienced more than one revolt on the same voyage. Shortly after the ship's departure from Angola in 1744, a rebellion killed one crew member and nineteen of the 293 slaves aboard before it was suppressed with assistance from another slave ship. Seven weeks later, when the *Baskenburg* ran aground on the Guyana Coast, the slaves rebelled again. After the crew fled in lifeboats, the Africans managed to reach shore. Finding it difficult to survive, however, they surrendered to a military expedition from the nearby colony of Essequibo. Their rebel leader was emancipated, but the others were re-enslaved and sold at auction.[17]

While the percentage of enslaved Africans killed in revolts varied, data suggest that about one percent of the overall number of slaves boarded for transport across the Atlantic—about one hundred thousand—died as a result of rebellion, either in the fighting or in the executions that followed.[18] While considerable, this was a much smaller proportion than those who died of illness during the voyage. Slaves were a valuable asset to slave traders, and although leaders of insurrections were usually executed, most ships that experienced revolts managed to reach the Americas with most of their captives alive. One tragic exception was the case of the Dutch ship *Middelburgs Welvaren* in 1751. Fourteen of their number had already died during the crossing when slaves gained control of the lower deck. The well-armed and trigger-happy crew on the upper deck shot indiscriminately on the rebels below and killed another 213. When the ship arrived in Suriname, only thirty of the 260 slaves boarded on the Guinea coast were landed and sold.[19]

Instigators and leaders of insurrections were usually executed brutally in front of the other slaves as a deterrent to further rebellion. In 1738, officers of the French ship *Africain* had rebel leaders flogged, their buttocks scarified, and then a concoction of gunpowder, lemon juice, and the brine of peppers rubbed into the wounds. After an 1845 rebellion on the *Kentucky*, an American ship being run by a Brazilian crew, forty-six men and one woman were sentenced to be hung. If the condemned person was in irons with others not slated for execution, he was separated from them by having his shackled leg chopped off. The hanging choked but did not kill any of the condemned, who were then shot and thrown overboard. The following day, twenty-two men and six women were flogged so severely that it killed all the women.[20]

One of the most successful shipboard insurrections took place on the *Amistad* in 1839. Forty-nine men, three girls, and one boy recently imported from West Africa were purchased by two Spaniards at Havana, Cuba, and placed aboard the chartered schooner for a short voyage to Puerto Principe. Led by Sengbe Pieh, who became known as Cinque (see Biographies), the captives freed themselves and easily took control of the ship. The captain and cook were killed, while the two crew members jumped overboard and disappeared, leaving only a teenaged cabin boy and the two Spanish purchasers on board with the Africans. The rebels forced the Spaniards to sail eastward toward Africa, but the men furtively kept the sails loose during the day, preventing the ship from making much headway, and steered northward at night, hoping to be rescued by a British patrol ship. The *Amistad* wandered the sea for seven weeks, while food and water ran out and ten of the Africans died. Anchored off Long Island, New York, while some of the Africans went ashore for provisions, the ship was seized on August 26 and towed to Connecticut. The Africans were jailed in New Haven while U.S. officials tried to determine what should be done with them.

Abolitionists hired an attorney, located an interpreter, and taught the Africans English so they could tell their story in court. In a trial before a U.S. district court in January 1840, government attorneys cited a 1795 treaty between the United States and Spain that required they return property seized on the high seas to its owner. But the defense countered that under an 1817 treaty between Spain and Great Britain banning the importation of slaves into Spanish colonies after 1820, the captives were not property, but free men. The court ruled in favor of the Africans and ordered them returned to their homeland. However, interceding on behalf of the Spaniards, President Martin Van Buren ordered the case to go to the U.S. Supreme Court. Former President John Quincy Adams joined in the defense, and in March 1841 the Supreme Court also ordered the Africans freed. Abolitionists raised money for their passage, and in January 1842, thirty-five of the original fifty-three *Amistad* captives were returned to Africa.[21]

Shipboard Revolts in the Indian Ocean Slave Trade

Slave traffic was much smaller in the Indian Ocean than in the Atlantic, and there were correspondingly fewer shipboard revolts. But results were similar. In 1766, the Dutch East India Company ship, *Meermin*, boarded 147 slaves at Madagascar for delivery at Cape Town, South Africa. Not far from their destination, the slaves broke free and killed half of the sixty-member crew with spears seized from the ship's cargo. Surviving crew members barricaded themselves in the lower quarters, but the rebels otherwise controlled the ship. In a ploy similar to that later staged on the *Amistad,* some of the crew agreed to sail the ship back to Madagascar but, while feigning to do so during the day, they reversed course at night. When land was spotted, half of the slaves took small boats to the shore of what they thought was Madagascar but which the crew knew to be South Africa. Local people killed or re-enslaved the rebels, and two rescue ships from Cape Town captured the remaining rebels and liberated the surviving crew.[22]

In 1783, another company ship, the *Slot ter Hoge*, had about thirty slaves among its passengers on the Batavia–Cape Town route. Midway through the voyage, a plot by twenty Indonesian slaves was discovered. After a perfunctory trial, the rebels were bound and thrown overboard. In 1790, a revolt took place on the small packet ship, *Haasje*, which was carrying seventeen Malayan slaves to the slave market at Cape Town. During the middle of a night, two slaves broke loose from their chains, obtained sabers, killed the captain and two other crew members, and wounded several others. They managed to hide in one of the cabins under cover of darkness, but after daybreak they were found and killed.[23]

Conclusion

As the modern era dawned, slavery had virtually disappeared in western Europe but remained a peripheral phenomenon in southern and eastern Europe. While continental Europe experienced no slave revolts after 1500, its peasantry, many of whom lived in slave-like conditions, staged major rebellions during the sixteenth century in the west and into the nineteenth century in the east. European maritime expansion after the fifteenth century created new slave systems and oceanic slave trades, which spawned slave revolts on slave ships, as well as in trading stations and colonies in Africa, Asia, and the Americas, which will be explored in the following chapters.

Notes

1. Jerome Blum, *The End of the Old Order in Europe* (Princeton, NJ: Princeton University Press, 1978), 270–276, 465–469; Orlando Patterson, "Foreword," in *Chronology of World Slavery*, ed. Junius P. Rodriguez (Santa Barbara, CA: ABC-CLIO, 1999), 59.

2. Thomas Robisheaux, "The Peasantries of Western Germany, 1300–1750," in *The Peasantries of Europe from the Fourteenth to the Eighteenth Centuries*, ed. Tom Scott (London: Longman, 1998), 137.

3. Hajo Holborn, *A History of Modern Germany*, vol. 1, *The Reformation* (Princeton, NJ: Princeton University Press, 1959), 60–64, 170–177.

4. Peter Kolchin, *Unfree Labor: American Labor and Russian Serfdom* (Cambridge, MA: Harvard University Press, 1987), 2, 40–52.

5. Edgar Melton, "The Russian Peasantries, 1450–1860," in *Peasantries of Europe*, 265.

6. Kolchin, *Unfree Labor*, 7, 9, 36–37, 204–249.

7. For the Russian peasant rebellions, see Paul Avrich, *Russian Rebels, 1600–1800* (New York: Schocken Books, 1972).

8. Stephen Clissold, *The Barbary Slaves* (New York: Barnes & Noble, 1992). See also L. P. Harvey, *Muslims in Spain, 1500 to 1614* (Chicago: University of Chicago Press, 2005).

9. For a recent assessment of Barbary piracy, see Robert C. Davis, *Christian Slaves, Muslim Masters: White Slavery in the Mediterranean, the Barbary Coast and Italy, 1500–1800* (Basingstoke, UK: Palgrave Macmillan, 2003).

10. Clissold, *Barbary Slaves*, 69–70, 74, 75.

11. Ibid., 25–27, 69–73.

12. David Richardson, "Shipboard Revolts, African Authority, and the Atlantic Slave Trade," *William and Mary Quarterly* 58 (January 2001): 74.

13. Ibid., 76.

14. Johannes Postma, *The Dutch in the Atlantic Slave Trade, 1600–1815* (New York: Cambridge University Press, 1990), 167.

15. Ibid., 166–168, 243.

16. Eric Robert Taylor, *If We Must Die: Shipboard Insurrections in the Era of the Atlantic Slave Trade* (Baton Rouge: Louisiana State University Press, 2006), 104–105, 119–122.

17. E. W. van der Oest, "Vergeten Kolonies: Handel en Scheepvaart op de kolonies van Essequibo en Demerary, 1700–1791" (master's thesis, University of Leiden, 1992), 66–67.

18. Richardson, "Shipboard Revolts, African Authority," 72.

19. Postma, *Dutch in the Atlantic Slave Trade*, 167–168.

20. Robert L. Stein, *The French Slave Trade in the Eighteenth Century* (Madison: University of Wisconsin Press, 1979), 105–106; Robert E. Conrad, *Children of God's Fire: A Documentary History of Black Slavery in Brazil* (Princeton, NJ: Princeton University Press, 1983), 39–42.

21. Howard Jones, *Mutiny on the Amistad: The Saga of a Slave Revolt and Its Impact on American Abolition, Law, and Diplomacy* (New York: Oxford University Press, 1987).

22. Sharon LaFraniere, "Combing for the Shipwreck of a Slave Rebellion," *International Herald Tribune*, August 25, 2005.

23. J. R. Bruijn and E. S. Van Eyck van Heslinga, "Wij Hebben Amok in ons Schip," in *Muiterij: Oproer en Berechting op Schepen van de VOC* (Haarlem: De Boer Maritiem, 1980), 123–147.

CHAPTER 3

SLAVE AND PEASANT REBELLIONS IN ASIA AND AFRICA

Searching for an ocean route to the Far East, Europeans of the fifteenth century explored the African coastline and rounded Africa's Cape of Good Hope into the Indian Ocean, opening for their exploitation and colonization regions in which slavery was common and rebellion rare. Over the next two centuries, as Portuguese, Dutch, British, and French merchants established commercial operations along the African and Indian ocean littorals (coastlines), they interacted with, and sometimes took over, indigenous slave systems. Although they employed hundreds of thousands of slaves, collaborative resistance remained rare until the nineteenth century, when a convergence of influences, including growing antislavery sentiment in Europe, propelled some Asian and African slaves to try to throw off their bonds.

Rebellions in East Asia

European trade activity reached all the way to the coasts of China, Japan, and Korea, known in Europe as the Far East. In China and Japan, slaves were such a small minority of the population that they were in no position to stage revolts. However, peasant uprisings were common in both countries. Korea, by contrast, had a large slave population and experienced several slave rebellions.

Peasant Wars in China

Impoverished peasants, burdened by heavy taxation and plagued by famine (see Primary Document 3), far outnumbered China's slaves, who were used primarily as domestic servants and concubines. With most of the land owned by a very small minority, most of China's peasants were tenants or owners of very small plots and were exploited by both the large landowners and the government. It was not uncommon for landowners to require peasants working their land to surrender more than half of their harvests, in addition to paying land rents and other dues. Peasants were also required to perform unpaid labor service for landowners or the government. Throughout China's history, frequent peasant revolts, some large enough to be called wars, sought to win social and economic improvements. One of these contributed to the fall of the Ming Dynasty (1368–1644), and a long series of revolts during the nineteenth century undermined the succeeding Manchu Dynasty and paved the way for the dissolution of the Chinese Empire in 1912.[1]

China's first great peasant war began in 1627 in the northern province of Shensi after a serious drought and subsequent famine devastated the peasantry in that region. Rising taxes, imposed to combat a Manchu invasion from the north, also contributed to peasant unrest. Begun by small bands of peasants led by deserting soldiers, the rebel forces numbered over two hundred thousand by 1634. With many in their ranks being experienced horsemen, they used hit-and-run tactics against superior government armies and by 1636 had gained control over several provinces in central China. Imperial armies succeeded in halting the rebel advance until 1641, when two leaders who had survived earlier battles—Li Tzu-ch'eng and Chang Hsien-chung—took charge of separate regions.

Taking advantage of a Manchu invasion from the north, Li's forces took control of Peking in 1644, after the last Ming emperor had committed suicide. However, triumphant Manchu forces reinforced by soldiers from the defeated imperial army retook the city after a few weeks, killing two hundred thousand rebels in the process. Another ten thousand rebels surrendered as Li fled the city. As the remnants of his army dispersed, Li himself disappeared and was never heard of again.

Meanwhile, Chang had established a separate rebel state, with the Szechwan city of Chengtu as its capital, and adopted an imperial title. This fragile state lasted only two years, however. Pressured by forces of the newly established Manchu Dynasty, Chang was forced to abandon Chengtu in the summer of 1646 and was killed in a final battle in January 1647. Having used terror and murder indiscriminately, Li and Chang left a legacy of brutality uncharacteristic of the noble ideals of social justice often espoused by peasant rebels.[2]

Two centuries later, foreign intervention and the so-called Opium Wars of 1839–1842 and 1858–1860 fueled a long series of peasant insurrections against Manchu rule. After an 1851 uprising in the Kwangsi Mountains, peasant armies conquered portions of southwestern China. Proclaiming himself emperor, their leader established a capital at Nanking in 1853. But his creation of a privileged class that heavily taxed the peasants led to factional conflict among his forces. After an unsuccessful rebel attack on Peking in 1854, Manchu rulers, with assistance from Western powers, crushed the rebellion in 1864.

Another peasant revolt that broke out in 1853 between the Yangtze and Yellow rivers, in thinly populated northern China, was waged by an army of peasants fighting in small guerilla units. Operating over large areas of northern China, they inflicted much damage on government forces before being subdued by imperial forces in 1868. Several smaller peasant insurrections occurred in western China, some led by ethnic minority groups that were often even more severely exploited. One of these, a Muslim rebellion in Yunan Province, lasted from 1853 to 1873. In defiance of government authority, many peasants joined secret societies or religious cults that staged revolts in 1854 and 1860.

These revolts achieved little and often led to even higher taxation, and their repression took the lives of millions of Chinese peasants. However, they provided the foundation for the Boxer Rebellion of 1897–1900, which hastened the demise of the Manchu Dynasty in 1912.

Peasant Protests and Rebellions in Japan

Prior to the mid-nineteenth century, between 80 to 90 percent of the Japanese population were peasants living under the Tokugawa Shogunate (1543–1867), a feudal system that was very slowly evolving into a market-driven money economy. Most peasants were severely exploited by state and noble agents through public work demands and crippling taxation. These were especially burdensome when failing crops forced peasants to the brink of starvation and were, therefore, the principal causes of peasant protests and uprisings.

Most of the three thousand peasant uprisings identified in Japan between 1590 and 1871 were local disturbances, and only a small percentage can be termed true revolts. Nevertheless, punishment meted out to rebel leaders was often brutal, especially before the eighteenth century. The memory of many peasant leaders was passed on through folklore, and some became heroes of legendary proportion. One peasant leader, Sakura Sōgorō, was executed in 1644 for petitioning the shogun, or ruler, to lower taxes. According to legend, he did this by intruding into an official procession, which was regarded as such a serious offense that both Sōgorō and his innocent wife were sentenced to death by crucifixion, and their four sons, the youngest only three years old, were beheaded in view of the condemned parents. Punishment for leaders of rebellions became less harsh over time, although decapitation remained a frequent punishment for leaders. Major uprisings took place in the 1720s, 1760s, 1780s, and 1860s, and although most were violently repressed by government forces, they often resulted in reforms the peasants sought.[3]

Slave Revolts in Korea

Unlike China and Japan, Korea had a sizable slave population, both state and privately owned, and experienced significant slave uprisings well into the modern era. With about 30 percent of the population enslaved, Korea was perhaps the only true slave society in Asia. Korean slaves had shown their inclination to rebel in previous times (see Chapter 1), but by the seventeenth century they were developing a radical ideology aimed at overthrowing the ruling class. Occasionally, slaves assaulted and killed members of the upper class. Using secret societies and religious cults, they advanced their cause in towns as well as in rural areas, and often gained the sympathy of free peasants and members of the urban middle class. When a foreign invasion seemed imminent in 1684, slaves rose against their masters and staged a massive escape from Seoul, Korea's seat of government. In 1688, cultist slaves developed a plot to take over the government and promised that the gods would intervene on their behalf. When the intervention failed to materialize, the rebellion collapsed and many slaves were captured and executed.

During the second half of the eighteenth and early nineteenth centuries, crop failures, epidemics, and famine caused much social unrest in Korea. After a series of small rebellions failed to win any improvement in their conditions, slaves increasingly fled and established their own settlements in remote areas, now called maroon communities (see Chapter 6), resulting in a gradual decline in the slave population. After Korea's sixty-six thousand state-owned slaves were emancipated in 1801, only wealthy upper-class families retained slaves until general emancipation was mandated in 1894.[4]

Slave Rebellion in the East Indies

Slavery and other forms of servitude were pervasive in the coastal regions and islands of the Indian Ocean that became known to Europeans as the "East Indies," as opposed to the "West Indies" of the Caribbean. Long a center of trade with the Middle East, the region was introduced to Islam in the thirteenth century by Muslim traders, for whom it was a source of slaves. As European powers—primarily Portugal, the Dutch Republic (officially, the United Provinces), Britain, and France—moved into the region beginning in the early sixteenth century, they interacted with and sometimes took over existing slave systems. Over four centuries, their "East India" trading companies and supporting private personnel employed hundreds of thousands of slaves at trading centers, plantations, mines, and other commercial ventures. In 1688, the Dutch alone had sixty thousand slaves working throughout the region, four thousand of whom were so-called *company slaves* working for the Dutch East India Company performing a myriad of trade-related duties from dock and warehouse work to construction of buildings and canals to service in homes and hospitals.

Although slavery undergirded European commercial and colonization activity in the East Indies, there is very little record of slave rebellion. Because the subject has attracted little scholarly attention so far, our knowledge of slave resistance in the East Indies is limited.

Resistance to Slavery in India

On the Indian Subcontinent, Britain's East India Company ultimately prevailed over competing interests from Portugal, the Dutch Republic, and France, gradually gaining control over most of the area. Known as British India, it remained a British colony until independence was granted in 1947.

Throughout India's colonial period, extreme poverty and destitution doomed the majority of its people to some form of servitude. Whereas New World slavery arose because resources were plentiful but labor was scarce, in India resources were too scarce to support its teeming masses.[5] Destitution forced some people to enter slavery voluntarily, and especially in times of famine, parents sold their children into slavery. By the terms of one 1727 contract, a man sold his two sons to be "bound as slaves ... from generation to generation," promising that if they absconded, he himself would take their place. Slaves were sold at public auction in many cities. Although a small minority of the population was actual chattel slaves, India's ancient caste system doomed many to a slave-like existence, and debt-bondage, while a separate and distinct form of labor obligation, was very much like slavery.[6]

With slavery considered part of the social order, sustained by both the Hindu and Muslim religions, and offering a measure of security, there was virtually no organized resistance to it. Even after

European colonials brought slaves from other Indian Ocean littorals, slave rebellion was unheard of. In a rare example of collaborative action to improve their conditions, a large number of slaves participated in an 1820 demonstration against the sale of slaves that led to the separation of family members.

After Britain abolished slavery in the 1840s, the law was often ignored or circumvented. To work recently established tea and coffee plantations, British colonials imported indentured laborers, whom they kept for years and treated much like slaves. They also shipped in unskilled contract laborers from China who were often treated as slaves. During the 1880s, Chinese laborers demonstrated against the brutal treatment of some in their ranks.[7]

Slave Rebellion in Indonesia

The Dutch East India Company ultimately predominated in islands that make up the Malay Archipelago between the Indian and Pacific oceans, establishing its headquarters at Batavia (now Jakarta) on the north coast of Java. At the beginning of the nineteenth century, the islands officially became a colony known as the Dutch East Indies. Achieving independence in 1949, the islands are now known as Indonesia.

The Dutch acquired some slaves through slave clauses of treaties signed with subdued peoples, but it purchased the vast majority of slaves used at its commercial operations from indigenous slave traders. Most of these slaves came from the Malayan Peninsula or islands such as Borneo and Bali that had little or no governmental structure to protect its inhabitants. The difference in geographic, ethnic, religious, and linguistic backgrounds prevented slaves from developing a common cultural identity, and this was one factor that made collaborative resistance virtually nonexistent in the Dutch East Indies. Other factors included the small size of slave-holding units, with few slave-holders having more than one hundred slaves, most far less; a slavery system that did not permit the rise of slave leadership; and the lack of social or political unrest that slaves could use to their advantage. Also, the geographical terrain provided ample opportunity for escape, making desertion easier and more effective than revolt.

Only three instances of revolt or planned revolt have been identified within Dutch colonies in the Indian Ocean. The first involved a 1689 plot to kill all Europeans at Batavia. Authorities learned of the plot and attempted to arrest its leader, a Muslim aristocrat who commanded a division of the company's army, but he escaped and began a campaign of plunder and murder. Although he was quickly captured and killed, his co-conspirators escaped into the island's interior. After a few months, fifty of the rebels were turned over to Dutch authorities by an indigenous ruler, and executed, while thirty slaves were exiled to the Dutch colony of Ceylon. In 1710, another conspiracy on a neighboring island was foiled.

In addition to slaves, Batavia had a large population of Chinese immigrants, many of whom were semi-free laborers known as *coolies*, who were often no better off than slaves. In 1740, a revolt by coolie sugar workers resulted in the massacre of an estimated seven thousand Chinese workers and townsmen. A plummeting sugar market had forced many of the colony's sugar planters into bankruptcy and thrown sugar coolies out of work, who, out of desperation resorted to plundering the countryside. To relieve the problem, Dutch authorities decided to transfer the workers to Dutch-run sugar plantations on Ceylon, but rumors spread that once out at sea, the coolies would be thrown overboard. Instead of boarding the ships, they broke into open revolt, robbing and killing in the countryside and attempting to break through the city walls. Suspecting that many of the city's five thousand Chinese sympathized with and might become involved in the revolt, authorities ordered a search of all Chinese homes and businesses. The search degenerated into a three-day massacre of most of the Chinese population. The governor was arrested and summoned before the company's directors in Amsterdam, but with his death in prison, the charges were annulled and the matter dropped.[8] After the Dutch East India Company dissolved in 1799, the Dutch government took control of the colony and abolished slavery in 1863.

Rebellion on Indian Ocean Islands

Until the nineteenth century, there was no recorded slave rebellion on the French plantation islands off the African mainland and Madagascar. France abolished slavery in its territories in 1794, but under pressure from French plantation owners in the Caribbean, Napoleon Bonaparte reestablished it in 1802. In 1811, an uprising at a sugar plantation on the French island of Réunion off Madagascar was quickly suppressed after betrayal of the plan forced it to start prematurely. Eighteen of the surviving 130 rebels tried under the French *Code Noire* (Black Law) were executed. In 1822, twelve years after Britain took neighboring Mauritius from the French, an exiled army officer from Malaysia led an ill-prepared rebellion that was also quickly put down and resulted in the execution of thirteen leaders.[9]

After the Second French Republic again abolished slavery in 1848, French plantations on the Comoro Islands began using contract labor, a disguised form of slavery that forced desperate workers to sign away rights and freedom in employment agreements. In 1856, these workers staged a minor rebellion on the Comoro island of Mayotte.[10]

Slave Rebellions in Sub-Saharan Africa

Although an estimated four million sub-Saharan Africans had been enslaved and transported across the Sahara Desert to the Mediterranean area before 1500, there is little historical record of slave resistance before Europeans began trading directly with sub-Saharan Africa in the fifteenth century. Restricted by African rulers to coastal trading stations, however, Europeans knew very little about the interior. Rebellion appears to have been rare among so-called *domestic slaves*, those retained in their own regions and assimilated into their new communities. Any resistance from *trade slaves*, those sold and exported, left little documentary evidence.

Once Europeans became involved in the trade, however, accounts of resistance began to be written down. We know from a slave trader's journal, for example, that in 1720 a Senegal chief named Tamba led an unsuccessful battle against coastal slave traders and then organized a shipboard revolt, during which he was killed.[11] Although accounts of uprisings at coastal trading stations are rare, the Dutch trading station at Cape Town, South Africa, developed into a slave-based colony that experienced minor slave rebellion during the late seventeenth century.

While previously little noted, rebellions within Africa's indigenous slave systems became more frequent during the nineteenth century, as increased warfare and a dissipating overseas slave trade created a burgeoning slave population, with slaves comprising more than 70 percent of the population of some West African states. Toward the end of that century and into the twentieth, as European nations began to conquer and colonize Africa, many slaves made use of the turmoil to flee to freedom.[12]

Slave Rebellion in South Africa

In 1652, the Dutch established a station on the southern tip of Africa to service their trade ships as they passed to and from the East Indies. Shortly thereafter, they imported slaves from India, Indonesia, and later East Africa to do domestic and agricultural work. Settlers spread out from Cape Town to establish large cattle and sheep ranches, forcing many local Khoisan-speaking people into servitude, and ultimately established a colony in which slavery and coerced labor were an integral part. While many slaves escaped to the interior and established their own communities, distribution over isolated estates generally prevented slaves from organizing collaborative resistance. Minor uprisings did occur at the village of Stellenbosch, east of Cape Town, in 1688 and 1690, but both were quickly quelled and no rebellions were reported during the following century.

By the time the British took control of the colony in 1806, talk of abolishing slavery was widespread and slaves had begun anticipating freedom. In the fall of 1808, a relatively peaceful protest occurred in the Cape Town area, led by a quasi-free mulatto tailor named Louis and two Irish men, James Hooper and Michael Kelley. Deciding that slaves should take collective action, they rode by wagon from farm to farm, subdued uncooperative owners, and gathered well over three hundred slaves for a march on Cape Town to demand freedom. When they arrived at the capital a few days later, the insurgents were met by an armed militia. No one was killed, but the marchers were arrested and tried. Five leaders, including Louis, Hooper, and Kelley, were executed.

A smaller but more violent uprising known as the Galant Rebellion took place in 1825. Galant was a 26-year-old slave who had enjoyed a privileged status as a household slave on a farm in rural Bokkevelt, northeast of Cape Town, until his mistress died and he was passed to her resentful son, Willem van der Merwe. Galant had reason to hate his master. Besides having himself received several brutal beatings from Van der Merwe, one of his six children had died as the result of a beating. But Galant also believed rumors that Britain had abolished slavery, and so believed that Van der Merwe and other masters continued to hold slaves in defiance of that official action. Threatening to wrest control of all ranches in the area, Galant and a number of supporting slaves and Khoisan servants succeeded in taking control of his and a neighboring ranch, killing Van der Merwe and two guests. Another guest escaped, however, and alerted neighbors who organized a posse that quickly subdued the rebels. While small compared to other rebellions, Galant's uprising terrified the region's slaveholders. After a biased trial, as most slave trials were (see Primary Document 4), Gallant and two co-conspirators were sent to the gallows.[13]

Slave Rebellion in West Africa

Starting in the late eighteenth century and lasting several decades, a wave of Islamic renewal and expansion swept through the West

African interior. The relentless warfare created several new states, the most powerful of which was the Sokoto Caliphate (Empire) in northern Nigeria, which incorporated many states as it expanded southward, including the large state of Oyo in southern Nigeria. The warfare greatly increased the number of enslaved prisoners of war, but at the same time provided opportunities for others to escape from slavery—either by fighting for one side or the other or by using the upheaval to flee.

At the same time, a coalition of countries led by Britain gradually suppressed the export of slaves from West Africa. Many African merchants and rulers who benefited from the slave trade kept up an illicit traffic that continued many years before an effective naval blockade could put an end to it.[14] To make use of the surplus slaves, Africans gradually developed slave-based plantation agriculture, which was profitable but also increased slave unrest. During the 1850s, a slave revolt on state-owned plantations in Dahomey (now Benin) was suppressed with considerable difficulty, teaching Dahomey's leaders the danger of concentrating too many slaves in one area.

The larger numbers and greater concentration of slaves in West Africa continued to breed rebellion. In 1848, slaves took advantage of a local succession conflict to gain control over a town in the Niger Delta region, which they held for three years. Additional slave rebellions occurred in the region during subsequent years. About that time, city slaves in Calabar, on the Nigerian coast, organized mass demonstrations to improve their conditions. In 1866 in Liberia, where formerly only trade-slaves had been marketed and sold, plantation slaves seized control of both their plantation and the neighboring town to protest the unprecedented sale of domestic slaves.[15]

Instances of group flight also increased during this period. Sometimes fugitives were granted asylum by neighboring peoples, as were ethnic Zawo slaves in the 1820s by the Vai people in what is now Liberia. Sometimes large groups fled into forested areas and established maroon settlements (see Chapter 6), which they then had to defend against attack by slaveholders. In 1785, the escape of up to a thousand slaves from their Mandingo masters in what is now Guinea precipitated a maroon war that lasted ten years. In what has become known as the Mandingo Rebellion, fugitives defended a mountain stronghold that served as a refuge for other runaway slaves until it was destroyed in 1796. Another maroon community established in Upper Guinea in 1838 was a serious threat to area slaveholders until they signed a treaty with its leader in 1870.[16] Around 1860 a large group of plantation slaves in the vicinity of Wase, Nigeria, rebelled against their Muslim ruler and received assistance from neighboring non-Muslim tribes. After moving from place to place and negotiating treaties with other communities, they eventually established their own community and negotiated a truce with their former masters. In 1870, about seven hundred slaves escaped from the Bauchi area in central Nigeria and established a town, called Yuli, and maintained their freedom until 1902, when they gained protection from Britain.[17]

Slave Rebellion in East Africa

Africa's eastern coast had been dominated for centuries by Arabs, who settled in the area and established a string of coastal trading stations from which they exported slaves. Trading caravans sent into the interior brought thousands of enslaved Africans to the coast. By the early nineteenth century, the sultans of Oman in Arabia had gained control over all of the northern East African coast and developed lucrative clove plantations on the coastal islands of Zanzibar and Pemba. In 1840, Sultan Sayyid Said moved his capital from Arabia to Zanzibar and made it the largest slave market in East Africa, exporting an estimated seventy thousand slaves annually during the 1860s. Thousands more slaves were kept to work the numerous clove plantations on Zanzibar and Pemba. With plantation slaves alone comprising more than 50 percent of the islands' populations (without counting household and urban slaves), these islands became true slave societies. Major slave rebellions broke out on both islands in 1840, the year Sayyid Said moved to Zanzibar. They were quickly suppressed, but many slaves escaped to the mainland and established maroon settlements in sparsely populated areas.

During the middle of the century, Britain began sending anti–slave-trade ships to the East African coast, extending its efforts to suppress slave trade in the Atlantic, and in 1873 it succeeded in getting a treaty from Zanzibar's sultan, agreeing to end slave exportation. Perhaps aware of Britain's antislavery activities, slaves in the Zanzibar Sultanate staged several uprisings during the late 1860s and in 1873, resulting in the formation of a number of maroon communities along the coast of today's Tanzania and Kenya (see Chapter 6). After additional revolts during the early 1880s, Zanzibar lost control over slaves on the mainland as Germany colonized the area in 1884.[18]

Slave Rebellion and the European Conquest of Africa

In 1870, slavery and slave trade were still very much alive on the African continent, 90 percent of which was controlled by African rulers. The abolition of slavery was a core rationale for the imposition of European colonial rule over Africa from 1870 to 1914. So as European powers occupied African territory, many slaves used the upheaval to flee their masters' control in anticipation of freedom.

After 1885, half a dozen European powers scrambled to stake out African colonies. Occupying forces tried to maintain order in West Africa by discouraging slave flight but succeeded only in confusing and frustrating the slaves. Believing the British would grant them the freedom denied by the French, slaves in the Senegal–Gambia border area rebelled in 1894, and slaves in northeastern Senegal rebelled in 1895–1896. To prevent a drain of workers from the region, French administrators compromised and persuaded some rebels to return as tenant farmers. Many other slaves took advantage of the turmoil to enlist as soldiers in a special African division of the French Army.[19]

Despite being urged to remain on their estates, many slaves fled as British troops moved into central and northern Nigeria in 1897 and 1900. In the bordering Bida kingdom, slave rebellion led to mass desertion of farms, looting and plundering, and flight to British-controlled areas. Officials urged slaveholders to return to their lands and reclaim their slaves but warned that while Britain did not intend to interfere with slavery, mistreated slaves would, as the Koran instructed, be set free. Officials also urged freed slaves to return to work and not remain idle, but most slaves were by then beyond control.

In 1903, Britain conquered the Sokoto Caliphate that had ruled northern Nigeria for nearly a century. In 1905–1906, radical Muslim clerics who opposed both European colonialists and African aristocracy led a massive rebellion in Nigeria and in French-controlled Niger to the north. Demanding emancipation and an end to exploitative taxation, they attracted thousands of runaway slaves and poor peasants. Although they were defeated and two thousand rebels were killed in the fighting, an estimated two hundred thousand slaves escaped during the rebellion.[20]

By 1912, most of Africa had fallen into European hands. While colonial officials succeeded in curtailing the enslavement of Africans, they moved slowly toward abolition, allowing African rulers and slaveholders to retain their slaves in order to maintain order and minimize resistance.

Conclusion

While slavery was common in modern-era Asia and Africa, slave rebellion was rare. In some places, such as China and Japan, slave populations were too small to take collaborative action. Occasional revolts by impoverished peasants usually failed but in China helped bring about the downfall of dynasties. In European colonies on the Indian Ocean littorals, slaves came from such a variety of geographic and ethnic backgrounds that they did not develop the common cultural identity that scholars consider a prerequisite for mass rebellion. Many Indian Ocean islands, as well as the interior of Africa, provided forested or hilly regions that made escape a more viable option than revolt (see Chapter 6). In many regions, slave rebellion increased during the nineteenth century, partially because of growing antislavery sentiment. Africa saw a final outbreak of revolt during the late nineteenth and early twentieth centuries, as European powers colonized the continent. As Europeans succeeded in abolishing chattel slavery in their colonies, however, it was often replaced by other forms of bondage and exploitation that subsequently produced anticolonial revolts throughout Asia and Africa.

Notes

1. Jean Chesneaux, *Peasant Revolts in China, 1840–1949* (London: Thames and Hudson, 1973), 7, 10, 17–18.

2. James Bunyan Parsons, *The Peasant Rebellions of the Late Ming Dynasty* (Tucson: University of Arizona Press, 1970), 50, 161–164, 178.

3. Anne Walthall, ed., *Peasant Uprisings in Japan* (Chicago: University of Chicago Press, 1991), 35–75; Herbert P. Bix, *Peasant Protest in Japan, 1590–1884* (New Haven, CT: Yale University Press, 1986); Stephen Vlastos, *Peasant Protests and Uprisings in Tokugawa Japan* (Berkeley: University of California Press, 1986).

4. Bok-Rae Kim, "Korean Nobi Resistance under the Chosun Dynasty, 1392–1910," *Slavery and Abolition* 25 (August 2004): 54–60; Takashi Hatada, *A History of Korea* (Santa Barbara, CA: ABC-CLIO, 1969), 87.

5. Howard Temperley, "New World Slavery, Old World Slavery," in *Serfdom and Slavery: Studies in Legal Bondage*, ed. M. L. Bush (London: Longman, 1996), 151.

6. Tanika Sarkar, "Bondage in the Colonial Context," in *Chains of Servitude: Bondage and Slavery in India*, ed. Utsa Patnaik and Manjari Dingwaney (Madras: Sangam Books, 1985), 97–98, 109.

7. Sarkar, "Bondage in the Colonial Context," 99–126, 119–120.

8. Markus Vink, "'The World's Oldest Trade': Dutch Slavery and Slave Trade in the Indian Ocean in the Seventeenth Century," *Journal of World History* 14 (June 2003): 160–167, 171–175; A. R. T. Kemasang, "The 1740 Massacre of Chinese in Java: Curtain Raiser for the Dutch Plantation Economy," *Bulletin of Concerned Asian Scholars* 14 (1982).

9. Deryck Scarr, *Slaving and Slavery in the Indian Ocean* (London: Macmillan, 1998), 76–77; Anthony J. Barker, *Slavery and Anti-Slavery in Mauritius, 1810–1833* (London: Macmillan, 1996), 112–114.

10. Gwyn Campbell and Edward A. Alpers, " Introduction: Slavery, Forced Labour and Resistance in Indian Ocean Africa and Asia," *Slavery and Abolition* 25 (August 2004): xvi–xix.

11. Boubacar Barry, *Senegambia and the Atlantic Slave Trade* (Cambridge: Cambridge University Press, 1998), 121.

12. Paul E. Lovejoy and Jan Hogendorn, *Slow Death of Slavery: The Course of Abolition in Northern Nigeria, 1897–1936* (New York: Cambridge University Press, 1993), 8.

13. Robert Ross, *Cape of Torments: Slavery and Resistance in South Africa* (London: Routledge & Kegan Paul, 1983), 12, 96–116; Vink, "World's Oldest Trade," 172–173.

14. In 1820, an Asante ruler met with a representative of the British government to protest the closing of the slave trade. See Johannes Postma, *Atlantic Slave Trade* (Westport, CT: Greenwood Press), 149–151.

15. Patrick Manning, "Slave Trade, 'Legitimate' Trade, and Imperialism Revisited: The Control of Wealth in the Bights of Benin and Biafra," in *Africans in Bondage: Studies in Slavery and the Slave Trade* (Madison: University of Wisconsin Press, 1986), 222–223, 237.

16. See Ismail Rashid, "A Devotion to the Idea of Liberty at Any Price: Rebellion and Antislavery in the Upper Guinea Coast in the Eighteenth and Nineteenth Centuries," in *Fighting the Slave Trade: West African Strategies*, ed. Sylvia A. Diouf (Athens: Ohio University Press, 2003), 132–147; Suzanne Miers and Igor Kopytoff, eds. *Slavery in Africa* (Madison: University of Wisconsin Press, 1977), 29–42, 291, 321.

17. Paul E. Lovejoy, "Problems of Slave Control in the Sokoto Caliphate," in *Africans in Bondage: Studies in Slavery and the Slave Trade* (Madison: University of Wisconsin Press, 1986), 261–262.

18. G. A. Akinola, "Slavery and Slave Revolts in the Sultanate of Zanzibar in the Nineteenth Century," *Journal of the Historical Society of Nigeria* 6 (1972): 215–228.

19. Martin Klein, *Slavery and Colonial Rule in French West Africa* (New York: Cambridge University Press, 1998), 97–104.

20. Lovejoy and Hogendorn, *Slow Death of Slavery*, 22–45, 54–61.

CHAPTER 4

SLAVE REVOLTS IN SPANISH AMERICA AND THE CARIBBEAN

European Expansion to the Americas

In opening the Western Hemisphere to European colonization, Christopher Columbus's discovery of America in 1492 also set the stage for a vast expansion of slavery. Just two years after Columbus landed on an island in the Caribbean Sea and claimed the land for Spain, a treaty between Spain and Portugal—the two most powerful maritime states of the time—settled a dispute over rights to explore and colonize new lands. The dividing line agreed upon in the 1494 Treaty of Tordesillas gave Spain rights to most of the Western Hemisphere, while Portugal received rights in Africa, the Indian Ocean, most of South and East Asia, and the as yet undiscovered eastern bulge of South America that became part of Brazil. During the following century, Spain seized control over many islands in the Caribbean Sea and Spanish war bands known as conquistadors conquered the Aztec Empire in Mexico and the Inca Empire in South America. While the Portuguese established sugar plantations in Brazil, patterned after their successful enterprises on the Madeira Islands, Spaniards concentrated on taking precious metals from the conquered Amerindians and establishing gold and silver mines.

Both the Spaniards and Portuguese enslaved Amerindians to work in their mines and plantations, transporting many from their native areas to other parts of the Caribbean where labor was needed. But the harsh conditions involved in mining and sugar agriculture produced extremely high mortality rates among Amerindian slaves, and diseases such as smallpox and influenza, to which native Americans had no resistance, took a high toll on the indigenous populations. The combination of enslavement, exportation, ill treatment, and disease killed large numbers of native Americans and nearly annihilated the Arawak and Carib populations of the Caribbean.[1] Government and church officials urged Spanish authorities to intervene to protect the natives, but the solution proposed in 1514 by Spanish priest Bartolomé de Las Casas—that Spain look to Africa for its New World labor needs—may have doomed another people to American slavery. Spaniards had brought a few African slaves to Hispaniola as early as 1502 and imported a large shipment of 250 slaves from Lisbon in 1510. Some African slaves were shipped directly from Africa to Santo Domingo and Cuba in 1519 and 1520 respectively, but the direct traffic from Africa became a regular practice after 1528, with Portugal—which had monopoly rights to Africa—serving as shipper. When Spain abolished Amerindian slavery in 1549, the slave trade from Africa to Spanish America increased rapidly.[2]

During the seventeenth century, other European states moved into the Caribbean, conquering territories from Spain and settling areas it had not colonized. France, England, the Dutch Republic (officially, the United Provinces), and Denmark established trading stations and plantations on several Caribbean islands and the northern coast of South America, known as the Guiana Coast. Initially these plantations produced a variety of tropical crops including coffee, cotton, and tobacco, but increasingly they turned to sugar production, which required large numbers of slave laborers. Between 1510 and 1867, ten to eleven million Africans were enslaved and transported across the Atlantic to the Americas.[3]

New World Slavery

The slavery introduced by Europeans into the New World differed from both that of pre-Columbian America and that of Asia and Africa. Many plantation societies in the Americas included more black slaves than free European colonists—in extreme cases the ratio was more than twenty to one. Unlike slave systems in Europe, Asia, and Africa, New World slavery increasingly became based on race and provided little opportunity for improvement or emancipation. In most cases, it lasted a lifetime, and slave status was passed from parent to child. American slavery was one of the most clearly defined systems of servitude and has shaped our conception of slavery everywhere.[4]

There were, however, variations in the practice of slavery throughout the Americas. The type of work required, regional climate, the character of the master, and the culture and values of the master class influenced the practice and experience of slavery. Slavery in Spanish and Portuguese colonies provided more opportunity for emancipation than in British colonies, as evidenced by the sizable free-colored communities in Latin America. Slavery in Spanish America was influenced by thirteenth-century Spanish law codes of *Siete Partidas*, which provided slaves more protection than Anglo-Saxon law did. Although Spanish slaves were considered property, quite a few enjoyed the right to earn money and purchase their freedom. The *Siete Partidas* gave slaves the right to be part of the religious community and to receive church sacraments. They also gave slaves the right to marry (although few were actually married by the church), and most slaves were denied many other protections of the code. The French established a harsh code of law for slaves, known as the *Code Noir*, or Black Code, but it also provided some security for slaves that allowed the growth of a sizable free black population in French colonies.[5] In Spanish colonies, both government policy and Catholic authorities urged settlers to proselytize among indigenous and black people, but Protestant settlers often feared that religious instruction and education would undermine slave discipline and encourage resistance.

Slave Rebellion in Spanish America before 1790

Although scholars have identified more than three hundred Amerindian village riots and uprisings against Spanish oppression in Central and South America from 1700 to 1900, there is very little record of Amerindian slave rebellion during the fifty years before Spain outlawed enslaving natives. One rare occurrence was a joint rebellion of Amerindian and African slaves in Puerto Rico in 1527. With slaves comprising only about 10 percent of Puerto Rico's population, that island experienced few other rebellions.

The first revolt of African slaves in the Americas occurred on Christmas Day 1521 at Santo Domingo, today's Dominican Republic. About twenty slaves on the estate of Governor Diego Colón, son of Christopher Columbus, staged an insurrection that caused the death of several whites. The rebels had been shipped directly from Africa and wanted to establish an African state, but they were quickly defeated by men on horseback, and several rebels were either killed or captured and brutally punished. Within weeks, the government issued the Ordinances of 1522, which set the standard of strict control over the slaves in the New World.[6]

Because the Spanish used forced labor primarily in its gold and silver mines, many early slave rebellions in the Americas involved miners. During the sixteenth century, mining slaves revolted in Cuba, Panama, Colombia, and Peru. In Colombia's Chocó region along the western coast, black mining slaves joined native Chocó Indians in a revolt against the Spanish in 1684, and staged another revolt in 1728. Although rumors of slave conspiracies continued, few developed into insurrections.

Mexico experienced at least four slave rebellions between 1527 and 1570, and slave riots occurred in Mexico City in 1624 and 1692. Conspiracies were thwarted in Mexico City in 1537 and 1612. In the latter case, an uprising had been planned for Christmas Day in response to the excessive punishment of a female slave. Many slaves were arrested, thirty-five of whom were executed, including seven women. Spanish America saw fewer slave revolts during the eighteenth century, probably because slaves increasingly gained their freedom through manumission and self-purchase.[7] The establishment of maroon communities by fugitive slaves was also very common in Mexico (see Chapter 6 and Primary Document 5).

Slave Rebellion in the Non-Spanish Caribbean before 1790

Other European countries began intruding on Spain's monopoly of the New World early in the seventeenth century. France started colonial expansion in the Caribbean in the 1620s and by the end of the century had established slave plantations on several islands, including major settlements on Guadeloupe, Martinique, and in Saint-Domingue. The English claimed the unsettled island of Barbados in 1627, seized Spanish Jamaica in 1655, and acquired several small islands from France—Grenada, Dominica, Saint Vincent, Saint Lucia, and Tobago—by treaty in 1763. The Dutch Republic established colonies on three islands off the coast of Venezuela—Aruba, Bonaire, and Curaçao—and on three islands in the northern Antilles—Saint Eustatius, Saba, and a portion of Saint Martin. Along with France and England, the Dutch Republic also established colonies in the Guiana region, on the northern coast of South America. In 1671, Denmark gained a foothold in the Caribbean by acquiring Saint Thomas, and went on to acquire Saint John and Saint Croix, collectively known as the Virgin Islands.

In the so-called sugar revolution of the seventeenth century, the cultivation of sugar cane spread from Brazil throughout the Caribbean region, increasing demand for slave labor and enticing English, French, and Dutch shippers to join the Portuguese in the transatlantic slave trade.[8] Altogether, nearly four and a half million enslaved Africans were taken to the Caribbean islands and the Guiana region, which was more than 40 percent of all slaves taken to the Americas. In general, slavery in the Caribbean was probably harsher than anywhere else in the New World. The labor regimen involved in sugar cultivation was intensive, and mortality rates were extremely high among the workers. In addition, Caribbean slaveholders were often absentee owners who entrusted the management of their plantations to overseers who had little vested interest in the well-being of the workers. It was seemingly easier and cheaper to replace workers with new imports from Africa than to establish practices that might promote healthier and longer slave lives. As a result, slaves were often worked to death. It is not surprising, therefore, that slave rebellions and fear of uprisings became widespread in the region.

England's Caribbean Colonies

At first, the English settlers of Barbados imported Irish and Scottish indentured servants to supply their labor needs, but as they changed from small-scale tobacco to large-scale sugar agriculture, they increasingly turned to slave labor. With nearly half a million African slaves imported to the island during the seventeenth century, the colony soon had twice as many black slaves as white colonists.

In the early years, while there were still forested areas, some slaves fled to the interior and established maroon communities. But during twenty-five years, from 1675 to 1701, four major conspiracies, or plots for rebellion, were discovered. The use of the word *conspiracy* by whites to refer to slaves' secret plans to escape bondage through flight or revolt shows that they did not accept slaves' right to resist enslavement, and considered such attempts both unlawful and sinister. After the island's first widespread conspiracy in the summer of 1675, more than one hundred suspected conspirators were arrested. Of the fifty-two executed, six were burned alive and eleven were beheaded. Five escaped brutal execution by committing suicide in jail. This violent reaction by the authorities indicates how severely the white community felt threatened.[9]

Another conspiracy discovered in 1686 prompted authorities to mandate precautionary measures such as limiting slave gatherings and guarding firearms more stringently. Despite these precautions, another widespread slave conspiracy was discovered in 1692. Three of its leaders, named Ben, Sambo, and Hammon, were arrested and, before being executed, were tortured into revealing that the rebels had organized military units with appointed leaders from among their ranks. Their aim was to capture firearms, horses, and ships, and then take control of the entire island and kill most of the white men. After another conspiracy was thwarted in 1701, no major slave revolts or conspiracies occurred in Barbados for more than one hundred years.

Another important British colony was established on Jamaica, which was captured from Spain in 1655. More than one million African slaves were imported to Jamaica, and by 1712, slaves outnumbered the colony's free whites ten to one. On Jamaica, hardly a decade passed without a revolt. The first plantation revolt took place in 1673, when two hundred slaves rose up and killed fourteen whites.[10]

One of Jamaica's worst insurrections of the eighteenth century started in the northeastern part of the island in April 1760 and rapidly spread westward, attracting perhaps as many as thirty thousand rebels. Like their leader, Tacky, nearly all of the rebels were African-born Akans—called Coromantees in Jamaica—from the West African coast then known as the Gold Coast, now Ghana. While destroying property and creating panic among the whites, the rebels avoided outright battles with army regulars and militia. The military forces were supported by many of the island's maroons, who had gained their freedom by promising to assist authorities in putting down slave revolts and returning fugitives. After more than a year of fighting, the combined force of soldiers, militia, and maroons defeated the rebels in the summer of 1761. Many rebels, including Tacky, were killed before the revolt was suppressed. Sporadic fighting continued in western Jamaica for months, and martial law was maintained until October 1761. By the time the last rebels surrendered, between three hundred and four hundred rebels had been killed, along with sixty whites and sixty free blacks. About 350 rebels were arrested, of whom about one hundred were brutally executed—some were slowly burned and others suspended and starved to death. Several rebels committed suicide rather than submit to torture and a more brutal death, and many were deported to the penal colony in British Honduras (now Belize).

After several years of relative quiet, another serious plan for rebellion was uncovered in Jamaica's western county of Hannover in July 1776. This time, the conspirators, including both African-born and creole slaves, planned to enlist the support of maroons and gain control of the whole island. Although well planned, the plot quickly unraveled after a rebel was caught with weapons in his possession. Suspected leaders were quickly arrested and tried, and six were executed. Trials of another 135 suspects continued for several months, after which another seventeen were executed, forty-five deported, and others severely flogged.[11]

Conspiracies and rebellions occurred on several other British islands. A major slave conspiracy was discovered on Antigua in 1736, organized by an African-born slave and a creole, both of whom held positions as slave drivers, or foremen. The betrayal of their plan, which called for capturing the whole island and creating an African-style kingdom, resulted in the execution of one hundred suspects and deportation of another forty-seven.[12]

A 1774 slave rebellion on Tobago killed three whites before being suppressed. Although some rebels escaped, thirty were captured, of whom seven leaders were tortured and burned alive, while minor participants were severely flogged.[13]

Dutch Caribbean West Indian Settlements

None of the Dutch Caribbean islands became important plantation colonies, but both Curaçao and Saint Eustatius, which served as centers in the Dutch slave trade, experienced slave revolts. The sole uprising on Saint Eustatius, which never had a large slave population, occurred in 1688 and was quickly suppressed.[14] Curaçao, whose few plantations served to provide food and shelter for slaves in transit, experienced its first revolt in 1716, when slaves newly arrived from Africa tried unsuccessfully to gain their freedom. In 1750, a revolt erupted spontaneously on the Hato plantation, during which slaves killed an unpopular slave driver, the plantation manager and his wife, and several slaves who opposed the uprising. A small military force dispatched by the governor quickly dispersed the rebels. Between sixty and one hundred rebels were killed or committed suicide during the conflict. Of those taken captive, thirty-four were executed, including thirteen women.[15]

The Dutch also established sugar plantations in its Guiana region—one on the Suriname River and smaller settlements in the valleys of the Berbice, Essequibo, and Demerara rivers, in today's Guyana. Here, black slaves outnumbered whites sometimes as much as twenty to one, and slave conditions were extremely harsh. Rebellion was a constant threat, and slaves escaping into the wilderness was a common phenomenon.

The Dutch acquired Suriname (formerly spelled Surinam and still pronounced in English as *soor-i-nam*) from the British in 1667 and expanded the plantation colony extensively. Although African slaves greatly outnumbered Europeans, there were surprisingly few slave revolts there, perhaps because of a sizable military presence and the opportunity for escape provided by the vast tropical rain forest. There were a number of single-plantation revolts, including one in 1750 that, although planned for a larger area, remained limited to the Bethlehem plantation. Motives for the rebellion included heavy workloads and harsh treatment, but also a personal grievance. The owner had demanded sexual favors from a slave woman who was the partner, or common-law wife, of a slave driver named Coridon, the leader of the rebellion. The rebels killed the owner and his assistant but were subdued before they could take the revolt further. Thirty-four slaves, including eleven women, were found guilty and sentenced to die, and several were executed in a most gruesome manner.

The last slave revolt in Suriname occurred in 1757, when 150 slaves stopped work at a lumber mill plantation and fled into the forest, where they found refuge in a maroon community. The incident prodded the colonial government to negotiate a treaty with the maroons a few years later (see Chapter 6).[16]

Berbice was the smallest of the Dutch Guiana settlements, with a 1760 population under six thousand, of whom only 275 were white colonists. Nearly all blacks were slaves, and another 250 were enslaved Amerindians. An epidemic of yellow fever, to which those of African descent were less susceptible, had killed many whites during the late 1750s. While slaves had attempted several conspiracies and six minor revolts in 1733 and 1762–1764, they staged a major revolt in 1763 that nearly drove out all white colonists.

In 1762–1763, Berbice had again been plagued by an epidemic of yellow fever that disabled or killed many in the white community. Taking advantage of the weakness of their oppressors, slaves planned an insurrection that began in February 1763 and quickly spread from plantation to plantation. Many whites fled to Fort Nassau, seat of the colonial government on the lower Berbice River, and those unable to escape were either massacred or taken captive. Because the fort did not guarantee safety, however, the refugees crowded onto three merchant ships and drifted downstream to take refuge at the estuary.

From among several rebel leaders, the insurgents elected as their chief a skilled slave named Kofi (Coffy by the Dutch, Cuffy by the English—see Biographies), who established a headquarters at Fort Nassau and set up a governance structure similar to that of the colonists. Rejecting the advice of more aggressive rebels who wanted to drive all whites from the colony, Kofi chose not to attack the refugees and instead, with the aid of captive secretaries and Amerindian messengers, tried to negotiate a peaceful settlement with the colonial governor, offering to divide the colony into two symbiotic entities—the interior controlled by the blacks, and the seaside by the colonists. Stalling for time while awaiting reinforcements from neighboring colonies and the mother country, the governor kept communications going with feigned interest in Kofi's proposal.

In August, rebel leaders who wanted to rid the entire colony of whites and thus disapproved of Kofi's strategy moved against him. One rival leader, named Accra (Akara), attacked a white settlement while another, named Atta, managed to depose Kofi as head of the rebel government. But the governor's military reinforcements began arriving about that time, and during the final months of 1763 troops dealt the rebels repeated defeats. Prevented by inhospitable Amerindians from finding safe haven in the forest, most surviving rebels returned to their plantations or were forced to surrender. The revolt effectively ended in March 1764.

The suppression of the rebellion and the reprisals that followed were marked by extreme cruelty. At four mass executions, at least 128 rebels died torturous deaths. When white control was completely reestablished in June 1764, the slave population had been reduced from about four thousand to twenty-five hundred, and the colonists were reduced from 350 to 116.[17]

Rebellion in the 1790s

The year 1791 was a watershed in the history of American slave rebellions. In that year, the largest and most successful of all slave revolts broke out in the French colony of Saint-Domingue. A turbulent time followed, with several slave revolts and conspiracies in the Caribbean and elsewhere. Several factors contributed to the increase in slave revolts, among them the human rights ideology that grew out of the eighteenth-century European Enlightenment and the reform movements it spawned, including a critical appraisal of slavery. Some of the slaves could read, domestics overheard conversations, and some slaves maintained contacts with free blacks who were often as well informed as white colonists. But the most significant catalysts for American slave revolts after 1790 seems to have been the French Revolution (1789–1799), with its ideology of liberty, equality, and fraternity, and the abolition of slavery in the French Empire in 1794.[18]

The Saint-Domingue Revolt and War of Independence

Located on the western third of Hispaniola, in what is now Haiti, Saint-Domingue was ceded to France in 1697. By the second half of the eighteenth century, it was a leading exporter of tropical staple crops, with a population of about half a million slaves, thirty thousand free blacks (often called mulattoes), and forty thousand white colonists. The revolt that began in 1791 was a complex and many-faceted series of events, influenced in part by the American Revolution (1775–1783), during which some Saint-Domingue mulattoes joined other Frenchmen in fighting against the British. In 1790, two years after the French Revolution began, Saint-Domingue's mulattoes staged a revolt that government troops quickly quashed. But the following year, an act of the French National Assembly extended citizenship to a large proportion of the colony's mulatto population and, in addition, it began debating whether slavery should be abolished in the French Empire.[19]

While the National Assembly moved slowly on the issue of abolition, the slaves of Saint-Domingue took their fate into their own hands. Led by a voodoo spiritual leader named Boukman, they rose against their masters in August 1791 and soon gained control over much of the northern countryside near the town of Le Cap (present-day Cap Haitien). Intending to destroy all plantations, they set fire to buildings and crops and created a cover of smoke so dense that for nearly three weeks, according to a contemporary source, the people of Le Cap could barely distinguish day from night. The rebels killed whites indiscriminately in revenge for the cruelties many of them had suffered, and government forces responded in like manner. According to historian C. L. R. James, twenty to thirty captured slaves were daily "broken at the wheel" (a form of execution in which the condemned was tied to a five-pronged table while each of his limbs was broken with an iron bar, after which he was killed with a blow to the chest). And as was sometimes the custom for executed criminals, their severed heads were placed on pikes along the road to Le Cap.[20]

Despite the brutal punishment, thousands of slaves as well as mulattoes and even some whites joined the rebellion. Boukman was killed in an early skirmish, but other leaders such as Jean François and Georges Biassou took over the leadership. They were soon joined by Toussaint de Bréda, a recently emancipated slave with uncommon intelligence and leadership ability. Toussaint distinguished himself by training fugitive slaves into effective soldiers and serving as an able negotiator for the rebels. A genius at organization and tactics, he quickly became a key leader of the rebellion, known as Louverture, meaning *the opening*, in recognition of his valor in creating a gap in the ranks of the enemy. By 1794 he had a large following, including several mulattoes and some white officers.

The early years of the rebellion were chaotic as patriots (defenders of the French Revolution) and royalists (its opponents) fought each other, as did wealthy planters and poor whites. Even free mulattoes, many of whom owned slaves and opposed abolition, vied with slaves for leadership of the rebellion. Under the leadership of André Rigaud, the mulattoes gained control over southern and western parts of Saint-Domingue, while Toussaint's forces temporarily formed an alliance with the Spanish of Santo Domingo and gained control over the northern and central regions of Saint-Domingue.

As the French Revolution progressed, its leadership became increasingly radical. By 1792 the monarchy was replaced by a republic, which declared war against Britain and Spain the following year. Most of Saint-Domingue's colonists and many mulattoes welcomed the twenty-five thousand invading British troops who captured the island's coastal ports and fortifications and defended slavery. But when tropical diseases killed over half of the British soldiers, Toussaint was able to drive the surviving troops from the island and then conquer neighboring Spanish Santo Domingo. When the revolutionaries abolished slavery in 1794, Toussaint declared his loyalty to the French Republic, which in turn appointed him deputy-governor and commander of the island's army.

Despite the official abolition of slavery, conflict in Saint-Domingue continued between whites and blacks and between mulattoes and emancipated slaves. By 1800, however, Toussaint had secured his leadership and was recognized as governor of the colony by France. But when Toussaint's government produced a constitution that established him as governor for life, it greatly irritated Napoleon Bonaparte, who ruled France in various capacities for much of the period 1799–1815. After making peace with Britain in 1801, Napoleon openly turned against Toussaint, rescinded the abolition of slavery, and sent nearly fifty thousand troops to reestablish his authority over Saint-Domingue. Lured into a meeting with French authorities, Toussaint was arrested and deported to France, where he died in prison in April 1803. Meanwhile, black generals led by Jean-Jacques Dessalines defeated the French troops in Saint-Domingue and permanently secured the colony's independence. Crowned emperor in 1804, President Dessalines gave the country its new name—Haiti.

The Haitian Revolution had widespread repercussions. Although it cost some two hundred thousand lives—mostly African Americans, but also at least fifty thousand European settlers, soldiers, and sailors—the rebellion produced "the world's first example of wholesale emancipation," bringing freedom to nearly half a million slaves. It also brought the greatest degree of social and economic change of any slave revolt, leaving the most productive colony of the day in ruins, eliminating its ruling class, and establishing an independent black state.[21] And for years to come, so-called French slaves and free blacks from Haiti participated in rebellions throughout the Caribbean region.[22]

Rebellion Spreads

Slaves on the French islands of Martinique and Guadeloupe were also influenced by the revolution in their mother country. As the French revolutionaries became more radical, rumors spread among Martinique's slaves that their emancipation was at hand and slaves became increasingly insubordinate. In the spring of 1793, slaves in Guadeloupe staged a violent revolt that killed twenty-two white colonists and damaged several plantations. These events on Martinique and Guadeloupe stimulated the French National Assembly to abolish slavery the following year.[23]

Undoubtedly encouraged by the rebellion in the French colonies and France's moves toward abolition, slaves in several other Caribbean colonies attempted revolts during the 1790s. None of these efforts, however, met with the success that ultimately came to Haiti.

Saint-Domingue's neighbor on Hispaniola was Santo Domingo, which Spain had continued to hold along with Puerto Rico and Cuba despite losing most of its Caribbean islands. Dramatically drawn into the Haitian Revolution, Santo Domingo experienced attempted slave revolts in 1795 and 1796. The first attempt, known as the Hinche Conspiracy, resulted in the arrest of nineteen suspected conspirators but no executions. But the following year, when an uprising at the large plantation of Boc Nigua killed a soldier and seven slaves, authorities sentenced its leaders, Tomas Congo and Ana Maria, to death by hanging, and other participants to severe flogging and several years of hard labor in irons.[24]

On the island of Grenada, slaves sought to win their freedom by joining free blacks in an attempt to throw off British rule in 1795–1796. Named for its free black leader, Julien Fédon (see Biographies), the Fédon Rebellion succeeded in establishing a short-lived republic patterned after the Republic of France, which had abolished slavery the previous year.

After Britain gained control over Grenada in 1783, a steady growth of manumissions, coupled with large-scale immigration of white French Roman Catholics, caused the free black class to grow to more than half the colony's free population. However, the personal freedom and aspirations of the free blacks were undercut by the British-controlled legislature. To Fédon and his fellow revolutionaries, the only way to guarantee their rights was to throw off British rule. Influenced by the French and Haitian revolutions and supported by France, which wanted to regain its lost eastern Caribbean empire, the revolutionaries raised a vast army of free blacks, slaves, maroons, and a few pro-French whites. In March 1795, Fédon appealed to all Grenadians to surrender to the republican forces. British refusal to capitulate resulted in sixteen months of military conflict, during which the revolutionaries took control of most of the colony and established a republican government.

By June 1796 the revolution was over. But it took ten thousand troops, including German mercenaries and a corps of military slaves, to subdue the rebels, restore British authority, and reestablish slavery. Many rebels escaped into the interior, including Fédon, who was never apprehended. But an estimated seven thousand revolutionaries died in action, and another four hundred were tried in special courts. Blacks convicted of rebellion were condemned to death, while convicted whites were exiled to the penal colony at British Honduras.[25]

Slave unrest also increased during the 1790s in British Dominica, whose free black population outnumbered slaves nearly two to one. Resistance to slavery on Dominica had usually taken the form of slaves escaping and hiding in the island's interior. In 1791, when officials denied slave demands for more free days to work their private plots, the slaves revolted and received support from many of the island's maroons. Nevertheless, the rebels were quickly overpowered by the militia. During the following years, as rebellions raged on other islands, Dominica's slaves' demands for improved working conditions gradually met with success.

In addition to this slave uprising in Dominica, black soldiers in a West India regiment stationed at the island mutinied in 1794, acting on a rumor that the regiment was to be disbanded and they were to be returned to work as plantation slaves. After the mutiny was suppressed, a court-martial resulted in six leaders being shot. The remaining 184 soldiers convicted of mutiny were distributed among other West India regiments.[26]

After many years of relative quiet, a major slave revolt broke out in the Dutch colony of Curaçao in 1795, influenced by both the rebellion then progressing in Saint-Domingue and the recent French takeover of the Dutch Republic. In August 1795, the Saint-Domingue revolutionary André Rigaud visited the plantation Knip, in the western part of Curaçao, and met with a slave named Tula (or Toela; see Biographies). Reasoning that French rule over Holland should also apply to Dutch colonies, Tula immediately started planning a revolt to force colonial authorities to abolish slavery. On August 17, about forty-five of Knip's slaves, insisting that French law made them free, refused to go to work. The uprising quickly spread. In less than a week as many as two thousand slaves took control of the plantations of western Curaçao, but colonial forces blocked them from moving to the more populated eastern side of the island.

After the rebels spurned officials' offer of general pardon if they surrendered, colonial authorities unleashed a force of several hundred militia, regular soldiers, and some free blacks against the insurgents. By the end of the month, the rebels were defeated. Colonial forces summarily executed armed rebels, and either imprisoned unarmed captives or cropped one of their ears for identification. Most of those who evaded death or capture returned to their plantations, while some went into hiding. About one hundred slaves had been killed during the fighting, and at least another sixty-four, including Tula, were tried and executed.[27]

Rebellions in the Nineteenth Century

After the turbulent decade of the 1790s, African Americans continued to rebel against slavery in Spanish America and the Caribbean until the institution was abolished throughout the region. The British Caribbean experienced conspiracies and revolts until 1831, and slaves rebelled in Spanish America in 1812 and 1835. A large slave riot in the Danish Caribbean led to emancipation in 1848.

The British Caribbean

Trinidad experienced its only attempted slave revolt in 1805. Although the island had been a Spanish possession until ceded to Britain in 1797, it had been settled and developed primarily by the French, whose treatment of slaves was relatively mild compared with that of other colonizers. But, influenced by events in Haiti and by slaves coming into the colony with masters fleeing that conflict,

Trinidad slaves planned a rebellion of their own. The plot was uncovered a few days before Christmas Day 1805, when the revolt was scheduled to commence, and was quickly quashed. Four suspected leaders were executed, and five other conspirators were deported after having their ears cut off.[28]

Also influenced by Haiti's success was a major revolt in Barbados, which had not experienced serious slave unrest since several conspiracies were suppressed at the turn of the eighteenth century. But in 1815, a rumor spread among the slave population that all slaves would be emancipated at the beginning of 1816. When this did not happen, resentment and tension deepened, and several craftsmen and other slave leaders organized a massive protest to demand their freedom on Easter weekend. Known as Bussa's Rebellion after its reputed leader, the rebellion quickly spread over the southeastern third of the island. Although they used guerilla tactics and a sophisticated strategy, the rebels were no match for British soldiers and militiamen. On just the second day of the uprising, a pitched battle that claimed the lives of only two soldiers but at least 120 slaves, including women and children, broke rebel resistance. Approximately three hundred slaves were tried for rebellion, of whom 144 were executed and 132 deported to British Honduras.

In 1823, a major insurrection occurred in Demerara, a colony ceded to Britain by the Dutch in 1814 along with neighboring Berbice and Essequibo, which together became known as Guyana. With a total slave population of about forty thousand, Demerara's and neighboring Essequibo's white settlers were outnumbered twenty to one. Although Demerara had experienced local slave revolts in the 1770s and in 1795, it had never had a major uprising. The 1823 rebellion, with an estimated nine thousand to twelve thousand participants, was one of the largest slave uprisings in the region.

Several factors contributed to heightened slave discontent during the summer of 1823. Demerara was gradually shifting from coffee and cotton to sugar cultivation, which required a much harsher work regime. During the early 1800s, work among the slaves by the London Missionary Society had increased slave literacy, enhanced slaves' sense of self-worth, and given some slaves positions of leadership as teachers and deacons. A May 1823 decree requiring slaves to receive written permission from their masters before they could attend religious services angered the large number of Christianized slaves. Also aware of the Haitian Revolution and Parliament's deliberations concerning the abolition of slavery, some slaves believed that British legislation recently received in Demerara concerning the treatment of slaves was actually an emancipation law.

A group of slaves, including a mild-mannered church deacon named Quamina (see Biographies) and his more aggressive son, Jack Gladstone, began planning a protest in case the governor and planters did not soon honor the law they believed ordered their freedom. They planned to disarm and constrain the whites and then send the governor their demand for the "new law." When some of the leaders suggested that violence would be unavoidable, Quamina, who had insisted that no whites be harmed in the uprising, made a last-minute attempt to call it off. Jack, however, ordered it to proceed.

On Monday, August 18, slaves took control of nearly forty plantations on the east coast of the colony, less than a tenth of Demerara's estates. They locked up owners and managers, many in stocks, and after confiscating any guns and ammunition they could find, fled to the plantations' back areas. Later that day, a group of about forty armed slaves marching to Georgetown to demand their rights encountered the governor, who had been out investigating rumors of a rebellion. Dismissing the slaves' demands, the governor ordered them to drop their arms and return to work. As the slaves continued to press their demands, their ranks grew to over two hundred. Finally making a quick dash for safety, the governor and his party rode off to Georgetown. After sending about five hundred soldiers from the colony's garrison to the area of turmoil, he declared martial law and ordered all colonial men to report for militia duty. On Wednesday more than two thousand armed rebels led by Jack Gladstone surrounded the military unit and again presented their demands. When they refused to obey an order to put down their arms and disperse, the military opened fire and killed around 250 fleeing slaves.

Hoping to break the rebellion more peacefully, the governor issued proclamations offering a pardon to those slaves who returned to their plantations and surrendered their arms but promising severe punishment to those who did not. Over the next few days, the soldiers went from one plantation to the next liberating imprisoned whites and executing randomly chosen slaves, disregarding both the promise of pardon and the degree to which individuals had participated in the uprising. Although there had been very little violence on the slaves' part—only three whites were killed during the conflict—retribution was brutal.

Many rebels went into hiding but fugitives were eventually captured or killed. More than one hundred slaves were imprisoned, including many wounded who received no care or treatment. Even as the military continued its plantation executions, rebel trials began in Georgetown. Although the legal system condemned fifty-one slaves to death, it actually executed only thirty-three. Also tried on grounds of encouraging the revolt was missionary John Smith (see Biographies). Convicted and sentenced to death, he was granted clemency by the British government but died in prison before news of the pardon reached Demerara. The 1823 Demerara Rebellion failed, but the brutal repression of the slaves and the death of a white clergyman invigorated antislavery debate in the British Parliament and influenced its passage ten years later of an emancipation act.[29]

Another revolt that influenced Parliament's deliberations occurred in Jamaica, Britain's most important sugar colony, in 1831–1832. The colony had experienced considerable slave unrest for several decades, as a declining sugar market forced many plantations to cease production, go into bankruptcy, or sell to new owners. Slaves on operating plantations were worked increasingly hard, while those on collapsed plantations were hired out for onerous tasks or left to provide for themselves. Revolutionary turmoil in other colonies and antislavery debates in Parliament strengthened slaves' expectations of freedom and heightened tension between them and their masters, who vehemently opposed emancipation and resisted all measures aimed at ameliorating slave conditions.

In 1831, believing that emancipation was near but that slaveholders were determined to prevent its implementation, a network of about twelve elite slaves on Jamaica's west side began planning mass action to force planters to grant them their freedom. With the sugar crop ready for harvest in December, leaders called for a general work stoppage after Christmas, urging slaves to claim their right to freedom and refuse to work without pay. The plan was carried to slaves across the western part of Jamaica by parish leaders, including an eloquent lay-preacher named Samuel Sharpe (see Biographies), the rebellion's paramount leader. On the night of December 27, fires across the horizon signaled the beginning of the insurrection. Slaves had been instructed simply to sit down and refuse to work, and if they were attacked, to retaliate by burning buildings, not by harming persons or crops. But they had also been urged to drive whites off the plantations if they could, and to seize weapons for their own protection. As sixty thousand slaves joined the rebellion, many resorted to plunder, intimidation, and fighting. Panicking whites fled to the towns as local militias, imperial soldiers and sailors, and maroons loyal to the government subdued the rebels. Only fourteen whites, most of them soldiers, were killed in the fighting, testifying to the rebels' restraint. However, approximately two hundred slaves were killed.

Although sporadic fighting continued into February, the uprising was quelled within two weeks. Government retaliation was severe. Approximately 630 rebels, including seventy-five women, were arrested and tried before military tribunals, and all but twenty-five were convicted. At least 350 rebels were shot or hanged, often immediately following the verdict, and fifteen were deported. The uprising became known as the Christmas Rebellion or, because many of its leaders were members of the Baptist church, the Baptist War. A few white ministers sympathetic to the slaves traveled to England to testify on their behalf at parliamentary hearings that contributed to adoption of Britain's Emancipation Act in 1833.[30]

Spanish South America and Cuba

The largest concentrations of slaves in Spanish America were in the mining areas of Colombia, Venezuela, and Peru, all of which experienced slave rebellions from the sixteenth through the eighteenth centuries. Increasing numbers of slaves gained freedom through manumission and self-purchase early in the nineteenth century, but some slaves still sought emancipation through rebellion. In 1812, uprisings occurred in all three of these Spanish colonies, and during the 1820s slaves joined the colonists' struggles for independence, especially when promised freedom in return for their collaboration. However, after independence was won, many slave owners continued to oppose abolition and refused to honor the promises of freedom. As a result, the mines of Colombia and Venezuela saw slave rebellions again in 1843. The abolition of slavery in Spanish South America came through a gradual process that was completed during the 1850s.[31]

Cuba's initial reliance on small-scale agriculture and ranching required relatively few slaves, and Spanish law made slave self-purchase both possible and frequent. As a result, a sizable free black population that enjoyed considerable rights and social mobility comprised nearly 20 percent of Cuba's population by 1812. However, with the rise of sugar plantation agriculture during the 1790s, Cuban planters imported enormous numbers of enslaved Africans—three hundred thousand during the thirty years between 1790 and 1820—increasing the island's slave population from 38,000 in 1773 to 436,000 in 1841. By 1843, slaves comprised 43 percent of the island's population.[32]

Cuba's transformation into a true slave society eroded the rights and privileges of the island's primarily creole free blacks, sharpened the division between them and the white population, and increasingly pushed them to identify and ally with the new African-born slave population. Free black urban artisans took a leading role in what became known as the Aponte Rebellion of 1812, a series of revolts and conspiracies in four Cuban cities. Slaves revolted on five plantations in Puerto Principe (now known as Camaguey), in the central part of the island on January 15 and 16. Arrests and interrogations enabled authorities to prevent rebellions planned for the eastern cities of Bayamo and Holguin. And on the western end of the island, military force kept revolts on three plantations outside Havana on March 15 and 16 from spreading and becoming the first stage of an attack on the capital city itself.

In all three areas, slave and free black organizers used the holiday season starting in December 1811 to hold secret meetings and recruit participants. In each area the plan was to the same end: liberate slaves on outlying plantations and then form battalions to attack and take control of the cities themselves. Recruitment was aided by rumors that slaves had been freed by royal decree, which the island's masters were suppressing, and that revolutionaries from Haiti would be assisting their efforts.

In Puerto Principe, slaves killed eight whites and destroyed much plantation property before military forces suppressed them. Scores of slaves escaped to the mountains, however, and were rumored to be headed east to Bayamo and Holguin. Amid growing hysteria, authorities moved white people from the countryside into the cities, stationed patrols, and searched for runaways from Puerto Principe. Interrogations led to the betrayal of plans in both cities in February and March.

On March 15, as plantation uprisings on the outskirts of Havana killed ten whites and completely razed one estate, a declaration of independence was tacked to the door of the Havana home of a high-ranking Spanish official, proclaiming the slaves' intention of ending "this empire of tyranny." Authorities later learned that the rebellion's urban leaders had diagrams of the forts protecting Havana's entrances and had planned to arm liberated plantation slaves with weapons and ammunition seized there. But a combined force of standing army, militia, and armed citizens quickly suppressed the plantation insurrections and forced the rebels to flee into the countryside. Over the next several months, most were hunted down and captured.

Trials and executions quickly followed the incidents in all three regions. Through extensive trial testimony, authorities learned that most of the organizers of Havana's revolt were free black artisans, and that a large number were members of Havana's free black militia. They also concluded that all of the uprisings and conspiracies were part of a single island-wide rebellion planned by José Antonio

Aponte, a retired captain of the free black militia and a pensioned veteran (see Biographies).

Of the nearly four hundred persons convicted of participating in the rebellions, thirty-four leaders were executed and nearly two hundred others lashed at public ceremonies that also awarded freedom to informants and slaves who had helped suppress the uprisings. Despite the attempt to convince slaves that loyalty to masters and obedience to the existing order would benefit them more than resistance, rumors of slave plots became common. Authorities suspected involvement by persons connected with the Aponte Rebellion in a number of incidents that occurred during the 1830s and 1840s, particularly a major conspiracy in 1844 that resulted in the deportation of hundreds of slaves and free blacks and brutal lashing of thousands more. Authorities also reacted with a harsh repression against slaves, free blacks, and abolitionists.[33] Although Cuba continued to import slaves until 1867 and did not abolish slavery until 1886, there were no further slave uprisings on the island.

Danish Saint Croix

Among the last of the Caribbean slave uprisings was a dramatic event on the Danish island of Saint Croix in 1848. Denmark had been a minor participant in the Atlantic slave trade, and the slave population of its Caribbean colonies was relatively small before 1790. In 1792, Denmark outlawed the slave trade, with the ban to take effect in 1802. Slave importation was brisk during that last decade and resulted in a slave population in the Danish islands of about thirty-two thousand in 1815, compared with only three thousand whites and five thousand free blacks. Most of the population lived at Saint Croix.

Slave rebellions had been rare in the Danish Caribbean. The only significant uprising before the nineteenth century had been a revolt in 1733, during which more than a hundred slaves seized control of the island of Saint John for several months, without much violence on either side. Then a dramatic revolt took place at Saint Croix in 1848, a year after Denmark began abolishing slavery through a gradual process of emancipation. Under the plan of gradual abolition, children born to slaves were to be henceforth free, but adults were required to serve an "apprenticeship" of up to twelve years. But the slaves did not want to wait that long. Influenced by events in the nearby French Caribbean, Saint Croix slaves planned to revolt if they could not achieve immediate emancipation through peaceful demonstration. On July 3, 1848, nearly half of the island's slave population refused to go to work. Led by a plantation driver named Gotlieb Bordeaux, also known as General Buddoe, several thousand slaves gathered in front of the government building at Frederiksted to demand their freedom. The island's Governor-General Peter von Scholten, who had encouraged considerable amelioration of slave conditions since the 1820s, feared that slaves might set the town on fire and many lives would be lost if he was not conciliatory. Addressing the crowd, he unexpectedly announced: "Now you are free, you are hereby emancipated."[34]

Slaves met the nonviolent grant of freedom with elation, but long pent-up resentment, along with doubts that slave owners would honor the governor's edict, erupted into rioting that lasted for three days. With police unable to halt the looting and destruction of property, Von Scholten suffered a nervous collapse and became unable to discharge his duties. His successor declared a state of emergency, called for assistance from naval units, and brought in 530 soldiers from Puerto Rico to restore order. More than one hundred blacks were arrested and taken before a specially created commission of justice, which convicted seven persons of felonies and sentenced them to death. General Buddoe, the leader of the demonstration, was deported.[35]

Conclusion

From the beginning of their enslavement in America, African slaves tried to gain their freedom through various acts of insubordination, including insurrection. In the face of almost certain failure and brutal punishment, miners, plantation workers, craftsmen, and domestic slaves repeatedly rose in spontaneous or well-planned revolts. Although some slaves won their freedom through escape or self-purchase, only one rebellion—the Haitian Revolution—brought lasting freedom to a large number of slaves. Enlightenment ideals and the example of the French Revolution inspired a growing number of slave revolts, which bolstered the abolition movement and terminated slavery in much of the Caribbean region and the Spanish American mainland.

Notes

1. Hilary Beckles, "Kalinago Resistance to European Colonization of the Caribbean," in *Caribbean Slavery in the Atlantic World*, ed. Verene Shepherd and Hilary Beckles (Kingston, Jamaica: Randle Publishers, 2000), 117–126.

2. See Bartolomé de Las Casas, *The Devastation of the Indies: A Brief Account. Translated by Herma Briffault with an introduction by Bill M. Donovan* (Baltimore: Johns Hopkins University Press, 1992); *General History of the Caribbean*, vol. 2, *New Societies: The Caribbean in the Long Sixteenth Century*, ed. P. C. Emmer and Germán Carrera Damas (London: UNESCO Publishing/Macmillan Education, 1999), 159–179.

3. See Philip D. Curtin, *The Rise and Fall of the Plantation Complex* (New York: Cambridge University Press, 1990). For Atlantic slave trade statistics, see Johannes Postma, *The Atlantic Slave Trade* (Westport, CT: Greenwood Press, 2003), 36.

4. Howard Temperley, "New World Slavery, Old World Slavery," in *Serfdom and Slavery: Studies in Legal Bondage*, ed. M. L. Bush (London: Longman, 1996), 145.

5. Herbert S. Klein, *African Slavery in Latin America and the Caribbean* (New York: Oxford University Press, 1986), 190–196.

6. Lynne Guitar, "Boiling It Down: Slavery on the First Commercial Sugarcane Ingenios in the Americas," in *Slaves, Subjects, and Subversives: Blacks in Colonial Latin America*, ed. Jane G. Landers and Barry M Robinson (Albuquerque: University of New Mexico Press, 2006), 49–52.

7. William F. Sharp, "Manumission, *Libres*, and Black Resistance: The Colombian Chocó, 1680–1810," in *Slavery and Race Relationa in Latin America*, ed. Robert B. Toplin (Westport, CT: Greenwood Press, 1974), 89–107; Klein, *African Slavery*, 205–207; Ida Altman, Sarah Cline, and Juan Javier Pescador, *The Early History of Greater Mexico* (Upper Saddle River, NJ: Prentice Hall, 2003), 215; and *Chronology of World Slavery*, ed. Junius P. Rodriguez (Santa Barbara, CA: ABC-CLIO, 1999), 152, 159, 173–174, 176, 179, 182.

8. Curtin, *Plantation Complex*, 73–85.

9. See Michael Craton, *Testing the Chains: Resistance to Slavery in the British Caribbean* (Ithaca, NY: Cornell University Press, 1982), 105–124, 254–266, for slave conspiracies and revolts at Barbados.

10. See Orlando Patterson, "Slavery and Slave Revolts: A Sociohistorical Analysis of the First Maroon War, 1665–1740," *Social and Economic Studies* 19 (1970): 289–325; *Chronology of World Slavery*, 159–160.

11. For Tacky's Revolt and the Hannover Plot, see Craton, *Testing the Chains*, 125–139, 172–179.

12. Ibid., 115–124; David Barry Gaspar, *Bondmen and Rebels: A Study of Master-Slave Relations in Antigua* (Baltimore: Johns Hopkins University Press, 1985).

13. Craton, *Testing the Chains*, 140–158.

14. Cornelis Ch. Goslinga, *The Dutch in the Caribbean and the Guianas, 1680–1791* (Assen, Netherlands: Van Gorcum, 1985), 129.

15. H. P. van Weeren, "De Slavenopstand van 1795 op Curaçao" (master's thesis, University of Amsterdam, 1978), 19–21; Goslinga, *Caribbean and the Guianas*, 81, 113, 128.

16. Rudi Otto Beeldsnijder, '*Om Werk van jullie te hebben;*' *Plantage-slaven in Suriname, 1730–1750* (Utrecht: BSA Series, University of Utrecht, 1994), 231–235; Goslinga, *Caribbean and the Guianas*, 301, 392–393.

17. See Hilary Beckles and Verene Shepherd, eds., *Caribbean Slave Society and Economy: A Student Reader* (Kingston, Jamaica: Randle Publishers, 1991), 378–381; and Goslinga, *Caribbean and the Guianas*, 461–494.

18. See David P. Geggus, "Slave Resistance in the Spanish Caribbean in the Mid-1790s," in *A Turbulent Time: The French Revolution and the Greater Caribbean*, ed. David Barry Gaspar and David P. Geggus (Bloomington: Indiana University Press, 1997).

19. For an assessment of the revolt, see Laurent Dubois, *Avengers of the New World: The Story of the Haitian Revolution* (Cambridge, MA: Harvard University Press, 2004); and David P. Geggus, *Haitian Revolutionary Studies* (Bloomington: Indiana University Press, 2002).

20. C. L. R. James, *The Black Jacobins: Toussaint L'Ouverture and the San Domingo Revolution*, rev. ed. (New York: Vintage Books, 1989), 88, 96.

21. Geggus, *Haitian Revolutionary Studies*, 5; and David P. Geggus, ed., *The Impact of the Haitian Revolution in the Atlantic World* (Columbia: University of South Carolina Press, 2001), Preface, ix.

22. Geggus, *Impact of the Haitian Revolution*, xii.

23. Laurent Dubois, *A Colony of Citizens: Revolution and Slave Emancipation in the French Caribbean, 1787–1804* (Chapel Hill: University of North Carolina Press, 2004), 31–50, 62–98.

24. Geggus, "Slave Resistance in the Spanish Caribbean," 131–155.

25. Curtis Jacobs, "The Fédons of Grenada, 1763–1814" (paper presented at the Grenada Country Conference, Grenada, January 2002); Edward L. Cox, "Fédon's Rebellion, 1795–1796: Causes and Consequences," *Journal of Negro History* 67 (Spring 1982): 7–19.

26. Craton, *Testing the Chains*, 140–145, 169, 183, 224–233.

27. Cornelis Ch. Goslinga, *The Dutch in the Caribbean and in Surinam, 1791/1795–1942* (Assen, Netherlands: Van Gorcum, 1990), 1–20; Van Weeren, "De Slavenopstand van 1795 op Curaçao."

28. Craton, *Testing the Chains*, 224–238.

29. For a detailed account and analysis of the Demerara revolt, see Emelia Viotti da Costa, *Crowns of Glory, Tears of Blood: The Demerara Slave Rebellion of 1823* (New York: Oxford University Press, 1994).

30. For the Baptist War, see Craton, *Testing the Chains*, 291–321; and Richard Hart, *Slaves Who Abolished Slavery: Blacks in Rebellion* (Jamaica: University of the West Indies, 1985), 221–273.

31. Dubois, *Colony of Citizens*, 91–92; Altman, Cline, and Pescador, *Early History of Greater Mexico*, 215; and *Chronology of World Slavery*, 159, 173–174, 176, 179, 182.

32. Matt D. Childs, *The 1812 Aponte Rebellion in Cuba and the Struggle against Atlantic Slavery* (Chapel Hill: University of North Carolina Press, 2006); Franklin W. Knight, *Slave Society in Cuba During the Nineteenth Century* (Madison: University of Wisconsin Press, 1970), 22, 85–120.

33. Childs, *1812 Aponte Rebellion*; Herbert S. Klein, *African Slavery in Latin America and the Caribbean* (New York: Oxford University Press, 1986), 212–213.

34. Neville A. T. Hall, *Slave Society in the Danish West Indies*, posthumously completed and edited by B. W. Higman (Baltimore: Johns Hopkins University Press, 1992), 15, 208.

35. Ibid., 1–5, 11, 25–33, 62–63, 66–67, 208–227.

CHAPTER 5

Slave Revolts in Brazil and North America

Brazil and the United States, the two most populous countries in the Western Hemisphere, provide valuable similarities and contrasts in the discussion of slavery and slave rebellion. Both had a stable, resident slave-owning class, in contrast to the absenteeism of plantation owners in the Caribbean region. Some 40 percent of the enslaved Africans transported across the Atlantic were taken to Brazil, while only 4 percent were shipped to the North American areas that became the United States. Yet, African American populations became vital in both countries. The United States developed a strong racial division between whites and blacks, while Brazil was more tolerant of racial mixing, although degrees of color remained important factors in social and economic status.[1] Both Brazil and the United States experienced slave rebellions, but none as severe as those in the Caribbean region, and emancipation in both came later than in much of the Caribbean region.

Brazil

Portugal claimed Brazil after Pedro Alvares Cabral discovered its coastal regions in 1500, and began systematic colonization until the 1530s. Hoping to replicate the success of the Madeira Island sugar enterprises, Portuguese settlers established sugar plantations in the new colony and by the end of the century had made Brazil the leading sugar producer in the world. Along with Spanish American colonies during the early nineteenth century, Brazil declared its independence in 1822 but continued to be governed by a member of the Portuguese royal family, Emperor Pedro I. In 1889, Brazil became a republic, which it remains to this day. With more than four million slaves imported between 1538 and 1851, the institution of slavery played a crucial role in Brazil's economy and society. Not until 1888, a year before adopting a republican form of government, did Brazil abolish slavery—the last country to do so in the Western Hemisphere.

Slavery

As in Spanish America, the Portuguese initially enslaved indigenous Amerindians to work their New World plantations but quickly turned to Africa to supply its labor needs. Enslaved Africans began arriving in Brazil in 1538 and by 1600 outnumbered the colony's Amerindian slaves. Approximately four million Africans arrived in Brazil over the next two hundred years, many of whom intermarried with the indigenous population or, to a much lesser extent, European immigrants. By 1800, Brazil's indigenous people had been reduced significantly, while Africans and those of African ancestry comprised approximately half of the colony's population. About 80 percent of the African Brazilians were slaves.[2]

Although Brazilian slavery has sometimes been described as having been more benign than that of North America, historian Robert Conrad has concluded that "the physical condition endured by slaves in Brazil made life there considerably more precarious and uncomfortable—in the physical sense—than it was for most slaves in the United States." Perhaps due in part to the low standard of living that existed throughout the land, slave mortality rates were very high in Brazil. An 1818 report to the Portuguese king described the relationship between masters and slaves as "a state of domestic war."[3] Although intermarriage and manumission were quite common, racial prejudice remained strong. Skin color was a vital criterion for social status, keeping free blacks as well as slaves in a state of subjugation.

Slave Conspiracies and Revolts

Except for a few local slave uprisings in the coastal sugar-growing province of Bahia in 1607, Brazil had no significant slave uprisings during its first 150 years. Perhaps the lack of open resistance was due to the opportunity slaves had to liberate themselves by fleeing into untamed hinterlands and establishing communities that were difficult to reach and suppress. Even when slaves rebelled, as they did again in Bahia in 1695 and 1719, the uprisings enabled large numbers of slaves to gain their freedom through flight. One of the colony's earliest maroon communities, which in Brazil were called *quilombos,* was Palmares, which lasted from about 1605 to 1694 and sheltered thousands of self-emancipated African Brazilians (see Chapter 6). While offering sanctuary to fugitives, *quilombos* sometimes encouraged and assisted the slave rebellions that became more prevalent during the eighteenth and nineteenth centuries.

In 1719, a major conspiracy was discovered in Brazil's interior province of Minas Gerais, where slaves who worked in the region's gold mines vastly outnumbered the free population. In plotting the overthrow of their masters, the rebels established their own cadre of leaders, including a king and a military commander. Once the plot was uncovered, though, the rebel leaders were quickly arrested and punished. Though suppressed, the conspiracy illustrated the region's vulnerability to slave uprisings. As the governor reported to the king of Portugal: "Since we cannot prevent the remaining blacks from thinking, and cannot deprive them of their natural desire for freedom ... it must be concluded that this country will always be subjected to this problem" (see Primary Document 7). Indeed, another conspiracy was uncovered in this mining region in 1756.

Undoubtedly stimulated by the great slave revolt in Haiti, Brazilian slave unrest increased so significantly after 1800 that fear of rebellion became endemic among slaveholders. Bahia experienced a series of revolts and conspiracies beginning in 1804, when slaves from a large plantation in the southern part of the province fled into the surrounding forest, from which they harassed and plundered the plantation for two years, effectively stopping all production. In 1806, a group of seventeen rebels went to the owner's home to negotiate an end to hostilities, proposing to return to work in exchange for improved working conditions and a letter of manumission for their leader, Gregoria. Pretending to agree, the owner directed the men to the nearby government office, where they were promptly arrested. Gregoria was imprisoned to await trial, and his fate is unknown; but his companions were re-enslaved and exiled to another province.[4]

In 1807, an elaborate plot to capture ships and sail to Africa was foiled in Bahia's capital, Salvador. Of thirteen conspirators arrested, two were executed and the others severely flogged. Others escaped to maroon communities and, despite repressive measures enacted to deter rebellion, succeeded in launching a revolt in 1809. However, their initial attack on the town of Nazaré das Farinhas failed, and while many rebels again escaped to maroon communities, nearly a hundred were captured, and their fate is unknown.

In 1810, Bahia received a new governor, the Count of Arcos, who hoped to end the wave of rebellions with a more enlightened policy that mandated improved treatment of slaves, milder punishments, and opportunities for slaves to practice their African religions and traditions. Despite these measures, three slave revolts occurred during Arcos's eight years in office. Slave rebellion reached a crisis point in 1814, when several hundred slaves escaped from Salvador into the outlying country, attacked plantations and fishing villages, and killed several white overseers as well as slaves who refused to join their ranks. During a fierce battle with cavalry units dispatched to quell the rampage, fifty-eight slaves and fourteen soldiers were killed. While most rebels managed to escape, four captives were sentenced to death and many others were publicly flogged. Several free blacks who had supported the insurrection were deported to Portuguese stations in Africa.[5]

A petition from Bahia merchants to Brazil's ruler, Prince Dom João, reveals the intense anxiety and fear that gripped the white population after the 1814 uprising. According to the petitioners, slaves, who greatly outnumbered whites and free mulattoes, had killed many whites and would kill all if the government did not take measures to control them. The petition claimed that while slaves of different ethnicity had often quarreled in the past, they had cooperated with each other in this rebellion, coordinating attacks against their masters. The merchants also feared that escaped rebels had established many more *quilombos*, especially in the vicinity around Salvador.[6] Four years later, another revolt took place in Bahia that killed several whites and destroyed much property. After Brazil gained its independence in 1822, five minor revolts occurred in quick succession between 1823 and 1830, but none of these were as dramatic as one that followed.

The Malê Urban Revolt of 1835

During the early decades of the nineteenth century, Bahia imported thousands of slaves from the Bay of Benin region, through the Nigerian port of Lagos. Many were Muslims of Hausa and Yoruba ethnicity who had been enslaved as prisoners of war. These newcomers increased the young African-born segment of Bahia's population, especially in and around Salvador, and thus also the propensity for slave rebellion there. Their impact is evident in the numerous revolts and conspiracies between 1806 and 1835.

Prior to 1835, revolts in Brazil occurred primarily in rural areas. But in 1835, Salvador experienced a revolt carried out essentially by urban slaves, who were less regimented than mining or plantation slaves and many of whom were often hired out as specialists. Muslims were prominent among the rebellion's leadership, and many of the rebels—slave and free alike—were also Muslims. Some wore amulets into battle that contained folded Koranic verses written in Arabic. This revolt, therefore, became known as the Malê (Muslim) Rebellion.

The rebels planned to take over the police barracks, seize weapons and ammunition, and take control of the city before moving on to plantations to free the slaves there. Authorities learned about the planned revolt on the evening before it was scheduled to start and, in a search of suspects' homes, broke in upon a meeting of rebel leaders that included its chief leader, Ahuna. Two rebel groups took to the streets calling for others to join them and rallied an estimated four to five hundred rebels who, despite having been forced to act prematurely, gained control over the inner-city streets. However, a well-armed militia and government troops defended strategic buildings and by early morning had forced the rebels to scatter.

About seventy rebels were killed in the conflict and many more subsequently died of wounds. Of more than one hundred arrested and tried, eleven were sentenced to death for leadership roles. Other rebels were sentenced to imprisonment or forced labor, but most were sentenced to flogging. Many of those flogged received more than a hundred lashes, and some received as many as one thousand—a brutal punishment that few survived. Most of the free men convicted of supporting the rebels were deported to Africa. And many slaves, convicted simply of being of Hausa or Yoruba ethnicity or of possessing a knife or documents written in Arabic, were sold and exported to other provinces.

The defeat of the Malê rebels was followed by repressive decrees and legislation in Bahia and other provinces that affected both slaves and free African Brazilians. Monitored by special inspectors, forced to pay a special tax, placed under strict curfews, and required to wear identity tags, slaves and free blacks lived in a virtual police state. Dancing and other African cultural expressions were forbidden. But the laws were not always strictly applied, and the cultural repression and ethnic persecution may actually have strengthened the common identity of all people of African descent, slave and free.[7]

Only a few slave rebellions took place in Brazil during the following half century: the so-called Balaiada movement in northern Brazil in 1838, three localized conspiracies in 1854, and a revolt at Campinas in São Paulo in 1882. And finally, one year before slavery was abolished in Brazil in 1888, slaves abandoned plantations in São Paulo en masse, forcing slaveholders to grant them their freedom.

North America

Colonial North America was initially quite diverse. In addition to the English settlements in New England and along the East Coast from Pennsylvania to Georgia, Spain had settlements in Florida and Georgia and also acquired the French colony of Louisiana. The Dutch colonized what is now New York City and part of Connecticut, and Swedes had a settlement in the Delaware Valley. While indentured servants were a significant element of the workforce in the English colonies, all of these settlements contained slaves. A few Amerindians were initially enslaved, especially in the Spanish colonies, but as elsewhere in the Americas, Africans eventually became the sole enslaved class in North America.

Compared to the other regions, however, the importation of enslaved Africans into the area that became the United States was relatively small—about four hundred thousand, or about 4 percent of the aggregate number brought to the Western Hemisphere. The first African slaves imported to the North American continent went to Spanish settlements in what are now Georgia and Florida during the sixteenth century. In the following century, in 1620, a shipment of twenty Africans was sold to the English settlement at Jamestown, Virginia, probably contraband from a captured Portuguese or Spanish ship. By 1700, the slave population in British North America reached about twenty-eight thousand, of whom twenty-three thousand lived in the southern colonies. In 1800, the total United States population of 5.3 million persons included slightly more than one million African Americans, of whom about 90 percent were slaves. Twenty-five years later, the slave population had nearly doubled and represented 36 percent of all slaves in the Western Hemisphere. In contrast to many other American regions, the natural increase of the slave population in North America was very high, and American-born, or creole, slaves quickly outnumbered African-born. Among the causes of this rapid increase in slave population were the temperate climate and the absence of absentee landlords. Undesirable as the slave's lot was, North American slaves were generally better off than those in many other parts of the Americas.[8]

Revolts in Colonial North America

Although few details survive concerning early slave insurrections and conspiracies in North America, Herbert Aptheker, the first historian to conduct a serious scholarly study of slave revolts in this region, found records of approximately 250 rebellions, conspiracies, or rumors of conspiracies that involved ten or more slaves from the seventeenth century through the Civil War.[9] The first recorded slave revolt in North America occurred in 1526, when several slaves at a Spanish colony in what is now Georgia rose against their masters and fled into the wilderness to find refuge among the Indians. The first slave conspiracy in British North America, in Virginia in 1663, involved white indentured servants as well as black slaves. One of the servants betrayed the plot and was rewarded with his freedom and five thousand pounds of tobacco, while his black co-conspirators were executed. Little is known about the few other slave conspiracies that occurred in Virginia and Maryland during the last three decades of the seventeenth century.

As the slave population of the southern colonies increased during the early eighteenth century, acts of resistance also increased. Some slaves escaped and fled to mountainous and marshy areas or to Spanish Florida, where in 1693 King Charles II offered freedom to slaves fleeing English colonies. Some used violence to attempt to gain their freedom, and others rebelled to protest overwork or cruel treatment.

In 1708, a small group of slaves revolted on Long Island, New York, killing seven whites before they were overpowered. Of the four slaves executed, one was a woman and another an Indian man. Another small-scale revolt occurred in New York in 1712, during which about twenty-five slaves armed with guns and clubs burned down houses on the northern edge of the city and killed nine whites. Soldiers killed some of the rebels in suppressing the revolt, and eighteen others were subsequently tried and executed. In 1711, a band of fugitive slaves terrorized a large area of South Carolina. Planned rebellions were thwarted in Virginia in 1709 and in South Carolina in 1713 and 1720; and in 1721–1723, rumors of conspiracies and a series of mysterious fires that destroyed buildings and crops spread fear of slave rebellion throughout the South. A serious plot quashed in Virginia in 1722 led the Virginia legislature to pass laws more severely restricting slave travel and assembly. In French New Orleans, a 1732 conspiracy of black slaves and Natchez Indians led to the execution of several slaves.

With the arrival of a new governor in Virginia in 1730, rumors spread among the slaves that he had brought an order from the king of Britain to free all Christian slaves but that their masters had suppressed it. A gathering of two hundred slaves chose officers to lead an insurrection, but the plot was quickly suppressed and four leaders were executed. Four years later, similar rumors prodded slaves near

Somerville, New Jersey, to plan a rebellion that would enable them to flee to nearby Indians. The plot was discovered and many slaves were arrested and punished, with one being sent to the gallows.[10]

In 1737–1739, local uprisings and assassinations in South Carolina enabled many slaves to escape to Florida. But one revolt, in early September 1739, resulted in death for nearly all its participants. Perhaps pushed to act before a security measure requiring all white males to carry arms on Sundays took effect on September 29, about twenty slaves met with Jemmy, also known as Cato, to plot how to seize their freedom. Under a banner proclaiming "Liberty!", they marched to the Stono Bridge south of Charleston, where they killed two guards and took guns from a warehouse. Continuing south toward Florida, they burned buildings, killed whites, and gathered recruits as they went. When armed whites caught up with the rebel band toward the end of the day, it numbered nearly one hundred fugitive slaves. Forty of the rebels were killed in the ensuing battle, along with twenty of their pursuers, and captured rebels were subsequently beheaded. After this revolt, which became known as the Stono Rebellion or Cato's Rebellion, the South Carolina legislature enacted a harsher slave code that forbade slaves to learn to read, assemble in groups, grow their own food, or earn money.

In spite of the repression, 150 to 200 slaves gathered near Charleston the following year to stage a rebellion, but betrayal of the plan enabled slaveholders to confront the slaves with armed force. At least fifty of the rebels were hanged. Suggesting that maltreatment and overwork may have contributed to the slaves' discontent, South Carolina subsequently passed laws requiring masters to provide slaves with more food and clothing and to reduce the workday to fourteen hours, fifteen during the summer.

In New York City, where slaves comprised one-fifth of the population, serious racial violence broke out in 1740. The following year, suspicions that slaves were planning to poison water supplies and burn buildings produced mass hysteria among whites. Dubious confessions obtained through torture led to the arrest of more than one hundred slaves and several white indentured servants. Five whites and thirty-one slaves were executed, either by being hanged or burned alive, and another seventy slaves were sold and deported.[11]

Slave unrest continued right up to the eve of the American Revolution, and maroon activity was particularly troublesome in South Carolina in 1765. In 1774, rebellions and the threat of rebellion caused much alarm in Georgia, Pennsylvania, and New Jersey.

The Revolutionary Period

Slaves in search of freedom fought on both sides of the American Revolution (1775–1783). After hundreds responded to Britain's promise of freedom to slaves or rebels who fought with British forces, General George Washington also promised freedom in return for military service. Around five thousand slaves from nearly every colony fought with the Continental Army. Taking advantage of the political conditions, some slaves fled to the back country and fought as guerillas with Loyalist forces, while others created much alarm by plotting or threatening violence in North and South Carolina, Virginia, Pennsylvania, New Jersey, and New York.

The ideals of liberty and equality advocated during the American and French (1789–1799) revolutions greatly undermined the system of slavery. After declaring their independence from Britain, the northern states began adopting various plans to abolish slavery, but southern states increased their importation of slaves, especially after the Constitution of 1787 banned importation of slaves after 1808. About half of the approximately four hundred thousand slaves ever shipped to North America arrived between 1780 and 1810. During the 1790s, the French Revolution and the Saint-Domingue slave rebellion precipitated great unrest among slaves not only in the Caribbean region, but throughout the Americas, including colonial Louisiana and the fledgling United States. Thousands of French planters fled the turmoil in Saint-Domingue and resettled on the North American mainland with their slaves. As many as fifteen thousand Dominguan slaves were taken to Louisiana, and by 1795, around twelve thousand had entered the United States before some states, fearing their influence, began passing laws barring the entry of slaves from that island.[12] Throughout the decade of the 1790s, slave uprisings and conspiracies were prevalent in several southern cities, including Richmond, Norfolk, Charleston, Savannah, and Baltimore. And an inordinate number of suspicious fires were blamed on discontented blacks in New Jersey and New York, where slavery was being phased out, and in South Carolina, Georgia, Maryland, and Virginia.[13]

The Pointe Coupee Conspiracy

Slaves in Louisiana were especially influenced by the Saint-Domingue revolt and the abolition of slavery in French colonies in 1794. Although Louisiana was by then a Spanish colony, having been ceded by France in 1762, its population remained overwhelmingly French and maintained close social and economic ties with the mother country. During the Saint-Domingue rebellion, thousands of French planters resettled in Louisiana with their slaves. Although Spanish authorities tried to suppress revolutionary tendencies, slave control became increasingly difficult. After a conspiracy was thwarted in 1791 and a small revolt put down in February 1795, a major conspiracy was discovered in the parish of Pointe Coupee in April 1795. The slaves in that region had become convinced by reports from several sources that Louisiana slaves had been freed by order of the Spanish king but that plantation owners were pressuring the governor not to publish or enforce the decree. It was also rumored that plantation owners were planning to force their slaves to sign a petition renouncing freedom. Indignant at being deprived of liberty, slaves from several Pointe Coupee plantations conspired to kill their masters and then send one of their leaders to New Orleans to explain the reasons for the massacre. Although kept secret for a long time, the plan was betrayed just days before the uprising was set to begin. Patrols immediately raided the slave quarters and began making arrests. In the trials that followed, fifty-seven slaves and three whites were convicted of conspiracy. Twenty-three slaves were hanged and beheaded, and their heads were mounted on posts along the Mississippi River between Pointe Coupee and New Orleans.[14]

If the harsh display was intended to intimidate slaves and discourage further rebellion, it failed. Within a year another conspiracy was formulated by Grand Jean, a white craftsman from New Orleans, aimed at freeing slaves throughout the Mississippi Valley. When the conspiracy was betrayed and Jean arrested, confiscated pamphlets prepared by Jean revealed the influence of French revolutionary ideals. After the United States gained control over the Louisiana Territory in 1803, it restricted the importation of free blacks from French colonies.[15]

Gabriel's and the Easter Conspiracies

In Virginia, several factors had caused slaves in the 1790s to hope that the American Revolution might ultimately bring them freedom: the revolutionary-era rhetoric about liberty and equality, the antislavery movement that had emerged within evangelical Christian churches, the many manumissions granted after the war, and a new postwar labor system that permitted surplus field hands and skilled slaves to hire themselves out—a system that both relaxed old controls over slavery and enabled some slaves to purchase their freedom. A very ambitious program proposed in Virginia's General Assembly in 1795 also roused hopes for freedom, but two years later the lawmakers abruptly halted debate on emancipation and made it clear that slavery would be maintained.

In 1800, influenced by the successful Saint-Domingue revolt and taking advantage of a volatile division between Virginia's political leaders, a slave named Gabriel (often identified as Gabriel Prosser) planned a revolt to force state authorities already sympathetic toward emancipation to abolish slavery and establish a fairer wage-labor system for both blacks and whites. A literate and highly skilled blacksmith who was permitted to hire out his labor, Gabriel often worked in Richmond alongside white artisans whose political views he absorbed. As Gabriel's associates interpreted the political landscape, the Republican majority who were champions of freedom and equality were held in check by the Federalist minority, represented in Richmond by wealthy merchants who exploited the working class. Gabriel planned to amass an overwhelming force of slaves and free blacks who, with the aid of Richmond's white artisans, would take control of the state capital and then kill or take hostage enough whites to force authorities to grant his demands.

Although he had expected to recruit at least a thousand of the county's eight thousand slaves, Gabriel succeeded in enlisting only a few hundred. However, on the night appointed for the insurrection—Saturday, April 30, 1800—a violent rainstorm that flooded rivers and washed out bridges prevented all but a few recruits from reaching the rendezvous, forcing Gabriel to postpone the uprising. One recruit, fearing that the undertaking was doomed, informed his master of the plot, and within hours, authorities were rounding up implicated conspirators. After eluding capture for three weeks, Gabriel was arrested, tried, and executed along with twenty-six co-conspirators. Authorities learned of the conspiracy's magnitude and complexity through court testimony and wildly overestimated the potential of Gabriel's army, both in number and might. Moving to protect the state from another such threat, the General Assembly quickly revitalized Virginia's patrol system and state militia.[16]

The measures did little to quell blacks' yearning for freedom. One of Gabriel's soldiers who had eluded arrest, a boatman named Sancho, organized another uprising to take place on April 19, Easter Monday, 1802. Like Gabriel, Sancho expected the attacks on whites to be brief and to move authorities to quickly accede to his demands for freedom, a right to earnings, and an equitable distribution of property. To ensure greater security, he recruited only a small cadre of fellow boatmen who could each in turn quickly raise a number of men at the appropriate time. He limited enlistment to one or two men per family and let the date set for the uprising be known only to his inner circle. Despite these precautions, the conspiracy spread along Virginia's rivers and into North Carolina, splintering into three smaller plots over which Sancho and his lieutenants lost control. When rumors of insurrection reached the white population, renewed vigilance uncovered pieces of the plot that allowed authorities to trace the plot to Sancho. Reserving the death penalty for leaders of the conspiracy, Virginia authorities executed only Sancho and thirteen others while North Carolina executed eleven rebels. Other conspirators were whipped, branded, had their ears cut off, or were sold to slave traders and taken to New Orleans. After these two conspiracies, the Virginia Assembly tightened restrictions on blacks, banning the education of slaves and the practice of hiring slaves from their masters, and requiring free blacks to leave the state or face re-enslavement.[17]

The Louisiana Revolt of 1811

The United States purchased Louisiana from France in 1803, along with more than five hundred million acres of land west of the Mississippi River, and scheduled to admit her to statehood in 1812. In January 1811, perhaps goaded by the belief that any remaining chances for freedom might evaporate once Louisiana was a state, slaves on a sugar plantation several miles west of New Orleans initiated a rebellion aimed at ending slavery throughout the territory. Led by Charles Deslondes, a slave originating from Saint-Domingue, rebels attacked and burned several plantations as they moved westward towards New Orleans, where they planned to negotiate for their freedom. Although only one white man was killed in the attacks, many whites fled in fear for their lives to New Orleans, where a counteroffensive was organized. By January 10, local militia reinforced by American troops managed to halt the rebel force, which had grown to about five hundred. Many rebels were killed during the battle or afterwards in nearby woods and swamps to which they fled. Twenty-five rebels were hurriedly tried and executed, while two or three whites were killed in the revolt.[18]

Revolts in the Domestic Slave Trade

By 1800, a domestic slave trade had developed within the United States that relocated hundreds of thousands of slaves from the eastern and border slave states to the expanding cotton region of the Deep South. Slaves were shipped to New Orleans via the Ohio and Mississippi rivers or a coastal route around Florida and then transported to plantations in Louisiana, Mississippi, Alabama, and Texas.

Free states on the north side of the Ohio River beckoned slaves being sent "down river," but escape was rare. One flatboat revolt that did result in freedom for at least some of the rebels occurred about ninety miles west of Louisville, Kentucky, in 1826. After managing to kill the crew and sink the boat, seventy-seven slaves fled into Indiana. Although fifty-six of the fugitives were promptly recaptured, it appears that the remaining twenty-one succeeded in escaping.

Also during the 1820s, slaves aboard two ships taking the coastal route to New Orleans from Baltimore and Norfolk seized control of the vessels and redirected them to Haiti. Both ships were retaken, however: the *Decatur* by two other ships and the *Lafayette* by its own crew. But an 1841 revolt aboard the *Creole*, which was sailing to New Orleans from Richmond, succeeded in gaining freedom for most of the 135 slaves aboard. The revolt was led by Madison Washington, who had lived for some time as a fugitive in the North but was captured when he returned to Virginia to rescue his wife. After a four-hour nighttime battle, the slaves took control of the *Creole* and set sail for the Bahamas, where slavery had been abolished by Britain seven years earlier. Upon the ship's arrival at Nassau, British authorities arrested nineteen slaves thought to have led the revolt, to be sent to London for trial, but let the remaining fugitives go free.[19]

George Boxley and Denmark Vesey

As cotton cultivation spread across the South, slavery became even more entrenched as an integral part of the southern U.S. economy, and state legislatures tightened controls over slaves. Nevertheless, black and white opponents of slavery continued to plot ways to wrest slaves' freedom from their masters. In Virginia, several slave conspiracies were rumored in 1813, and in 1816 a white man named George Boxley organized an insurrection, intending to capture Fredericksburg with a following of armed slaves and then take the state capital at Richmond. But a slave woman betrayed the scheme. About thirty slaves were arrested, six of whom were hanged and another six deported. Boxley escaped and remained at large despite a large reward on his head.[20]

The leader of an 1822 conspiracy in Charleston, South Carolina, Denmark Vesey (see Biographies) was a former slave who had purchased his freedom in 1799 and become a respected member of Charleston's free black community. As a Bible teacher for the African

Methodist Episcopal Church, where four thousand slave and free blacks worshiped apart from white oversight, he argued that Africans' enslavement violated biblical edicts and exhorted slaves to resist their bondage.

Perhaps influenced by advertisements placed in American newspapers in 1820 by Haiti's newly elected president, inviting free African Americans to relocate to the black republic and promising them free land, Vesey planned an exodus of slaves to Haiti. His plan called for taking control of Charleston, seizing the ships docked in its harbor, provisioning them with supplies from city stores, taking gold from the bank, and, before outside forces could intervene, setting sail for Haiti with as many slaves as could be hurried aboard the confiscated ships. Although authorities later estimated that as many as nine thousand slaves from the city and surrounding plantations could have known about the plan, a much smaller number was actually recruited to carry out the insurrection that would enable the mass flight. Set for July 14, 1822, the plot was betrayed in late May, and authorities rounded up several implicated conspirators but had to release them for lack of evidence. Hoping to carry off the revolt before he could be tracked down, Vesey moved the date forward to mid-June, to no avail. He was arrested, tried, and hanged along with thirty-four of his followers. Another thirty-seven were deported.

Convinced that distortion of biblical teaching had influenced much of the support for the conspiracy, the South Carolina legislature banned autonomous worship by blacks. It also passed laws forbidding the teaching of slaves to read and write and restricting the movement of both slaves and free blacks.[21]

The Nat Turner Revolt

Undoubtedly the most violent slave revolt in U.S. history occurred in Southampton County, Virginia, in August 1831. During the two-day insurrection, rebels killed thirty-two white men and women and twenty-five children. Whites responded by killing scores of blacks who had nothing to do with the rebellion. The revolt was led by a thirty-year-old preacher named Nat Turner (see Primary Document 14), who was regarded by his fellow slaves as a prophet. Experiencing visions that he interpreted as messages from God, Nat believed he had received divine instruction to lead his people out of slavery and interpreted a solar eclipse in February 1831 as God's signal to act. Illness forced him to postpone an insurrection planned for the Fourth of July, and he interpreted a second solar eclipse, on August 13, as a divine command to move forward. In the early morning hours of August 21, Nat and a small group of followers killed his master's family as they slept. Then, moving on to other plantations, they methodically killed nearly every white person they found, regardless of gender or age. Although many of the slaves they liberated refused to join the revolt, the rebel force grew to around seventy-five as it approached the county seat of Jerusalem (now Courtland). A group of armed whites engaged the rebels in battle until militia units from other counties arrived and crushed the uprising. Although most rebels were killed in battle, nineteen were executed on the spot and seventeen were arrested and tried. Nat was among the few who escaped, but after hiding out for more than two months, he was captured, tried, and hanged on November 11, 1831.

Nat Turner's rebellion spread immense fear throughout Virginia and the other southern states which, in addition to passing even more stringent slave laws, banned talk of abolition for fear it would incite slaves to revolt. The culture of fear engendered by the rebellion polarized moderates and slave owners and sharpened the tension between northern and southern states.[22]

Decades before the Civil War

During the three decades leading up to America's Civil War, reports of "growing and dangerous insubordination," suspicious fires, numerous conspiracies and rebellions, and slaves killing masters poured out of nearly every state in the South. Reports of slaves arrested, whipped, and hanged, along with increasing activities of slave patrols, vigilance committees, and military interventions showed that African Americans were actively resisting their enslavement. Planters from outside New Orleans moved into the city after a plot was betrayed and arms were found in the possession of forty slaves in December 1835. Fifty-six slaves and three blacks were arrested in connection with another Louisiana conspiracy in 1837. Serious plots were uncovered in the District of Columbia in 1838 and 1840. In 1856, a conspiracy in Arkansas involved three hundred slaves from two counties, while a conspiracy in Texas resulted in the arrest and whipping of two hundred slaves. In the same year, slaves attacked Kentucky iron mills and cut telegraph poles, while in Tennessee an armed force broke up about 150 slaves marching toward a town to rescue four slaves slated for execution. In 1860, fourteen counties of Texas suffered a virtual six-week reign of terror, with cities burned, plots discovered, and rebels executed.

Many uprisings and conspiracies were attempts to escape to Mexico, free states, or Canada. In a plot uncovered in Missouri in

1836, slaves planned to kill their master and flee to Canada. Authorities quashed a large conspiracy in Louisiana in 1840, involving
slaves from seven Louisiana parishes—four hundred in one parish
alone—who planned to flee to Mexico. In Kentucky, even though
authorities discovered an escape plan in 1838, six slaves succeeded
in fleeing to Canada with the help of local whites. Ten years later,
seventy-five armed Kentucky slaves led by a white college student
tried to reach the Ohio River. In 1849, slaves in Georgia planned to
seize a steamboat and sail to British West Indies. In 1850, a large
number of slaves from Texas succeeded in reaching Mexico. In 1853,
a New Orleans plot involving twenty-five hundred slaves was
betrayed, but large numbers of slaves were reported missing and
apparently succeeded in escaping. One of many battles between runaways and their pursuers involved a group from Missouri who were
intercepted in southern Illinois in 1859. One fugitive was killed, two
were wounded and captured, but the others succeeded in escaping.

While the majority of slave rebellions were attempts to escape,
in one notable uprising on a Mississippi plantation in 1858, slaves
tried to change procedures of punishment. The rebellion occurred
on the Polk plantation, belonging to the widow of the eleventh President of the United States, James K. Polk, who had died in 1849.
Arming themselves with axes, scythes, stones, brickbats, and clubs,
the slaves barricaded themselves and announced to the overseer and
the handful of neighbors who had come to his aid that they would
no longer submit to whipping, that they would rather all die than
have any one of them whipped. The slaves succeeded in holding the
whites off for a few days but were subdued by a larger force that
came from surrounding communities. All the slaves were whipped,
and two were executed.[23]

John Brown's Raid

Many of the escapes during these decades were aided by a network of people who hid fugitives and transported them in stages
across the North to Canada in what became known as the *under-
ground railroad*. A radical antislavery movement encouraged both
blacks and whites to actively resist slavery, and while most abolitionists believed in using moral suasion rather than violence to end slavery, some considered violence justified for that purpose. One of these
was John Brown (1800–1859), who during the late 1850s developed
a plan to instigate a general liberation movement among slaves by
seizing arsenals of weapons and supplying slaves with the arms necessary to succeed.

With financial backing from a group of prominent abolitionists, he raised a band of twenty-one followers from various northern states and Canada, including five blacks and sixteen whites, three of whom were his own sons. On October 16, 1859, Brown's force captured the federal arsenal and several other buildings at Harpers Ferry, Virginia (now West Virginia). But the local citizens and militia acted quickly to pin him down until federal troops arrived two days later and brought a quick end to the siege. Ten rebels were killed in the fighting, and seven were captured, including the wounded leader. Five of Brown's followers managed to escape. Tried for treason against the United States, Brown conducted an eloquent self-defense that roused the sympathy of many Northerners. Brown's execution on December 2, 1859, made him a martyr to the antislavery cause, memorialized in song and legend. For more than a century, most historians viewed John Brown as a misguided fanatic, but it has been argued that his action and the response to it helped push the United States toward Civil War and the abolition of slavery in 1865.[24]

Slave Rebellion during the Civil War

Slaves contributed to the havoc experienced by the South during the Civil War and placed a serious strain on the Confederacy. Hundreds of thousands of slaves deserted their masters and sought freedom with the invading Union forces. Two hundred thousand of these fugitives worked for the Union Army, digging trenches, felling trees, driving wagons, and cooking meals. When they were finally allowed to fight, 120,000 former slaves became Union soldiers. Maroons and fugitive slave outlaws waged guerilla warfare over much of the South, and the insubordination and open defiance of slaves who remained on their estates added to the chaos. Many slaves refused to work and committed acts of sabotage and violence. Conspiracies and rebellions abounded, and in some places, armed forces had to be called in to keep order. Although the Confederacy initially exempted from military duty one white overseer for every twenty slaves, it was forced to change that to one for every fifteen slaves. Even so, Mississippi officials notified Confederate leaders in 1862 that they could send no more men to fight in the army because they were needed to control the slaves at home. The measures slaves forced the South to take to attempt to suppress unrest and maintain order seriously weakened the prowess of the Confederacy.[25]

Conclusions

Brazil and the United States, the two most populous countries in the Western Hemisphere, were greatly influenced by slavery and slave rebellion. While some slave revolts were dramatic, such as those by the Muslims in Bahia and the one led by Nat Turner, none were as violent as slave revolts in the Caribbean. The successful Haitian revolt encouraged slave rebellion in both Brazil and North America, but those revolts generally led to repressive legislation that impacted the lives of both slaves and free people of color. Despite several slave revolts and conspiracies, the abolition of slavery came much later in the United States and Brazil than in most of the Caribbean region.

Notes

1. See Carl N. Degler, *Neither Black Nor White: Slavery and Race Relations in Brazil and the United States* (New York: Macmillan, 1971).

2. Philip D. Curtin. *The Rise and Fall of the Plantation Complex* (New York: Cambridge University Press, 1990), 46–53; David Eltis, "The Volume and Structure of the Transatlantic Slave Trade: A Reassessment," *William and Mary Quarterly* 58 (January 2001): 45.

3. See Robert E. Conrad, *Children of God's Fire: A Documentary History of Black Slavery in Brazil* (Princeton, NJ: Princeton University Press, 1983), xvi–xvii, 359–361.

4. Conrad, *Children of God's Fire*, 398–400.

5. For early nineteenth-century rebellions, see João José Reis, *Slave Rebellion in Brazil: The Muslim Uprising of 1835 in Bahia* (Baltimore: Johns Hopkins University Press, 1993), 40–69.

6. Conrad, *Children of God's Fire*, 401–405; Stuart B. Schwartz, "Cantos and Quilombos: A Hausa Rebellion in Bahia, 1814," in *Slaves, Subjects, and Subversives: Blacks in Colonial Latin America*, ed. Jane G. Landers and Barry M. Robinson (Albuquerque: University of New Mexico Press, 2006), 147–166.

7. Reis, *Slave Rebellion in Brazil*, 231–232; Conrad, *Children of God's Fire*, 411–412, 487.

8. Eltis, "Volume and Structure," 45; Robert W. Fogel, *Without Consent or Contract: The Rise and Fall of American Slavery* (New York: Norton, 1989), 31–34, 114–153; Eugene D. Genovese, *Roll, Jordan, Roll: The World the Slaves Made* (New York: Pantheon Books, 1972), 57.

9. Herbert Aptheker, *American Negro Slave Revolts* (1943; reprint, New York: International Publishers, 1993), 162.

10. Ibid., 79–80.

11. Ibid., 162–202.

12. Douglas R. Egerton, *Gabriel's Rebellion: The Virginia Slave Conspiracies of 1800 and 1802* (Chapel Hill: University of North Carolina Press, 1993), 47.

13. Aptheker, *American Negro Slave Revolts*, 209–219.

14. Gwendolyn Midlo Hall, *Africans in Colonial Louisiana: The Development of Afro-Creole Culture in the Eighteenth Century* (Baton Rouge: Louisiana State University Press, 1992), 343–380.

15. David Barry Gaspar and David P. Geggus, eds., *A Turbulent Time: The French Revolution and the Greater Caribbean* (Bloomington: Indiana University Press, 1997), 216–217.

16. Egerton, *Gabriel's Rebellion*, 3–115.

17. Ibid., 119–165.

18. Gaspar and Geggus, *A Turbulent Time*, 204–220.

19. Eric Robert Taylor, *If We Must Die: Shipboard Insurrections in the Era of the Atlantic Slave Trade* (Baton Rouge: Louisiana State University Press, 2006), 161–162, 147–159.

20. Aptheker, *American Negro Slave Revolts*, 255–258.

21. See Douglas R. Egerton, *He Shall Go Out Free: The Lives of Denmark Vesey* (Madison, WI: Madison House, 1999); David Robertson, *Denmark Vesey* (New York: Knopf, 1999); and Edward Pearson, *Designs Against Charleston: The Trial Record of the Denmark Vesey Slave Conspiracy of 1822* (Chapel Hill: University of North Carolina Press, 1999).

22. See Scot French, *The Rebellious Slave: Nat Turner in American Memory* (Boston: Houghton Mifflin, 2004); and Kenneth S. Greenberg, ed., *Nat Turner: A Slave Rebellion in History and Memory* (New York: Oxford University Press, 2003).

23. Aptheker, *American Negro Slave Revolts*, 325–353.

24. See Evan Carton, *Patriotic Treason: Johan Brown and the Soul of America* (New York: Free Press, 2006); and Paul Finkelman, ed., *His Soul Goes Marching On: Responses to John Brown and the Harpers Ferry Raid* (Charlottesville: University of Virginia Press, 1995).

25. Aptheker, *American Negro Slave Revolts*, 359–367.

A recaptured slave in Sumatra. "A Tuba Slave in the Stocks," from
John Anderson, *Mission to the East Coast of Sumatra in 1823* (1823;
reprint, Oxford University Press, 1971).

A slave execution in Suriname. "A Negro Hung Alive by the Ribs to a Gallows," from John Gabriel Stedman, *Narrative of a Five Years' Expedition against the Revolted Negroes of Surinam: Transcribed for the First Time from the Original 1790 Manuscript*, ed. Richard Price and Sally Price (Baltimore: Johns Hopkins University Press, 1988). *(Courtesy of Richard and Sally Price)*

A Jamaican maroon leader, 1769. "Maroon Captain Leonard Parkinson," an engraving by Raimback. (*Courtesy of the National Library of Jamaica*)

Maroons attack a Jamaican estate, 1795. "Maroons in Ambush on the Dromilly Estate Trelawny," an engraving of a painting by J. Bourgoin. *(Courtesy of the National Library of Jamaica)*

Demerara slaves in revolt, 1823. "Retreat of Lt. Brady," from Joshua Bryant, *Account of an Insurrection of the Negro Slaves of Demerara, ... 1823* (Georgetown, Demerara, 1824), 24–25. *(Courtesy of the John Carter Brown Library at Brown University)*

Black Caribs negotiate for peace with British officials in St. Vincent, 1773. "Pacification with the Maroon Negroes," from Bryan Edwards, *The History ... of the British Colonies in the West Indies* (London, 1801), 529. (*Courtesy of the John Carter Brown Library at Brown University*)

Death of Capt. Ferrer, the Captain of the Amistad, July, 1839.

Don Jose Ruiz and Don Pedro Montez, of the Island of Cuba, having purchased fifty-three slaves at Havana, recently imported from Africa, put them on board the Amistad, Capt. Ferrer, in order to transport them to Principe, another port on the Island of Cuba. After being out from Havana about four days, the African captives on board, in order to obtain their freedom, and return to Africa, armed themselves with cane knives, and rose upon the Captain and crew of the vessel. Capt. Ferrer and the cook of the vessel were killed; two of the crew escaped; Ruiz and Montez were made prisoners.

Revolt aboard the *Amistad*, 1839. "Death of Captain Ferrer," from John W. Barber, *A History of the Amistad Captives* (New Haven, CT: E. L. and J. W. Barber, 1840). *(Courtesy of the Library of Congress)*

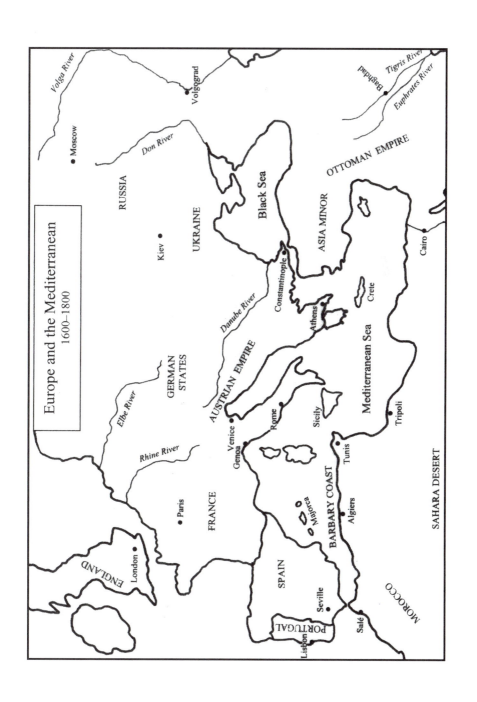

Europe and the Mediterranean
1600–1800

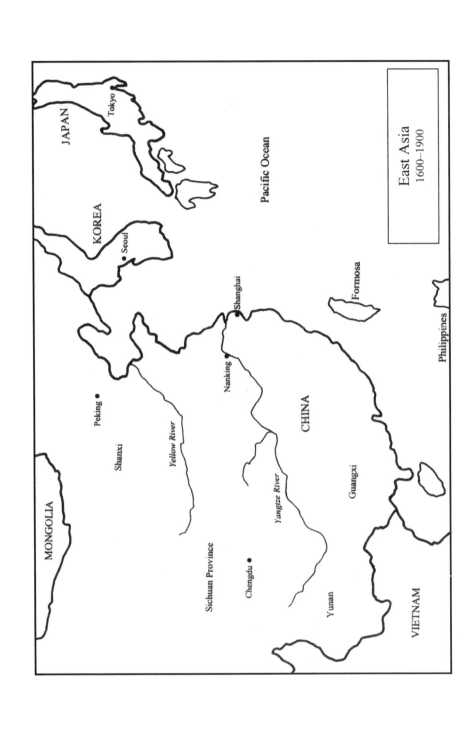

MONGOLIA

JAPAN

Tokyo

KOREA

Seoul

Shanghai

Nanking

Peking

Shanxi

Yellow River

CHINA

Yangtze River

Sichuan Province

Chengdu

Yunan

Guangxi

VIETNAM

Pacific Ocean

Formosa

Philippines

East Asia
1600–1900

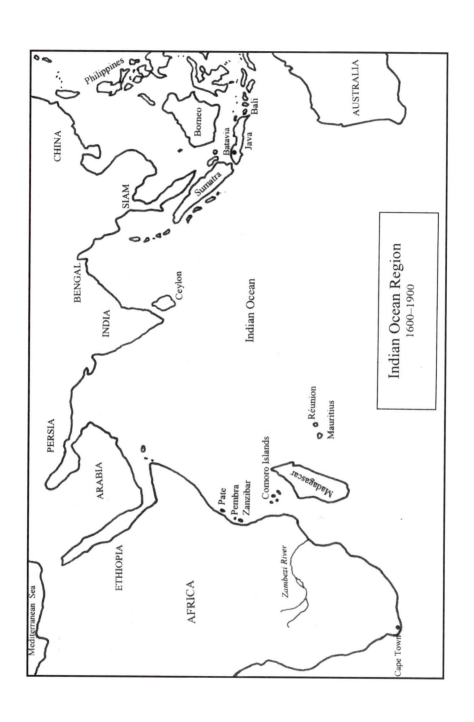

Indian Ocean Region
1600–1900

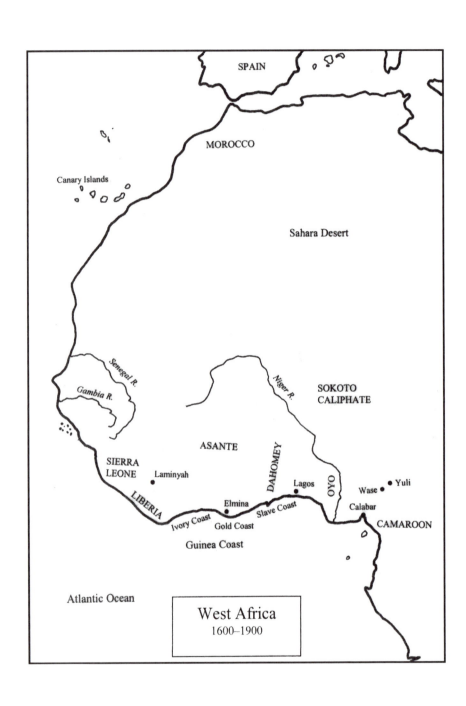

SPAIN

MOROCCO

Canary Islands

Sahara Desert

Senegal R.

Gambia R.

Niger R.

SOKOTO
CALIPHATE

ASANTE

DAHOMEY

OYO

SIERRA
LEONE

Laminyah

Lagos

Wase • Yuli

Calabar

LIBERIA

Elmina

Slave Coast

CAMAROON

Ivory Coast

Gold Coast

Guinea Coast

Atlantic Ocean

West Africa
1600–1900

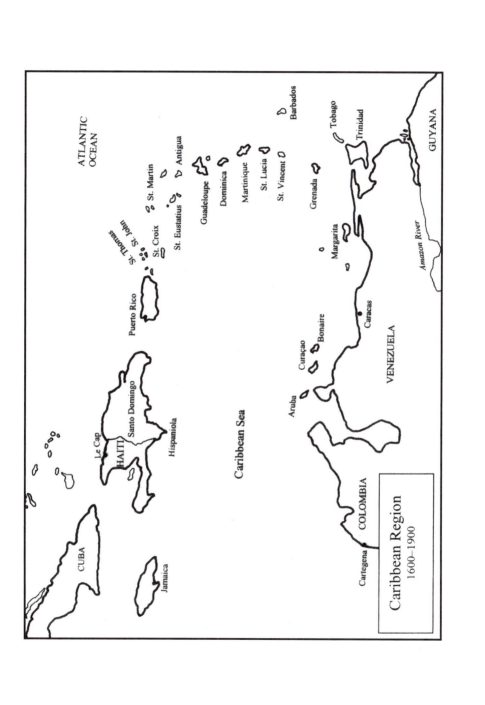

ATLANTIC
OCEAN

St. Martin

St. Thomas
St. John

Puerto Rico

St. Croix

St. Eustatius
Antigua

Guadeloupe

Dominica

Martinique

St. Lucia

St. Vincent

Barbados

Tobago

Trinidad

Grenada

Margarita

GUYANA

Amazon River

Le Cap

HAITI

Santo Domingo

Hispaniola

CUBA

Jamaica

Caribbean Sea

Caracas

Bonaire

Curaçao

Aruba

VENEZUELA

COLOMBIA

Cartegena

Caribbean Region
1600–1900

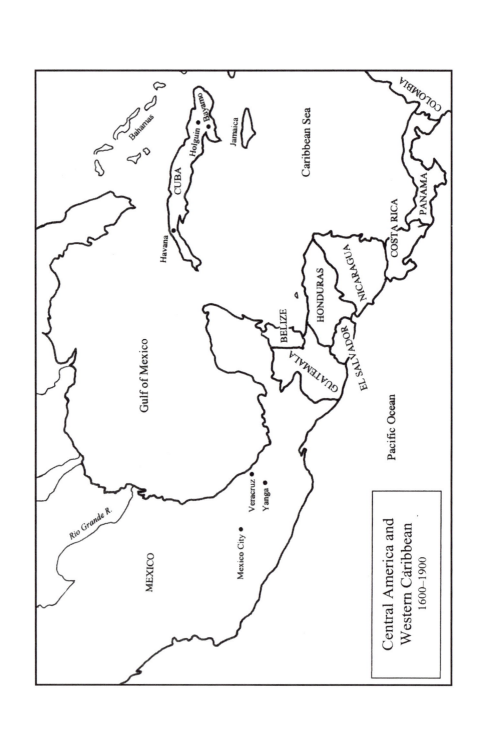

Central America and
Western Caribbean
1600–1900

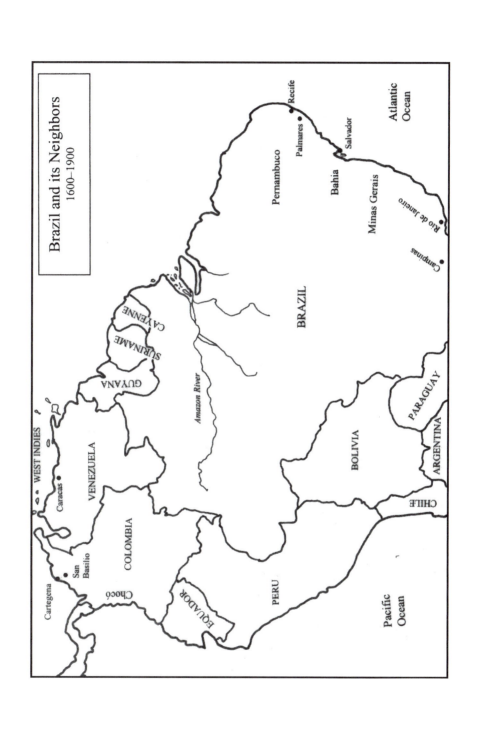

Brazil and its Neighbors
1600–1900

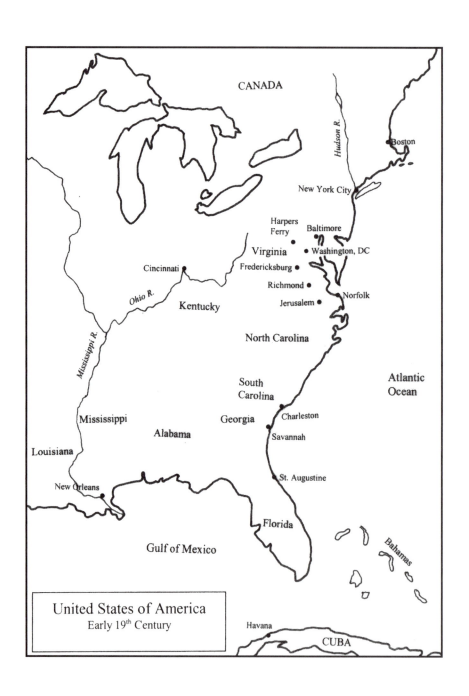

CANADA

Hudson R.

Boston

New York City

Harpers
Ferry

Baltimore

Virginia

Washington, DC

Cincinnati

Fredericksburg

Ohio R.

Richmond

Norfolk

Kentucky

Jerusalem

Mississippi R.

North Carolina

Atlantic
Ocean

South
Carolina

Mississippi

Georgia

Charleston

Alabama

Savannah

Louisiana

St. Augustine

New Orleans

Florida

Bahamas

Gulf of Mexico

United States of America
Early 19th Century

Havana

CUBA

CHAPTER 6

MARRONAGE: REBELLION THROUGH FLIGHT

Fleeing a master's control was a form of rebellion that took place wherever slavery existed. Escape was often spontaneous and temporary, with slaves sometimes running away to escape punishment but remaining near their estates, only to be recaptured or to return voluntarily because they missed family or could not survive on their own. Some slaves went further, trying to reach distant places where slavery was outlawed or, hoping only to escape the reach of their masters, fleeing to remote swamps, mountains, or forests. Away in these wilderness areas, fugitive slaves often joined up with others to form roaming bands or establish hidden settlements where they could help each other survive and defend themselves against attack by slaveholders and their armies. Such communities of escaped slaves existed in the Old World as well as the New, wherever slaves were a significant proportion of society and the geography was suitable.

Communities of runaways were especially common among plantation societies in the Americas because of the concentration of slaves and the abundance of uninhabited areas. The Spanish called these communities *palenques,* and the Portuguese, *mocambos* or *quilombos.* The French often referred to fugitive slaves as *marrons,* derived from the Spanish *cimarron*, a term first applied to escaped livestock. The English transformed this word into *maroons* and called runaway settlements maroon communities. The French noun *marronage* is widely used in English scholarly writing to mean the formation of such communities.

The motives for flight were much the same as for revolt: Slaves ran away when they faced the threat of punishment, feared they might be sold, were underfed and overworked, or were mistreated by a master or overseer. But flight required less planning and organizing than a revolt, and individuals were more likely to succeed if they could join a group of maroons. Revolts and marronage often occurred in conjunction with each other, with maroons encouraging and supporting slave insurrections, and escapees from suppressed revolts forming maroon bands or joining existing maroon communities.

Most runaway slaves were men, and because gender equilibrium could be maintained in their settlements only by capturing female slaves, maroons regularly raided plantations for women. They also stole food, supplies, and tools.

Marronage was a serious threat to the institution of slavery, and slaveholders tried to eliminate it by hunting down fugitives and destroying their settlements. Punishment for runaways included whipping, castration, pinching with glowing tongs, and cutting off ears, hands, feet, legs, or arms. Even crueler punishments were meted out to some. A group of captured Suriname maroons received the following sentences in 1730: "The Negro Joosje shall be hanged from the gibbet [gallows] by an iron hook through his ribs, until death.... Negroes Wierai and Manbote ... shall be bound to a stake and roasted alive.... Negro girls, Lucretia, Ambia, Aga, Gomba, Marie and Victoria will be tied to a cross, to be broken alive...."[1]

Invariably, maroons offered formidable resistance to being recaptured and developed sophisticated guerilla warfare techniques to fend off attack. Nevertheless, most maroon bands were eliminated before they could develop into settled communities. Once established, though, maroon communities often grew quite large and survived for many years. Occasionally, they developed commerce with free citizens. Some negotiated treaties with governments that granted freedom in exchange for returning other fugitives. A few maroon communities managed to sustain their existence for so long that they became unique ethnic groups, and some established towns that still exist today.[2]

Old World Marronage

Marronage had been common in ancient Greece and Rome, where bands of fugitive slaves frequently raided outlying towns. One early maroon community, on the third-century BCE trade-center island of Chios, became powerful enough that authorities were forced to negotiate a treaty with them. But by 1500, marronage was not a major factor in Europe, where slavery had ceased to be a significant system of forced labor, nor in the Muslim world, where a large proportion of slaves were women and children. In Eastern Asia marronage was prominent only in Korea, where the proliferation of maroon communities near the end of the eighteenth century has-tened the abolition of slavery in 1801 (see Chapter 3).[3]

While little is known about marronage within the indigenous slave systems of early Africa or the Indian Ocean region, certainly the preponderance of slavery and remote wildernesses of those regions made it probable, and Portuguese mariners discovered a large community of escaped African slaves on the island of Madagascar shortly after 1500. Marronage became prevalent on several Indian Ocean islands after European powers colonized them and introduced plantation slavery. Runaway settlements in the mountains of French-controlled Réunion survived for many years and inspired legends and literature about maroon heroes.[4]

From the beginning of their operations on the Indonesian islands of Java, Ambon, and Banda, the Dutch were harassed by bands of fugitive slaves. After a 1684 attack on the Dutch East India Company's headquarters at Batavia, officials sent repeated military expeditions into the jungles to root out the maroons. Despite these prolonged efforts, at least one maroon community survived until the end of the eighteenth century. Fugitive slaves and maroon commun-ities were a serious problem for the Dutch trading station at Cape Town, South Africa, from 1658, when its initial shipment of slaves escaped and were never recaptured. Over the next century and a half of Dutch control of the colony, many slaves imported from East Africa and Madagascar fled into the interior, where they assimilated into indigenous societies, or to the mountains northeast of Cape Town, where they established small maroon settlements. At least one of these survived until the British abolished slavery in South Africa in 1833.[5]

Marronage in sub-Saharan Africa has received little scholarly attention, but it appears not to have been uncommon (see Chapter 3). A slave revolt against Mandingo elites in West Africa in 1785 spawned the maroon town of Yangiakuri and several satellite com-munities, which sometimes attacked Mandingo towns and sold cap-tives as slaves. Neighboring Mandingo rivals, the Soso, initially tolerated the maroons but by 1795 had become so alarmed by the maroons' growing power that they allied themselves with the Man-dingo. Together they eliminated several maroon villages and, after a lengthy siege that killed most of the maroons, succeeded in destroy-ing Yangiakuri in 1796.

Another formidable maroon community called Laminyah, estab-lished in what is now Guinea in 1838, seriously threatened the stability of regional slave-owning states such as Soso and Temne. Founded by an escaped Muslim slave named Bilali (see Biographies), Laminyah became a magnet for fugitive slaves from throughout the region and was soon surrounded by several smaller communities. The region's major political leaders joined forces to destroy Laminyah and its satellites, but Bilali and his followers repelled their repeated attacks. The conflict raged for over three decades and involved military forces from nearly all the major governments in the region. The British colonial government in Freetown, Sierra Leone, upset by the conflict's recurrent closing of trade routes, intervened, first with military force and then by brokering negotiations. Finally, in 1870, Soso and Temne leaders ended their crusade against Bilali in return for his promise to stop granting asylum to fugitive slaves.[6]

After the slave trade from West Africa declined during the nineteenth century, Africans retained more slaves themselves, putting them to work on newly established plantations. This in itself increased the incidence of slave revolts and marronage, but the warfare that accompanied the spread of Islam also spurred slave revolts and escape. During the 1850s, fugitive slaves from today's Liberia were granted asylum by adversaries of their former masters, and in Sierra Leone, escaped slaves established several independent communities. One maroon leader from that region, Gumbu Smart, managed to become quite wealthy in later years—paradoxically as a slave trader.[7] During the 1860s, large numbers of recently enslaved Africans revolted in the Nigerian town of Wase and subsequently established their own settlement, called Yalwa. After several years of warfare, maroon leaders negotiated a treaty with Wase that recognized Yalwa's independence.[8]

In East Africa, marronage occurred both in the interior and on the coast. In Mozambique, various frontiersmen known as Chikunda were actually maroons who had escaped from nearby African Portuguese mini-states. In addition to the maroon communities established in Somalia and Kenya, the British explorer David Livingstone came upon two maroon communities in the Zambezi River valley in 1858, populated most likely by fugitives from the island of Zanzibar.[9]

Zanzibar experienced several slave revolts between 1840 and 1880 (see Chapter 3), during which many slaves escaped to the mainland and established at least six maroon settlements, mostly in river valleys near the coast. Most formidable was the strongly fortified maroon town of Watoro, located across from the island of Pate. Led by a former African chief named Sheikh Ahmad Simba, who had been deposed by the Zanzibar Sultan in 1863, Watoro had a population of five thousand in 1867, and it continued to attract fugitive slaves until the 1880s. Another maroon community, located on the Pangani River across from the island of Pemba, successfully repelled an attack by a Zanzibar force of three thousand in 1873. In 1875, Christian missionaries added to the allure of freedom by establishing a place of refuge for fugitive slaves near the mainland town of Mombassa.[10]

Marronage in Spanish America

Soon after Europeans began enslaving them, Amerindians began establishing maroon villages protected by stockades, which the Spanish called *palenques,* meaning palisades. The term came to be applied to all maroon settlements in Spanish America. Some early African slaves joined with native Americans in establishing maroon communities, but they also created their own hiding places, often in the isolated areas Amerindians had previously used. However, Amerindians sometimes viewed African runaways as rivals and assisted whites in locating and destroying their maroon settlements.[11]

In a 1546 report to the king of Spain, colonial officials of Santo Domingo (Hispaniola) stated that more than seven thousand maroons, divided into several *palenques,* were hiding in the island's forests and mountains. One of these settlements, led by a fugitive named Diego de Campo, periodically attacked plantations and caused considerable damage on the island. Fugitive African gold miners established *palenques* in what is now Venezuela, and escaped pearl divers created a *palenque* on the Venezuelan island of Margarita in 1549.

Panama had a large maroon community during the 1550s, ruled by a king named Bayano. When Spanish expeditions were unable to eliminate it, they negotiated a treaty with Bayano granting the maroons their freedom and their community the benefits and obligations of other colonial towns, but requiring maroons to return future runaway slaves to their masters. When the English Vice Admiral Francis Drake arrived there two decades later, he discovered a community of some three thousand fugitives, who joined his raiding expedition against Spanish settlers. During Guatemala's early colonial days, maroons on both the Caribbean and Pacific coasts disrupted convoys to the interior, blocking roads, robbing passengers, and persuading slave porters to desert and join them.[12]

Mexico's rugged terrain also facilitated marronage. As early as the 1560s, escaped mining slaves established maroon settlements in hidden mountain caves, and some of these communities collaborated with the Chichimeca Indians in fighting Spanish colonial rulers during 1550–1606. By 1600, several *palenques* existed in the mountainous hinterland of Veracruz, a major Mexican port that supplied Mexico City. One well-defended settlement, called Cofre de Perote and led for more than thirty years by an African-born fugitive named Yanga (see Biographies), staged numerous attacks on plantations and towns. Spanish troops attacked the settlement in 1608, but the maroons escaped and rebuilt elsewhere. After a larger force under Spanish commander Pedro Gonzalo de Herrera failed to defeat the maroons again the next year, he proposed a truce that led to a negotiated settlement with Yanga. The agreement granted individual freedom and autonomy to the *palenque* on condition the maroons return future fugitives to their masters (see Primary Document 5). The community eventually developed into the nearby town of San Lorenzo de los Negros, later known as San Lorenzo Cerralvo and then renamed Yanga in 1932.[13]

A very successful *palenque,* a fortified town named San Basilio, was established south of Cartagena in present-day Colombia at the beginning of the seventeenth century. Its founder was a runaway slave named Domingo Bioho, who claimed to have been a king in Africa and was known to his followers as King Benkos. Several expeditions tried to eliminate San Basilio, but Benkos was well organized and outsmarted them all. Eventually, the Spanish authorities negotiated a treaty with the maroons, but when Benkos plotted a new revolt in 1619, he was captured and executed. The community of San Basilio survived, however, and was incorporated as a town in the colonial system during the 1770s.

Cuba had several small *palenques* early in the sixteenth century, especially in the western part of the island. Some traded wax and tropical produce with neighboring islands and other outsiders, and some supplied provisions to pirates and other European enemies of Spain. In 1819, maroon leader Ventura Sánchez (aka Coba) also signed a treaty with Cuba's governor, securing the autonomy of his *palenque,* but shortly thereafter colonial forces treacherously attacked the village. Sánchez committed suicide rather than allow himself to be captured, and his community was destroyed. As the century progressed, hundreds of small *palenques* were established in Cuba, some of which developed into towns that still exist today. When Cubans began their long effort to throw off Spanish rule in 1868, many maroons joined the liberation forces.[14]

Marronage in Brazil

With its vast wilderness hinterland, Brazil provided ample opportunity for the establishment of maroon communities, which may explain why its large slave population staged few slave revolts before the nineteenth century. Increasingly referred to as *quilombos* after 1670, Brazilian maroon communities were generally quite small and usually close to the home plantation so that maroons could remain in contact with relatives and steal supplies from their former masters. But because Brazilian planters made determined efforts to eliminate *quilombos,* they were usually short-lived.

The maroon society called Palmares, which lasted nearly one hundred years, was an exception. Located in the province of Pernambuco, at its peak it spanned over an estimated eleven hundred square leagues and had a population of thirty thousand people living in a number of large towns surrounded by villages. It was led by an elected king, with its various regions governed by chiefs who were usually relatives of the king. With many African survivals evident in its culture, language, and political practices, Palmares was a virtual African state in the interior of Brazil.

Established about a decade before its first mention in a 1612 report about an expedition sent against it, Palmares became a substantial threat to the colony by frequently raiding plantations for women and attracting throngs of runaway slaves. In 1645, the Dutch, who controlled much of Pernambuco for two decades, dispatched an expedition against Palmares and destroyed two large centers, but an alert and mobile defense system enabled most maroons to flee in advance of the attack and rebuild after the soldiers withdrew. After the Portuguese regained control of the region in 1654, the maroons continued to defend Palmares against repeated attack, which intensified after 1672.

In 1675, the Palmares maroons elected as king Ganga Zumba, who three years later accepted a peace treaty that, while recognizing the freedom of maroons born in Palmares, required the return of all runaways, relocating to an area designated by the government, and submitting to government authority. An opposition faction led by Zumbi (see Biographies), commander of the *quilombo*'s army and Ganga Zumba's nephew, refused to abide by the treaty. In 1680, Ganga Zumba died in an apparent regicide, a practice widespread in Africa used to remove a weak or abusive ruler. Zumbi succeeded as king and, continuing to resist government control, defended Palmares against repeated attacks. After an intense two-year campaign, Palmares fell in February 1694. Two hundred maroons were killed in the final battle and another two hundred threw themselves off cliffs rather than surrender. At least five hundred survivors were sold at slave markets and exported from Pernambuco.[15]

Although no other *quilombos* matched the size and longevity of Palmares, Brazil had many other maroon communities. In 1787–1788, several slaves led by Gregoria Luís escaped from the sugar plantation of Santana, near Ilhéus, Bahia, and, operating as a band of maroons, regularly attacked the plantation, stole most of its equipment, and halted production. After the plantation had been idle for about two years, Gregoria and fifteen fellow maroons visited the owner, Manoel da Silva Ferreira, and offered to return if working conditions were substantially improved and Gregoria were emancipated. Pretending to agree, Ferreira signed Gregoria's emancipation declaration. But he tricked the maroons into presenting themselves at a governmental office, which led to the re-enslavement of all the maroons except Gregoria, who had been legally emancipated. While the others were exported from the province, he was imprisoned, and in 1806, he started a legal process that resulted in the preservation of the peace proposal he had made to Ferreira (see Primary Document 8).[16]

The countryside surrounding Bahia's capital of Salvador also harbored many small *quilombos* that, in a society with lax control over its slaves, functioned more as temporary getaways for city slaves. While some free blacks lived in these communities, many residents were slaves who came for a brief respite from their labors and to engage freely in African cultural activities before returning to their masters. These *quilombos* were subject to frequent raids by slave hunters and provincial police that forced residents to flee to other *quilombos* or into the bush. In 1826, however, apparently led by a woman named Zeferina (see Biographies), members of a *quilombo* called Urubu put up a fierce defense against a police attack. The maroons were quickly defeated and many were captured, including Zeferina. Before her trial, she told authorities that the *quilombo* had expected an infusion of slaves from Salvador and planned to invade the city on Christmas Day, and gain their freedom by killing the white population.[17]

Marronage in the Caribbean Region

The rugged mountains and dense forests of most Caribbean islands and the northern coast of South America provided inhospitable refuge for slaves escaping from British, French, Dutch, and Danish plantations. To survive, maroon settlements had to be located in areas virtually inaccessible to pursuing troops, but if those areas did not also provide water and enough good soil on which to raise crops, maroons had to rely on raiding plantations for the food and supplies they needed. The harsh environments of most Caribbean maroon bands never allowed them to completely sever their dependence on the plantations from which they had fled.

The British Caribbean

After Britain captured Jamaica in 1655, Spanish settlers defied the new government by releasing their slaves, who then organized into roaming bands that harassed the English colonizers. With the development of sugar agriculture on the island after 1670, planters imported large numbers of slaves, resulting in larger numbers of runaways. By the 1720s, the island's steep mountains harbored hundreds of maroons, who posed an increasing threat to the colony. Frequent military excursions against the maroons and their fierce resistance between the 1720s and 1739 became known as Jamaica's First Maroon War.

Deciding to deal with the maroon communities separately, colonial forces drove a military wedge across the island between the maroons on its western and eastern sides. By the 1720s, the Western, or Leeward, Maroons had unified under the autocratic leadership of a paramount chief named Kojo, now more frequently called Cudjoe. Not wanting trouble with whites, Cudjoe strictly enforced a proscription against attacks on white settlements. The maroons on the eastern, or windward, side, however, with a larger proportion of recent runaways who were unrestrained by a strong, unified leadership, made frequent plantation raids. Because the government perceived the Windward Maroons as both a greater threat and an easier military target, its campaign began in the east.

Reinforced by eight hundred new imperial soldiers, colonial forces attacked the Windward Maroons' most important center, Nanny Town. Severely challenged by the guerilla tactics of the town's military leader, a woman named Nanny (see Biographies), colonial forces captured Nanny Town in 1732 but lost it to the maroons again the following year. After a fierce five-day battle in 1834, colonial forces recaptured Nanny Town and burned both it and its outlying settlements to the ground. While some of Nanny Town's inhabitants trekked westward to join Cudjoe, a large group, including Nanny herself, reestablished the town at a new location eight miles away. The government, having suffered great losses of both men and money, shifted its focus to the west, but after five years of even more costly warfare with no progress made toward subduing the Leeward Maroons, the government signed a peace settlement with Cudjoe in

March 1739 (see Primary Document 10), and with the Windward Maroons four months later. In addition to treaties that granted conditional freedom and autonomy, the maroon communities were given land grants of varying sizes.[18]

Jamaica's white and maroon populations lived in uneasy partnership for the next half century. But the 1795 slave uprisings on nearby French islands made Jamaica's whites fearful of both slave revolt and the power their maroons possessed to assist rebelling slaves. Believing French agents were already on the island to promote rebellion, a newly arrived governor overreacted to incidents involving the maroons of Trelawny Town, formerly Cudjoe Town, that would have been considered minor incidents at any other time. His declaration of martial law and arrest of several Trelawny captains precipitated a new conflict in 1795 that became known as the Second Maroon War. Colonial forces suffered heavy casualties but succeeded in driving the maroons from their food supplies, and when they brought in one hundred attack dogs from Cuba, the Trelawny Maroons surrendered, apparently with the understanding that the government would listen to their grievances. The entire Trelawny population—more than six hundred men, women, and children— were deported to the barren Nova Scotia region of Canada, and after four years of hardship there, 550 survivors were allowed to emigrate to Sierra Leone in West Africa.[19]

Settlers on the British island of Saint Vincent were in conflict with a mixed population of indigenous Carib and African descendants who lived a maroon-like existence as the so-called Black Caribs. Although they negotiated a treaty in 1773, settler hostility led to the subsequent death or deportation of most Black Caribs.

On Dominica, maroons had harassed planters from the beginning of British colonization and, during the island's brief re-conquest by France, had been encouraged and armed to continue fighting the development of plantations. After the island returned to British rule in 1782, frequent attacks by maroons under a dozen different leaders, their rejection of amnesty, and colonial efforts to subdue them created a virtual maroon war. The killing of four of their leaders united maroons under a paramount leader named Pharcell (or Farcel), who unified and reorganized their forces. After Pharcell received a pledge of support from French Jacobin commissioners in 1794, the colonial Assembly negotiated a treaty with Pharcell, granting him and some of his followers freedom in return for their services as slave-catchers. During a French invasion the following year, Pharcell's maroons remained loyal to the colonial government, but after the French had been driven out, slaves and maroons intensified their resistance to the British. After Britain ended its participation in the slave trade in 1808, British planters became desperate to retain their slaves and stop mounting escapes. During 1809–1814, extensive and continuous efforts to subdue the maroons became another maroon war. In 1812, a new governor launched a campaign of eradication against the island's eight hundred maroons. He sent a message to Quashie, one of several maroon leaders, promising amnesty to all maroons who surrendered by a certain date, and certain death to those who did not. When Quashie rejected the offer and killed the messenger, the governor placed a price on Quashie's head, who, in turn, offered two thousand dollars for the governor's head. British command of the seas enabled colonial troops to mount surprise attacks on the maroons and keep them from receiving outside help. The conflict ended in 1814, after the surrender, capture, or killing of nearly six hundred maroons.[20]

The French Caribbean

As early as 1665, the French island of Martinique had a community of some five hundred maroons, led by Francisque Fabulé. Rather than risk a lengthy and costly campaign to subdue the maroons, colonial authorities negotiated an agreement with Fabulé, granting him freedom and his followers amnesty if they returned to their plantations. Although Fabulé agreed to the arrangement, he jeopardized his freedom by inducing other slaves to commit crimes with him. He was captured and sentenced to galley slavery for life.

On Guadeloupe, about six hundred escaped slaves formed four different maroon bands, which authorities gradually suppressed by 1726. Small maroon bands also operated in French Cayenne, on the Guiana coast, especially during the mid-eighteenth century, and some escaped slaves from neighboring Suriname were permitted to live as maroons in the colony (see Chapter 4).

In Saint-Domingue, marronage does not appear to have been an overriding problem but the great slave insurgency in the 1790s produced several temporary maroon bands of fugitive slaves, although their role in the revolt is not clear. Before the insurgency, maroon bands were a threat in the colony's southern peninsula during the first half of the eighteenth century. In the 1720s, the colonial government undertook a concerted effort to capture maroons and forced the mulatto population to assist in this effort. One maroon band was eliminated in 1730 when its leader, Plymouth, was killed, and two other bands were eliminated in 1734 and 1775 when their leaders were killed.

Mountain maroons in the rugged area on both sides of the border with Spanish Santo Domingo had survived repeated campaigns against them since 1702—including joint French and Spanish efforts in 1776—when a French settler whose estate was near maroon territory began efforts to negotiate with them in 1782. Using Spanish settlers who traded with the maroons as intermediaries, he persuaded them to surrender and live in a community sanctioned by the government. After four years of negotiations, the band of 130 French and Spanish maroons led by Santiago were granted their freedom and, although they ultimately refused to live in the agreed-upon area, they lived peaceably thereafter.[21]

Maroons in Dutch Suriname

Although small bands of fugitive slaves had operated during Suriname's early years under English rule, large numbers of slaves took advantage of the upheaval during the Dutch takeover in 1663, and again during a French attack in 1712, to flee to the unlimited tropical rain forest of the southern hinterland. Called Bush-Negroes by the colonists, the maroons raided outlying plantations for food, supplies, and women. Viewing marronage as a threat to the colony's survival, Suriname authorities paid increasingly higher bounties for the capture or killing of maroons, and for the discovery of maroon villages. Military expeditions succeeded in destroying some maroon settlements, but maroons quickly reestablished them, making such campaigns ineffective as well as costly in both lives and money.

A few maroon communities—including the Saramaka, Djuka, Aluku, Paramaka, Matawai, and Kwinti—developed into tribes or ethnic groups that survive to this day, with unique cultures, language, and social structure that reflect their African roots. The largest and oldest of these was the Saramaka community in the south-central river valleys, which formed in the mid-1600s and whose population increased to between fifteen thousand and twenty thousand during the following century. The colonial government negotiated peace treaties with the Saramaka in 1760, with the Djuka in 1762, and with the Matawai in 1767. Like most maroon treaties, these granted the maroons their freedom and autonomy but demanded assistance in capturing and returning other fugitive slaves. During his treaty negotiations, the Djuka chief, Araby, counseled colonial authorities that escapes would diminish if slaves were cared for more humanely and not left to mistreatment by drunken managers and overseers (see Primary Document 11).

In the early 1760s, several small maroon bands located in the northeastern part of the colony, near the border with French Cayenne, merged into a federation known as the Bonis, after their paramount leader Boni (or Bonny). In addition to plantations, the Bonis raided small military posts to get guns and ammunition, and they enticed many plantation slaves to join their ranks. Despite the recent treaties with the Saramaka and Djuka, Suriname authorities refused to negotiate with the Bonis and instead launched an intense campaign against them that became known as the First Boni War (1765–1783).

The extremely high financial and human costs of combating the maroons forced colonial authorities as well as the mother country to develop new strategies. To assist the citizen militia, authorities recruited Amerindians and in 1772 created a new military unit called the Black Rangers, a force of several hundred slaves granted freedom and other rewards in return for their service. That same year the Dutch Republic began sending professional soldiers—totaling seventeen hundred over the next four years—to combat the maroons. In a journal kept during his time in Suriname, one of the officers in this special force described the maroons' guerilla tactics that inflicted heavy casualty rates on the soldiers (see Primary Document 12). Despite their losses, the combined forces succeeded in destroying several maroon villages, including the Boni headquarters, and forced the maroons deeper into the forest. In 1775, the government began constructing a fifty-five-mile-long defensive cordon—a two-hundred-foot-wide clearing with intermittent military posts—to protect plantations against maroon attacks. This strategy succeeded. Prevented from getting supplies they needed for survival, the Bonis withdrew into French Cayenne in 1783.

Six years later, however, the reinvigorated Bonis moved back into Suriname, and their resumption of plantation attacks precipitated the Second Boni War (1789–1793). After colonial forces destroyed their headquarters in early 1793, the Bonis persuaded Djuka leaders to intercede on their behalf and arrange peace negotiations with the government. Chief Boni himself participated in the negotiations that produced a treaty, but continued demands to return fugitive slaves soon caused the shaky peace to fall apart. Caught between two opponents, the Djukas chose peace with the colonial establishment over friendship with the Bonis, and in March 1793, one of their military units killed Boni. About 350 surviving Bonis again retreated to French Cayenne, where some of their descendants live today.[22]

Marronage in North America

Shortly after the Spanish established a settlement in what is now South Carolina in 1526, about one hundred slaves revolted and fled into the wilderness. Mixing with the native American population, they created what was perhaps the first maroon community on the North American mainland.[23]

It was not unusual for escaping slaves to find refuge among native Americans. Responding to a 1693 offer of freedom by the king of Spain to any slaves who fled British America for Spanish-controlled Florida, many Carolina and Georgia slaves fled to Florida. While some lived in Spanish communities as free men, others took refuge among Florida's indigenous peoples or formed their own maroon communities. In French- and Spanish-controlled Louisiana, Choctaw Indians protected fugitive slaves, allowed some to intermarry with the tribe, and aided the establishment of small maroon communities in the region's tidewater marshes and cypress swamps.[24]

Several short-lived maroon settlements or bands also lived in the remote, swampy areas of the southern colonies along the Atlantic and Gulf coasts. Few were able to establish much permanence, but they were a persistent threat that kept colonial authorities busy. Believing that marronage incited slave insubordination and rebellion, slave masters regularly dispatched militia expeditions to capture fugitives and destroy their hiding places, and Virginia authorities offered bounties for captured maroons as early as 1672.

A few maroon groups were active in seventeenth-century British America, operating primarily as marauding bands and referred to in historical records as "bandits" and "outlaws." They established communities in the border region between Virginia and North Carolina, the so-called Dismal Swamp, and one of them was estimated to have had one thousand inhabitants. Maroons were especially active in South Carolina and Georgia during the years 1765–1771.[25]

Runaway slaves from South Carolina and Georgia also still had the option of finding freedom in Florida, and during the 1730s hundreds made their way, singly and in small groups, to join maroon settlements there. Again during America's Revolutionary War, many runaways went to Florida, which had fallen to British control in 1763. By the end of that war, when Florida was returned to Spain, its native American population had come to be known as Seminole, another derivation from the Spanish word *cimarrón*, meaning "wild," or "runaway." Including very few original indigenous peoples, the

Seminoles consisted primarily of Creeks and a few other Muskogean peoples who had moved down from Georgia during the 1700s, and the many African Americans who had taken up residence there, known as Black Seminoles.

Hundreds of these Black Seminoles fought against U.S. military forces in the Seminole Wars of 1817–1818 and 1835–1842. In the first conflict, Seminoles allied with Spain in a dispute over possession of West Spain, the coastal region stretching from today's Florida panhandle to the Mississippi River. After the United States purchased Florida in 1821, white settlers moved into the territory and established slave-based plantations. In 1830, Congress passed the Indian Removal Act, requiring all eastern Indians to relocate west of the Mississippi River. When several Seminole chiefs refused to go voluntarily, the United States military removed them forcibly in what became known as the Second Seminole War. At the start of this war in December 1835, hundreds of slaves escaped from new sugar plantations south of St. Augustine to fight with the Black Seminole Maroons. Most of those were captured and returned to slavery, as were some Black Seminoles. But most Black Seminoles who survived the war were forced to emigrate to Oklahoma with the Seminole Indians. To evade slave catchers during the 1850s, hundreds of Black Seminoles fled from Oklahoma to Mexico.[26]

As long as slavery existed in the United States, so, too, did marronage. During the Civil War, maroons in Virginia, the Carolinas, and Georgia attacked villages at night, retreated to their hiding places before daybreak, and in stealing from the rich and giving to the poor, earned the moniker "Black Robin Hoods."[27]

Conclusion

Maroon communities existed in many regions of the world, but especially where slaves constituted a significant proportion of the population and where the geographic environment offered refuge. Most runaway communities were small and short-lived because slaveholders and colonial authorities went to great expense and effort to eradicate them. But a few became quite large and survived many years, some continuing as autonomous communities into the twentieth century. Perhaps the most notable and successful maroon communities were Palmares in Brazil and the Djuka and Saramaka communities in Suriname. Marronage has received much less scholarly attention than slave revolts, but its effect on the institution of slavery was undoubtedly greater than violent uprisings. Although it has been called the "weapon of the weak,"[28] slaveholders regarded marronage as one of the greatest threats to their power because it made slaves aware that their bondage could be broken.

Notes

1. Richard Price, *The Guiana Maroons: A Historical and Biographical Introduction* (Baltimore: Johns Hopkins University Press, 1976), 26.

2. For a good overview of marronage, see Richard Price, "Introduction," in *Maroon Societies: Rebel Slave Communities in the Americas*, 2d ed. (Baltimore: Johns Hopkins University Press, 1979), 1–30.

3. M. I. Finley, *Ancient Slavery and Modern Ideology* (New York: Viking, 1980), 111–113; Bok-Rae Kim, "Korean Nobi Resistance under the Chosun Dynasty, 1392–1910," *Slavery and Abolition*, 25 (August 2004): 48–62.

4. Gwyn Campbell and Edward Alpers, "Introduction: Slavery, Forced Labour, and Resistance in Indian Ocean Africa and Asia," *Slavery and Abolition* 27 (August 2006): xvi–xix; Allan G. B. Fisher and Humphrey J. Fisher, *Slavery and Muslim Society in Africa* (Garden City, NY: Doubleday, 1971), 110; Edward A. Alpers, "The Idea of Marronage: Reflections on Literature and Politics in Réunion," in *Slavery and Resistance in Africa and Asia*, ed. Edward A. Alpers and Gwyn Campbell (London: Routledge, 2005), 20, 37–48.

5. Markus Vink, "'The World's Oldest Trade': Dutch Slavery and Slave Trade in the Indian Ocean in the Seventeenth Century," *Journal of World History* 14 (June 2003): 171–175; Robert Ross, *Slavery and Resistance in South Africa* (London: Routledge & Kegan Paul, 1983), 4, 11–12, 54–72.

6. Ismail Rashid, "A Devotion to the Idea of Liberty at Any Price: Rebellion and Antislavery in the Upper Guinea Coast in the Eighteenth and Nineteenth Centuries," in *Fighting the Slave Trade: West African Strategies*, ed. Sylvia A. Diouf (Athens: Ohio University Press, 2003), 137–151.

7. Suzanne Miers and Igor Kopytoff, eds., *Slavery in Africa* (Madison: University of Wisconsin Press, 1977), 48–55, 215, 291, 320–321; Ismail Rashid, "'Do Daddy Nor Lef Me Make Dem Carry Me': Slave Resistance and Emancipation in Sierra Leone, 1894–1928," in *Slavery and Colonial Rule in Africa*, ed. Suzanne Miers and Martin A. Klein (London: Frank Cass, 1999), 212–213.

8. Paul E. Lovejoy, ed. *The Ideology of Slavery in Africa* (London: Sage Publications, 1981), 229–230.

9. See Allen E. Isaacman and Barbara S. Isaacman, *Slavery and Beyond: The Making of Men and Chikunda Ethnic Identities in the Unstable World of South-Central Africa, 1750–1920* (Portsmouth, NH: Heinemann, 2004).

10. G. A. Akinola, "Slavery and Slave Revolts in the Sultanate of Zanzibar in the Nineteenth Century," *Journal of the Historical Society of Nigeria* 6 (1972): 215–228.

11. Price, *Maroon Societies*, 35–48, 82–102; Lynne Guitar, "Boiling It Down: Slavery on the First Commercial Sugarcane Ingenios in the Americas," in *Slaves, Subjects, and Subversives: Blacks in Colonial Latin America*, ed. Jane G. Landers and Barry M Robinson (Albuquerque: University of New Mexico Press, 2006), 49–52.

12. Paul Lokken, "A Maroon Moment: Rebel Slaves in Early Seventeenth-Century Guatemala," *Slavery and Abolition* 25 (December 2004): 44–58; Price, *Maroon Societies*, 41.

13. See Jane G. Landers, "Cimarrón and Citizen: African Ethnicity, Corporate Identity, and the Evolution of Black Towns in the Spanish Circum-Caribbean," in *Slaves, Subjects, and Subversives*, 111–132.

14. Price, *Maroon Societies*, 49–59, 74–81.

15. Ibid., 170–190; Aaron Myers, "Zumbi," in *Africana: The Encyclopedia of the African and African American*, ed. Kwame Anthony Appiach and Henry Louis Gates Jr., vol. 5 (New York: Oxford University Press, 2005), 515–516.

16. Stuart B. Schwartz, "Resistance and Accommodation in Eighteenth-Century Brazil: The Slaves' View of Slavery," *Hispanic American Historical Review* 57, no. 1 (1977): 69–81.

17. Price, *Maroon Societies*, 191–200. See also João José Reis, *Slave Rebellion in Brazil: The Muslim Uprising of 1835 in Bahia* (Baltimore: Johns Hopkins University Press, 1993), 55–59.

18. Michael Craton, *Testing the Chains: Resistance to Slavery in the British Caribbean* (Ithaca, NY: Cornell University Press, 1982), 81–96; Karla Gottlieb, *The Mother of Us All: A History of Queen Nanny, Leader of the Windward Jamaican Maroons* (Trenton, NJ: Africa World Press, 2000).

19. Craton, *Testing the Chains*, 211–223.

20. Ibid., 23, 140–153, 190–194, 224–232.

21. David P. Geggus, *Haitian Revolutionary Studies* (Bloomington: Indiana University Press, 2002), 69–74; Price, *Maroon Societies*, 107–142, 313–319.

22. Wim Hoogbergen, *The Boni Maroon Wars in Suriname* (Leiden: Brill, 1990); Price, *Guiana Maroons*, 1–39.

23. Price, *Maroon Societies*, 149.

24. Gwendolyn Midlo Hall, *Africans in Colonial Louisiana: The Development of Afro-Creole Culture in the Eighteenth Century* (Baton Rouge: Louisiana State University Press, 1992), 115–118, 203–212.

25. Price, *Maroon Societies*, 151–162.

26. Bruce Edward Twyman, *The Black Seminole Legacy and North American Politics, 1693–1845* (Washington, DC: Howard University Press, 1999); Kenneth W. Porter, *Black Seminoles: History of a Freedom-Speaking People* (Gainesville: University Press of Florida, 1996), 39.

27. Price, *Maroon Societies*, 152, 164–165.

28. Alpers, "The Idea of Marronage," 21.

CHAPTER 7

IDENTITY AND LEADERSHIP IN SLAVE REVOLTS

Only a relatively small percentage of slaves ever participated in slave uprisings, and for good reason: Failure was virtually a foregone conclusion, and torturous punishment or death was the likely outcome for its leaders. Why, then, did collective rebellions repeatedly occur, and why did their participants take such risks? Focusing primarily on the Americas, for this is the area for which most of the documentary record exists, this chapter explores who participated in slave revolts, and what their motivations were.

Certain conditions that preceded many revolts were beyond slaves' control. Most revolts occurred where there was a large slave population and where slaves outnumbered the free population by at least three to one. A concentration of slaves of the same ethnic group or speaking the same language increased chances for rebellion, because slaves could more easily communicate and organize. Social disorder created by warfare, political upheaval, economic crisis, or environmental distress such as famine or epidemic disease often produced opportunities for revolt. Excessive brutality or exploitation by managers sometimes broke slave forbearance, while the spread of political or religious ideology sympathetic to slaves sometimes strengthened slave motivation. The simultaneous existence of more than one of these preconditions multiplied chances of slave rebellion, especially if decisive leadership arose.[1]

Group Dynamics of Rebellion
The "African Phase"

Until about the second half of the eighteenth century, most slave rebellions involved African-born slaves rather than slaves born in the Americas and were characterized by certain aspects of African culture. Because of this, some scholars refer to the first 150 years of American slave rebellion as the "African phase."[2]

New arrivals from Africa, often called *bozals* or *saltwater slaves* by their contemporaries, had a difficult time adjusting to their new environment. They were often assigned the more arduous tasks and unless they were fortunate enough to have companions from their own country, they probably found it difficult to communicate with other slaves. Some suffered a melancholy that drove them to suicide, while others fell victim to New World diseases to which they had no immunity. But others refused to succumb to the regimented life of slavery and sought alternatives, especially if they had only recently been enslaved. Newly arrived slaves were notorious for running away within their first hours or days on American soil. Others eagerly joined in plots and insurrections. Shortly after the start of the 1763 Berbice Revolt, for example, a shipment of 350 slaves arrived from Africa, and as soon as they learned about the revolt, they escaped and joined the rebels.[3]

Before 1700, the great majority of maroon leaders on whom we have data were African-born, and the vast majority of slaves who sought liberty in America's wildernesses were African-born. Slaves born in the Americas, so-called *creole slaves*, who had never known freedom and who lived with or near family, were less likely to have been participants in early revolts. Many creoles worked as household servants and neither identified with the African imports nor wished to lose their privileged positions. Those who practiced a craft or trade or enjoyed a measure of trust as drivers were rarely willing to trade those positions for the primitive life of a maroon. Not until the eighteenth century, as creoles began to outnumber African-born slaves in many places, did they become involved in slave revolts on a large scale.

The goal of most early rebelling slaves was to either overthrow their white captors or escape from them so they could establish their own order based on the African traditions from which they had been alienated. They depended upon African forms of leadership and as a preliminary step to revolt, generally elected a king—and sometimes a queen as well, not necessarily the king's consort. For example, rebelling miners in Venezuela in 1555 and in Brazil in 1719 elected kings, and planners of Mexico City's 1612 conspiracy elected a king and queen. Co-leaders of Santo Domingo's short-lived 1797 revolt—Tomas Congo and Ana Maria—were proclaimed king and queen. In addition to choosing a ruler, rebelling slaves usually chose military leaders as well, often from among those in their ranks who had been warriors in Africa, many enslaved as prisoners of war.

African religious beliefs and practices were of paramount importance in slave revolts. Rebel leaders sought advice from African-born healers and mystical practitioners, known as obeah priests in West Africa, who performed complex rituals to prepare warriors for battle and protect them against injury. Some rebel soldiers wore magical amulets to make them bulletproof. Fighting strategies, guerilla techniques, and communication by drums and horns were adaptations from their African experiences.[4]

Maroon settlements established during the African phases were generally kingdoms structured after African models. To bolster their credibility, many leaders claimed descent from African kings or chiefs, and four major maroon leaders may have been African chiefs before their enslavement: Bayano in Panama, Domingo Bioho in Colombia, Yanga in Mexico, and Ganga Zumba in Brazil. Ganga Zumba, in fact, was apparently not the leader's name, but a title meaning *Great Lord*, derived from the Kimbangu language widely spoken in Angola.[5] After 1700, however, few maroon leaders claimed royal ancestry or established themselves as kings.

However, even in later stages of American slavery, major rebellions occurred in places where African-born slaves constituted a large segment of the slave population. The importation of thousands of enslaved Africans to Cuba and Bahia, Brazil, during the early decades of the nineteenth century was an important factor in Cuba's Aponte Rebellion in 1812 and Brazil's Malê Rebellion in 1835.

Ethnicity

With nearly a thousand different language and ethnic groups on the African continent, enslaved Africans were a highly diverse population. They came from all over Africa except the extreme north and south, with the majority, about 7.5 million, shipped from West Africa and another 3.5 million from across the continent's tropical midsection. Slave ships usually carried a mixture of ethnic groups, or nationalities, but American planters often preferred slaves from specific nations or areas, and depending on their access to the African coast (various European nations claimed monopolies on certain coastal regions), slave traders tried to accommodate them. The British and Dutch Caribbean colonies imported large numbers of slaves from West Africa, especially from the coastline of Ghana (then called the Gold Coast), Togo, and Ivory Coast, where various Akan languages were widely spoken. Contemporaries often referred to these slaves as *Coromantees* or *Elminas*, after the trading stations Cormantin and Elmina from which the ships sailed. The French imported slaves from nearly all of Africa's coastal regions, but primarily from Senegal, the Slave Coast (today's Togo, Benin, and western Nigeria), and Central Africa. Brazil received most of its slaves from Central Africa but also imported from the Gold and Slave Coasts of West Africa. During the early nineteenth century, it received large numbers of slaves from the Nigerian interior, many of them Hausa and Yoruba Muslims captured in the Sokoto Caliphate's expansion wars.

Slaveholders came to regard certain ethnic groups as more prone to rebellion than others. Akans from the Gold Coast, for example, initially preferred by Jamaicans for their purported loyalty, intelligence, and willingness to work, later gained a reputation for rebelliousness. Most slaves involved in the island's 1760 Tacky Revolt were said to have been Akans, and six years later, when a group of Akans newly arrived in Jamaica revolted and killed several whites, the Assembly considered prohibiting the importation of Gold Coast slaves.[6] Slaveholders regarded some ethnic groups, such as Igbos from the Niger Delta region and Bantu-speakers from Central Africa, as nonaggressive and less prone to rebellion. But both groups were minorities in American slave communities, and it was usually dominant groups who took the lead in rebellions.

Common origins, backgrounds, and language provided slaves a degree of cultural homogeneity and unity, eased communication, and fostered a sense of ethnic solidarity that facilitated group resistance. Members of the same ethnic group formed distinct fighting units in Berbice's 1763 revolt. Angolans from West Central Africa were a significant component of Brazil's maroon communities, and large numbers of Hausa and Yoruba Muslims staged rebellions in Brazil between 1807 and 1835. When Cuba began importing tens of thousands of enslaved Africans during the last decades of the eighteenth century, the island's large free black population formed ethnic-based fraternal societies, called *cabildos*, to help those who shared their ancestral, linguistic, and cultural backgrounds cope with their oppression. Investigations after the Aponte Rebellion revealed that these *cabildos* had been instrumental in planning at least the Bayamo phase of the rebellion.[7]

Other Group Ties

In addition to a common ethnicity, such ties as having been a combatant in an African war or having served in the same military, working the same African craft, or sharing the same religious background could promote mutual trust and a sense of kinship. Shared experiences since leaving Africa also fostered identity bonds. Travelers on the same slave ship often came to regard each other as relatives. Living and working at the same plantation, toiling in the same mine, or sharing the same skills fostered trust as well as facilitated communication and provided opportunity to meet, plot, and participate in collaborative action. After increasing numbers of slaves converted to Christianity in the eighteenth century, church membership and being part of a congregation often replaced old ethnic identities in forging solidarity of purpose and action.

Age and Gender

While most of those who participated in and led slave revolts were young men, slave rebellions cut across age and gender lines. Ettin, Galant, and Gabriel were in their twenties. Nat Turner was thirty; Fédon was thirty-six. Toussaint Louverture, often referred to as "Old Toussaint," was about fifty when he became a leader of the Haitian revolt. Fifty was probably very old for a slave, but other rebel leaders, such as Quamina and Vesey, had also reached that age.

Although the majority of slave rebels were men, women frequently played important supportive roles and sometimes took active part as combatants. As previously noted, rebellion was more frequent on slave ships that had a larger than usual proportion of women, who were not shackled and could move easily and obtain both information and weapons needed for revolt. Of the ninety-six slaves who escaped after the revolt onboard the *Little George* in 1730, two-thirds were women and children.[8] The execution of women after both shipboard and New World revolts suggests that they played leadership roles. One-third of those executed after 1750 revolts in Curaçao and Suriname were women. Seventy-five women were convicted of participating in the 1731 Baptist Revolt in Jamaica, of whom two were executed.

A few women have been mentioned as leaders of maroon communities. Both a military and a spiritual leader, Nanny of Jamaica was a symbol of unity and strength for her people during her lifetime and after (see Biographies). A woman named Filippa Maria Aranha led a maroon community in Amazonia, in the Brazilian interior, and managed to negotiate a peace treaty with the colonial government.[9] A woman named Zeferina appears to have led the defense of another Brazilian maroon community on the outskirts of San Salvador (see Biographies).

Leaders of Slave Revolts

As creoles became a larger proportion of America's slave populations, they increasingly became participants in and leaders of slave
revolts. Increasingly, rebel leaders needed to be both knowledgeable
about African traditions and skilled at understanding and dealing
with whites. Rebel leaders such as Toussaint Louverture, Gabriel,
and Denmark Vesey, for example, bridged both worlds.

Privilege

Especially after the mid-eighteenth century, rebel leaders frequently had what could be called "privileged" or "elite" status; that
is, they usually were literate, held positions of trust and responsibility, often were skilled craftsmen, and enjoyed considerable freedom
of movement. Some were no longer slaves, but freemen: Toussaint
had been emancipated, Vesey had purchased his freedom, and Fédon
and Aponte were free-born. Though a slave, Samuel Sharpe, leader
of Jamaica's Baptist War in 1831–1832, is said to have lived virtually
as a freeman.

Literacy and mastery of the written word not only served as
organizing tools for slave rebellions—enabling leaders to gain vital
information, communicate with each other, and forge passes—but
also were regarded by slaves as holding special powers that often
served as a criterion for leadership roles. Recognizing the power that
literacy had to both kindle and enable rebellion, colonial legislatures
repeatedly banned the teaching of slaves to read and write. Nevertheless, literacy became an increasingly common skill of rebel leaders.
By becoming an expert on biblical passages concerning slavery and
collecting antislavery articles and debates from a large number of
newspapers, Denmark Vesey used his ability to read to foment discontent and recruit soldiers. Written communications allowed Sancho and other leaders of the 1802 Easter Conspiracy to coordinate
activities over a widespread area, although they later helped authorities unravel the plot. Literate Muslims were prominent among the
leadership of Brazil's Malê Rebellion, and mastery of the written
word served to strengthen the movement. Some rebels carried written Koranic verses with them into battle.[10]

Slaves who led revolts generally held positions of responsibility
that allowed them to move about without supervision. The two leaders
of a 1736 rebellion in Antigua—one African-born and one creole—
were drivers, or foremen. Tula's position on his Curaçao plantation is

unknown, but it permitted him to travel to neighboring plantations to rouse support for a rebellion in 1795. Gabriel, mastermind behind the complex 1800 conspiracy in Virginia, was allowed to hire out his labor as a blacksmith and was influenced by the white artisans with whom he worked. By operating a ferry without supervision, Sancho was able to organize other slave boatmen in the widespread Easter Conspiracy. Members of Havana's free black militia, who enjoyed a large measure of rights and privileges, were prominent among the leadership of Cuba's 1812 Aponte Rebellion, and slave and free black artisans moved freely from Havana to countryside plantations to organize that city's phase of the revolt. Quamina, one of the planners of the Demerara Rebellion of 1823, was chief carpenter on his plantation and head deacon of the colony's church for blacks. Leaders of the Malê Rebellion were urban artisans. Vesey's status as a free black and church teacher enabled him to visit slaves in a sixty-mile radius around Charleston.

Rebel leaders were often more informed about world events than was generally assumed. Particularly by the early nineteenth century, most were aware of the French Revolution and France's abolition of slavery, of slave revolts in Saint-Domingue and elsewhere, of antislavery debates both in the British Parliament and in the Congress and state legislatures of the United States.

Motives for Slave Rebellions

For most of human history, slave uprisings were attempts to escape personal enslavement, protest abnormally cruel treatment, or gain improved working conditions. They were not attempts to overthrow systems of slavery. Slaves who succeeded in securing their own freedom did not necessarily object to the enslavement of others. In both Africa and the Americas, they sometimes became slaveholders or slave traders themselves. Some African maroons raided enemy towns and sold their captives as slaves. In the Americas, maroon settlements often held newcomers as slaves for a probationary period before wholly accepting them into the community.[11] And many maroon communities secured their own freedom and survival by agreeing to hunt down and deliver other runaways to colonial authorities. A notable exception in this pattern of maroon treaties was the faction of Palmares maroons led by free-born Zumbi, who refused to accept the treaty signed by Ganga Zumba because it required the return of maroons not born in Palmares. But not until the eighteenth century— when the philosophical revolution known as the Enlightenment gave birth to the concept of freedom as a natural right rather than a privilege of the elite—does there seem to have been deliberate attempts to destroy the institution of slavery.

Personal Freedom

Whether a Spartacus battling the legions of ancient Rome, a French Catholic trying to wrest control of a Mediterranean galley, a Zawo seeking asylum among a neighboring people in Liberia, an Indonesian fleeing into the interior of South Africa, or an African miner rising up against Brazilian overseers, most slave rebellions were attempts by enslaved persons to secure freedom for themselves. Flight was the most common form of slave rebellion, with violent combat used to overpower guards and effect escape. Once free of their captors, slaves tried to return to their homeland or, if that was not possible, to reach some other area beyond their captors' authority or control.

Response to Harsh Treatment

Some slave rebellions were not attempts to escape, but responses—either spontaneous or carefully calculated—to harsh treatment by a master or overseer, the withdrawal of a privilege or promise, or unfair or cruel punishment of a slave leader, woman, or child. Other insurrections, often in the form of work stoppages, sought to gain better working and living conditions. Frequently, grievances having to do with slave treatment triggered rebellions aimed at escape. The rebellion planned by Mexico City slaves in 1612 was a response to excessive punishment meted out to a slave woman. The 1750 revolt in Suriname was partially in response to the sexual abuse of the rebel leader's common-law wife. The fatal beating of his child was one of several cruel punishments that provoked South Africa's Galant to rebel in 1825. And in 1858, slaves on a Mississippi plantation united to try to end the use of whipping as a punishment.

Work stoppages intended to press for better working conditions or some other concession were generally regarded by slaveholders as insubordination and put down with force. Although striking slaves were usually severely punished, sometimes, as in British Dominica in 1791, their demands were granted. And the threat of rebellion moved some colonial authorities to enact laws mandating better treatment of slaves.

Emancipation and Abolition

During the eighteenth century, the secular concept of freedom as a human right rather than a privilege for the elite, and the religious concept of equality of all persons before God challenged the validity of slavery. Reaching the consciousness of America's slaves, these ideas raised hopes of emancipation. As early as 1730 and 1734, slaves in Virginia and New Jersey rose up to demand their rights when colonial masters did not free them in accordance with a rumored decree by the king of Britain. Such rumors and expectations led to similar slave uprisings in Louisiana in 1795, Cuba in 1812, Demerara in 1823, and South Africa in 1825.

Many rebellions were fueled by the democratic rhetoric and slogans that accompanied the American and French revolutions. Acting upon these revolutionary ideals, slaves on such Caribbean islands as Saint-Domingue, Grenada, Martinique, Guadeloupe, and Curaçao tried to free themselves by overthrowing colonial governments. In 1791, slaves and free blacks launched a thirteen-year struggle that won their independence and established Haiti as a free republic, demonstrating to the world's slaves that revolts could succeed. While the Saint-Domingue war was being waged, Grenada slaves succeeded in freeing themselves in 1795, but their independence lasted barely over one year. One of Saint-Domingue's rebel leaders visited Tula shortly before the outbreak of the 1795 revolt on Curaçao, and other leaders were rumored to have agitated revolt in such places as Jamaica and New Orleans. Having traveled throughout the Caribbean during the last two decades of the eighteenth century, José Antonio Aponte and another primary leader of Cuba's 1812 rebellion were influenced by events there. Participants in the revolt told authorities they had been shown portraits of Haiti's revolutionary leaders and told Haitian soldiers would aid them in their fight. Influenced by abolition in the British West Indies and on other Caribbean islands, slaves on Saint Croix staged a massive demonstration that enabled the governor to override planter opposition and declare immediate emancipation throughout the Danish West Indies in 1848.

Religion also influenced slave rebellion. By the early nineteenth century, many American slaves had been converted to the evangelical Christianity that had swept the Anglo-Protestant world, and they forged its teachings—particularly the belief in equality before God—into tools to attack slavery. During questioning after the Demerara rebellion, some rebels insisted that God had made them of the same flesh and blood as the whites.[12] While slaveholders used the Bible to defend slavery and called upon the New Testament admonition for slaves to obey their masters, slaves seized upon the Old Testament story of God's deliverance of the Israelites from slavery in Egypt and applied it to their own situation, believing that God would deliver them as well.

Churches also provided slaves places where slaves could congregate away from their plantations, meet with slaves from other plantations, express themselves, and develop leadership hierarchies apart from their plantation—all useful elements in organizing group action. Missionaries encouraged converted slaves and free blacks to conduct their own religious services, and in Demerara and Jamaica slaves turned Sunday services into organizational opportunities. Authorities in such places as Demerara and South Carolina so feared the influence of religious instruction and gatherings that they restricted attendance at religious services or banned slaves' autonomous worship.

The Christian Bible influenced several nineteenth-century attacks on slavery. Based on what he believed were orders from heaven, the white Virginian George Boxley tried to organize a slave rebellion in 1816. After using the Bible to rouse slave participation, Denmark Vesey planned an elaborate exodus of slaves from Charleston, South Carolina, in 1822. David Walker's 1829 *Appeal* insisted that God would surely raise up an agent to deliver slaves to freedom and urged slaves and free blacks to assist the divine work. Two years later, the Virginia slave Nat Turner led a revolt based on his belief that God had directed him to destroy slavery (see Primary Documents 13 and 14). And in 1859, acting upon his interpretation of biblical instruction, the white abolitionist John Brown tried to seize a United States federal arsenal as a first step in leading slaves of the American South to freedom.

Conclusion

Identity, personal roots, and experience affected the way enslaved Africans and African Americans responded to their condition. Certain ethnic groups, particularly Akans from West Africa, were prominent as leaders in early slave insurrections. African-born slaves, initially more prone than American-born slaves to rebel, patterned their rebellions and maroon communities upon African models. By the nineteenth century, with the advancement of creolization, American-born slaves became active in slave rebellions.

While harsh treatment and working conditions triggered some slave uprisings, most rebellions before the late eighteenth century were waged primarily to gain personal freedom. Rebellions based on human rights ideology and aimed at mass emancipation or the abolition of slavery began in the 1790s and helped end slavery in the Americas during the nineteenth century.

News of Parliament's ongoing debates especially showed slaves in the British Caribbean that they had allies in London, and they made use of that knowledge in recruiting participation in revolts.

Notes

1. For additional preconditions, see Eugene Genovese, *From Rebellion to Revolution* (Baton Rouge: Louisiana State University Press, 1979), 11–12.

2. See Michael Craton, *Testing the Chains: Resistance to Slavery in the British Caribbean* (Ithaca, NY: Cornell University Press, 1982), 99–104.

3. Cornelis Ch. Goslinga, *The Dutch in the Caribbean and the Guianas, 1680–1791* (Assen, Netherlands: Van Gorcum, 1985), 466.

4. Emelia Viotti da Costa, *Crowns of Glory, Tears of Blood: The Demerara Slave Rebellion of 1823* (New York: Oxford University Press, 1994), 194; Richard Price, ed., *Maroon Societies: Rebel Slave Communities in the Americas*, 2d ed. (Baltimore: Johns Hopkins University Press, 1979), 9–10.

5. R. K. Kent, "Palmares: An African State in Brazil," in *Maroon Societies*, 20, 36, 179.

6. Craton, *Testing the Chains*, 128–141, 173–183.

7. Matt D. Childs, *The 1812 Aponte Rebellion in Cuba and the Struggle against Atlantic Slavery* (Chapel Hill: University of North Carolina Press, 2006), 187–188.

8. Elisabeth Donnan, ed., *Documents Illustrative of the Slave Trade to America*, vol. 3 (Washington, DC: Carnegie Institution, 1931), 118–121.

9. Roger Bastide, "The Other Quilombos," in *Maroon Societies*, 197.

10. Childs, *1812 Aponte Rebellion*, 181.

11. Price, *Maroon Societies*, 17.

12. Da Costa, *Crowns of Glory*, 216.

CHAPTER 8

LEGACY OF SLAVE REVOLTS

Throughout the modern era, millions of people have been enslaved or held in some form of bondage across the globe—in indigenous slave systems in Asia and Africa, in slave systems of the Muslim world, and in slave systems established by European colonial expansion. Millions more have been held in other forms of servitude and unfree labor. Although pervasive, slavery and especially resistance to slavery have been sparsely noted in recorded history. In the past, those who recorded and interpreted history were members of elite upper classes, and what they chose to record and how they interpreted events and people reflected their experiences, interests, and values.

While Europeans and Americans protested the enslavement of thousands of Christian countrymen by the notorious Barbary pirates, few saw their own enslavement of Amerindians, Africans, and Asians in the same light. To Europe's and America's ruling and mercantile classes, slavery was a legitimate and necessary labor system that made use of criminals, prisoners of war who might otherwise have been executed, or peoples they considered inferior and barbaric. Not viewing slavery as a violation of universal human rights, they did not recognize any right of the enslaved to resist their condition.

Slaveholders found it nearly impossible to see slave rebellions as anything but criminal acts against a natural and lawful social order. In the Americas, rebellions by enslaved Africans and their descendants were often explained as eruptions of deep-seated, barbaric propensities to violence, motivated by desire to plunder, rape, and kill. However, especially in the nineteenth century, some masters maintained that the majority of their slaves were simple, meek beings who accepted their condition, and if they were incited to rebel, it was usually through some means of delusion. This myth of the "docile slave" dominated interpretation of slave history in the United States well into the twentieth century.[1]

Slaves and peasants saw things differently. To them and their descendants, rebellions were justifiable attempts to gain freedom, rights, or improved living and working conditions. Through the centuries, the names and deeds of many rebel leaders were handed down through legend and folklore and served as an inspiration to subsequent mass political action. In Asia and Europe, peasant leaders such as Japan's Sakura Sōgorō and Russia's Stepan Razin, both executed as criminals, became legendary heroes celebrated in story and song. A Shinto shrine was erected in Sōgorō's honor in the nineteenth century, and even today Japanese farmers fiercely protesting government seizure of land see themselves as following in his footsteps.[2] Razin's rebellion and others of that century and the next influenced the Russian Revolution of 1917. Even Spartacus, who to slaveholders symbolized the dangers they must protect against, remained alive in the minds of peasants as a symbol of justifiable struggle against oppression. Calling itself the Spartacist League, a 1918 German political group promoted mass revolt of "wage-slaves" against the capitalist establishment.

In the Americas and other parts of the globe affected by European colonial expansion, slave rebellion produced lasting effects in political organization, geography, and culture. The establishment of Haiti as an independent nation was the direct result of a slave rebellion. Many of the maroon communities established by self-liberated slaves in Africa, on the islands of the Indian Ocean, and throughout the Americas survived until their respective colonies or countries abolished slavery, and some continue today either as Maroon societies or as ethnic groups. And over the last fifty years, historical and cultural reassessment has been placing slave rebellions within the long history of oppressed people taking justice into their own hands to throw off their oppressors.

Haiti, the Product of Slave Rebellion

Arguably the most dramatic and successful slave insurrection in modern history, if not the whole of human history, was the thirteen-year struggle of slaves and free blacks in the Caribbean colony of Saint-Domingue, who seized their liberty by force, overthrew French rule, repelled British invasion, and established Haiti as an independent nation. The slaves' revolution was not hailed by most of the contemporary world as a positive development, however. Surrounded by nations and colonies with the world's foremost slave regimes, the fledgling Haitian Republic was feared as an incendiary influence. And indeed, as we have seen, the Haitian Revolution inspired slave rebellions throughout the region.

Although the slave rebellion succeeded in abolishing slavery in the new country of Haiti, it resulted in great loss of life, flight of population—especially among the educated and skilled—and enormous destruction of property. The country faced the daunting tasks of rebuilding its infrastructure and creating a sustaining economic system based on free labor. Without needed aid from the international community, Haiti became an impoverished country that, with many other former colonial states, is often characterized as underdeveloped or "third world." Nevertheless, Haiti survived, and today 90 percent of its population is descended from self-liberated African slaves.

Contemporary Maroon Cultures

With the abolition of slavery in Mexico, the United States, Brazil, and other areas with maroon activity, most maroon communities disappeared as their populations assimilated into the larger societies around them. But some left behind a testament to their existence in towns they established and mountains named after them. In Veracruz, Mexico, for example, the town Yanga established as a maroon community during the late sixteenth century still exists today. Granted its freedom and autonomy in 1609, it was known for most of the following three centuries as San Lorenzo de los Negros but was renamed Yanga in 1932. On the Indian Ocean island of Réunion, a former French plantation colony, the names of mountains bear the names of maroon leaders who once hid in their valleys—Dimitile, Anchain, Cimendef. In Africa, a few towns established by maroon societies, such as Yalwa and Yuli, survive to this day.

In the Americas, some Maroon cultures continue to live as separate communities or distinct ethnic groups, embracing and preserving their unique heritage. Probably the best known of contemporary Maroon peoples are those of Jamaica, descendants of the island's Leeward and Windward Maroons. Jamaica's Maroons live, for the most part, autonomous and separate from Jamaican culture in the villages of Moore Town, Scotts Hall, Charles Town, and Accompong. Just as children in the United States memorize passages from the Declaration of Independence, so Jamaica's Maroon children recite passages from the 1739 treaty that granted freedom and autonomy to their forebears. A festival that celebrates the birthday of maroon captain

Cudjoe, whom the maroons consider their founding father, draws thousands of visitors each year.

Six Maroon peoples survive on the northeastern coast of South America: the Saramaka, Djuka, Paramaka, Matawai, Kwinti in Suriname, and the Aluku (descendants of the Boni maroons who fled from Suriname in 1776–1777) in French Guiana. Having lived for centuries isolated in the interior rain forests, these peoples have preserved much of their original African culture and music. Another Maroon people, the Palenqueros, live in the village San Basilio De Palenque in northern Colombia. About half of its three thousand residents still speak a language unique to that village.

Mexico's Costa Chica Maroons live in the mountainous region in Guerrero and Oaxaca after which they are named. Living in isolation here, their ancestors, fugitives from Spanish estates along the Pacific coast, were able to preserve their liberty until Mexico abolished slavery in 1829.

Known as Seminole Maroons or Black Seminoles, many descendants of the slaves who fled from South Carolina and Georgia to live in Spanish Florida with the Seminole Indians and who were exiled with them to Oklahoma, now live in Oklahoma, Texas, the Bahamas, and the northern Mexican state of Coahuila. Although scattered, these Maroons have succeeded in preserving their ethnic identity.

These Maroon peoples have preserved a cultural heritage that reflects both their African roots—in language, customs, and arts—and their pride in their forebears' victory over enslavement.

Historical and Cultural Reassessment of Slave Revolts

The historical record of slave resistance uncovered over the last fifty years, and continuing to be uncovered, refutes the idea that most slaves accepted their condition. Resistance was endemic among enslaved peoples, and collaborative armed revolt was more frequent than formerly averred. And the record shows that the overriding objective of slave rebellion was, quite simply, to secure liberty.

In the last several decades, a movement has arisen among the peoples and governments of the Caribbean region that embraces slave rebellions as emancipation wars and celebrates rebel leaders as courageous resistance leaders and freedom fighters. Less than two decades after Jamaica became independent from Great Britain in 1962, its government formally declared Samuel Sharpe, leader of the island's 1831–1832 slave rebellion, and the legendary maroon leader Queen Nanny to be national heroes, and placed their images on denominations of the island's currency. The market square on which Sharpe and other rebels were executed is now named Sam Sharpe Square, and in the center of that public space stands a group of statues honoring Sharpe as a teacher and leader of his people. Rejecting the names by which Sharpe's rebellion was known to white colonists—the Baptist War or Christmas Rebellion—the Jamaica National Heritage Trust has erected a monument to the Emancipation War of 1831–1832, listing the names of over six hundred men and women who were tried after the rebellion.

The government of Barbados commissioned a larger-than-life reproduction of a sculpture titled "Slave in Revolt" and placed it in the center of Emancipation Roundabout as a tribute to Bussa, the reputed leader of the island's 1816 slave revolt, now considered a national hero. In Grenada, hikers climb Mt. Fédon to visit the outpost that served as headquarters for Julien Fédon, leader of the island's 1795 rebellion.

In Brazil, both Ganga Zumba, king of the *quilombo* Palmares, and his successor, Zumbi, are considered national heroes. The day of Zumbi's execution is observed as a national day of pride, and Zumbi's image has appeared on both currency and postage stamps. In Guyana, where the beginning date of the Berbice Rebellion is celebrated as a national holiday, a monument in Georgetown honors Kofi, the rebellion's primary leader.

In the United States, honoring leaders of slave rebellions as freedom fighters is controversial. Sites connected with the two men whose names were used as rallying cries during the Civil War—John Brown and Denmark Vesey—have been designated as official historical sites. Brown's farm in New York is a state historical site, and Vesey's Charleston home is a National Historic Landmark. But fierce opposition met the proposal to erect a monument in Vesey's honor in downtown Charleston.

However, a new appreciation for slave resistance as justifiable attempts for liberty has stimulated much literary and artistic interest in rebel and maroon leaders. In addition to a flood of biographies of various rebel leaders, historical novels or stage plays have been written about Vesey, Gabriel Prosser, Nat Turner, the Amistad Rebellion, the 1741 conspiracy in New York City, and about Haiti's Toussaint Louverture and South Africa's Galant.[3] The Amistad Rebellion was the subject of a major 1997 Hollywood motion picture, and in Brazil, Ganga Zumba is the hero of the movie *Ganga Zumba* (1972), adapted from a novel by Joao Felicio dos Santos. Another movie, *Quilombo*

(1986), depicts the rise and fall of Palmares and honors both Ganga Zumba and Zumbi as courageous resistance leaders. Even on the island of Réunion, a former French colony in the Indian Ocean, a vibrant literary and artistic interest in the island's maroon heritage over the past three decades has established the maroon as a figure of dignity and the embodiment of liberation.[4]

Of course, the impulse toward popular reinterpretation of slave rebellion carries with it risks of inaccuracy and exaggeration, just as did previous myths based on perceptions of the slavocracy and historical neglect. However, the historical and cultural reassessments of slave rebellion are creating a new appreciation for the men and women who sought to liberate themselves from slavery, by whatever means available to them. Demonstrating this radical change in perception, Virginia's Governor Tim Kaine issued a symbolic pardon to Gabriel Prosser in 2007, honoring his devotion to "the fundamental Virginia values of freedom and equality" and "the ideals of the American Revolution—it was worth risking death to secure liberty." He also noted that "the slave rebel's cause"—whether perceived as a collective effort to overthrow slavery or an individual attempt to escape the system—"has prevailed in the light of history."[5]

Notes

1. See texts cited by John H. Bracey, "Foreword," in Herbert Aptheker, *American Negro Slave Revolts*, 50th anniversary ed. (New York: International Publishers, 1993), 4; John Hicks, *The Federal Union: A History of the United States to 1865* (Boston: Houghton Mifflin, 1937), 495; Samuel E. Morison and Henry S. Commager, *The Growth of the American Republic*, vol. 1, 3rd ed. (New York: Oxford University Press, 1942), 537–539; Alan Nevins and H. S. Commager, *A Short History of the United States* (New York: Modern Library, 1956), 237–238; Samuel E. Morison, *The Oxford History of the American People* (New York: Oxford University Press, 1965), 505–507.

2. Anne Walthall, "Japanese *Gimin*: Peasant Martyrs in Popular Memory," *American Historical Review* 91 (December 1986): 1076.

3. Vesey: *Denmark Vesey: Insurrection* by Julian Wiles (2007); Gabriel: *Black Thunder* by Arna Bontemps (1936); Turner: *The Confessions of Nat Turner* by William Styron (1963); *Amistad Kata-Kata* by Charlie Haffner (1988); New York conspiracy: *The Great Negro Plot* by Mat Johnson (2007); Toussaint: *The Black Jacobins* by C. L. R. James, which appeared as a stage play in 1936 before being rewritten a novel two years later; *Drums at Dusk* by Arna Bontemps (1939); *The Kingdom of this World* by Aléjo Carpentier (1957); and *All Souls' Rising* by Madison Smartt Bell (1995); Galant: *A Chain of Voices* by André Brink (1982).

4. Edward A. Alpers, "The Idea of Marronage: Reflections on Literature and Politics in Réunion," in *Slavery and Resistance in Africa and Asia*, ed. Edward A. Alpers and Gwyn Campbell (London: Routledge, 2005), 43–44.

5. "Kaine Issues Pardon in Slave Revolt," *Richmond* (Virginia) *Times-Dispatch*, August 31, 2007.

BIOGRAPHIES

José Antonio Aponte (ca. 1757–1812)

A retired captain of Havana's free black militia, José Antonio Aponte was determined by Cuban authorities to have been the primary leader of a planned island-wide rebellion in 1812 (see Chapter 4).

Although the date of his birth is not known, Aponte retired from the militia in 1800 after twenty-three years of service, during which he served with Spanish forces trying to Drive the British out of the Gulf of Mexico during the American Revolution. His father and grandfather also had long careers in the black militia, his grandfather having received a medal for meritorious service during the Seven Years' War.

Aponte's home, located outside the fortified walls of Havana where many of the city's free and slave artisans lived, doubled as a carpenter shop where, in addition to practicing his trade, he trained apprentices and taught them to read and write. One of his instructional methods was to have the apprentices write out copies of royal decrees delineating the rights and benefits of black militiamen.

After Aponte was identified as being involved in the Havana Rebellion of March 1812, authorities searched his home and found a *libro de pinturas*, or book of paintings or drawings, that became a major piece of evidence against him. It included sketches of his father, grandfather, and other black soldiers defeating white soldiers, as well as autobiographical drawings of his own military service. It also contained maps of Havana's streets and various military garrisons. According to trial testimony, Aponte had showed this book, along with portraits of Toussaint Louverture and other leaders of Haiti's revolution, to members of the black militia and to slaves and free blacks who met in his house to plan the rebellion.

During his trial, Aponte confessed to dictating the declaration of independence posted in Havana on March 15, 1812, that declared the slaves' revolutionary intentions. He was hanged on April 9, 1812.

Bilali (ca. 1805–after 1872)

Called a "New Spartacus" by the British who admired his valiant efforts to defend the freedom of his followers, Bilali was the leader of a large maroon community in West Africa during the mid-nineteenth century (see Chapter 6). Born around 1805 in Kakuna, a Soso (or Susu) state in today's Guinea and Sierra Leone, Bilali was the son of the king of Kakuna, Almamy Dumbuya, but inherited the slave status of his concubine mother. Almamy Dumbuya ensured that Bilali received an extensive Muslim education as well as military training and promised that, according to custom, his son would be emancipated upon his death. When the king died in 1837, however, his successor refused to grant Bilali his freedom, and Bilali fled with his family and supporters to a neighboring country, where he was granted refuge and land upon which to settle.

Bilali banned slavery from Laminyah, the community he established, and granted asylum to runaway slaves from across the region, incurring the wrath of the region's slave-holding political leaders, who repeatedly tried to destroy the town. But as Bilali's reputation for steadfastness in protecting the liberty of his followers grew, so too did his power. For thirty years he succeeded in defending his free communities from attack by the region's slave-holding powers. But in 1870, as the price of peace, he agreed not to accept any more fugitive slaves in Laminyah. Nothing more is known of Bilali's life after these negotiations.

Joseph Cinque (Sengbe Pieh) (1814–1879)

Captured in what is today Sierra Leone and shipped across the Atlantic aboard a Portuguese slaver, Sengbe Pieh was given the Spanish name Joseph Cinque by Cuban purchasers shortly before he led the shipboard revolt that became a legal case before the United States Supreme Court and established his place in history (see Chapter 2).

The son of a Mende village leader, Cinque was twenty-five years old and the father of three children when he was captured, marched three days to the West African coast, and boarded onto the Portuguese slaver *Tecora*. After a two-month voyage during which over one-third of the ship's five hundred captives died, Cinque and fifty-two other survivors were purchased at Havana in June 1839 and placed aboard the schooner, *Amistad*, for a short voyage to the home of their purchasers, Pedro Montes and Jose Ruiz. On their third night out, Cinque picked the lock of his shackles with a nail he had found, freed his companions, and quickly gained control of the ship. Knowing the *Tecora* had sailed toward the setting sun, Cinque forced Montes to sail eastward, toward Africa. But Montes reversed direction at night, and the *Amistad* ended up off the coast of Long Island, New York, where, desperate for food and water, Cinque and a few companions went ashore for provisions. Officers from a U.S. naval vessel seized the *Amistad* and after returning Cinque and his companions to the ship, towed it to Connecticut, where the Africans were imprisoned to await trials that would determine their fate.

Murder charges against Cinque and the other rebels were dismissed for jurisdictional reasons, but a civil case was filed to determine whether they should be returned to the Spaniards. Abolitionists mounted a defense and won their release, but the verdict was appealed to the Supreme Court, which also ruled in favor of the Africans. In January 1842, Cinque arrived at Freetown, Sierra Leone, along with other captives who had survived the long ordeal. He returned to his people, but found that both his village and his family were gone. He later became an interpreter at the mission of Kaw-Mende, where he died in 1879.

Essjerrie Ettin (ca. 1740–1769)

One of a very few African shipboard insurrectionists whose name survives in ship records, Essjerrie Ettin was an Asante (an Akan subgroup) from the interior of what is today Ghana who led an uprising on the Dutch slave ship *Guineese Vriendschap* on October 31, 1769 (see Chapter 2). Interrogated with nine other rebels at the Dutch West India Company's headquarters at Elmina, he was determined to be the primary leader and was sentenced to death. While there is no record of the actual execution, he was to have had his right hand severed (his left arm had been maimed during battle) and then be hung from the mast of the *Guineese Vriendschap*, his body abused and broken by the crew until he died, and then thrown into the ocean.

Julien Fédon (ca. 1750–after 1796)

A free black planter who himself owned one hundred slaves, Julien Fédon led a revolt against British rule of Grenada that temporarily liberated the island's slaves and established a short-lived black republic (see Chapter 4).

The son of a white French immigrant and free black woman, Fédon became a member of Grenada's emerging free black elite in 1791 when he purchased a plantation that made him one of the island's largest landowners. However, as a French Catholic mulatto, his personal freedom, economic aspirations, and political rights were undercut by legislation designed to control the free black population, limit land ownership by non-British subjects, and exclude French Roman Catholics from public affairs. Under an act that required free blacks to prove their free status or be sold as slaves, Fédon's wife had been detained in 1787 until witnesses verified her freedom.

Wanting to protect their freedom and rights, and influenced by the French and Haitian revolutions, a group of rebels made plans to overthrow the British government. By the summer of 1794 when they were visited by an emissary from the French Republic, preparations were well under way, with Fédon elected leader and his mountain plantation chosen as headquarters. In addition to providing both military and diplomatic assistance, France commissioned Fédon as a general. The revolution started on March 4, 1795, when Fédon called on the island's inhabitants to yield to the revolutionary forces or face the scourges of war. British colonists and a few French supporters refused to surrender, and the revolutionary forces quickly took control of most of the island.

Fédon governed the island for nearly a year from his plantation in central Grenada before his revolutionary forces were defeated in the summer of 1796. Along with many of his followers, Fédon escaped into the wilderness, and although rebels continued to be captured for several years thereafter, Fédon was never found. After an upturned canoe was found with Fédon's compass nailed to the bottom, many believed that he had drowned. But one scholar has pointed out that the canoe and compass could have been deliberate signs in African tradition that Fédon had made his escape.[1] His uncertain fate has added to the mystery surrounding this legendary folk hero, whose mountain plantation in central Grenada is today a popular tourist attraction.

Gabriel (1776–1800)

A skilled blacksmith who absorbed the political views of the white artisans with whom he worked, Gabriel was a Virginia slave who engineered a complex conspiracy in 1800 aimed both at forcing state authorities to abolish slavery and at establishing a system of fair wage labor for both blacks and whites (see Chapter 5).

Although historians often identify him as Gabriel Prosser, contemporary records refer to him only as Gabriel and there is no evidence that he ever used the surname of his master, Thomas Prosser. Born in 1776 on a tobacco plantation north of Richmond, Virginia, Gabriel was influenced by the pervasive rhetoric about natural rights, freedom, and equality that marked the revolutionary period of his youth. He benefited from a postwar labor system that permitted skilled slaves such as he to hire out their labor and worked part of each month in the state capital of Richmond, where he became aware of the bitter political feud between Republicans and Federalists. Intending to take advantage of this schism, Gabriel planned to take control of Richmond and force authorities to grant his demands.

However, a violent rainstorm delayed implementation, and an informant alerted authorities. Two of Gabriel's brothers were among the first conspirators executed. Gabriel himself evaded arrest for three weeks, until he was captured aboard a schooner docked in Norfolk some ninety miles down river from Richmond. Ironically, he had been aided by a sympathetic white captain but betrayed by one of the ship's black slaves. He was executed on October 10, 1800.

Kofi (aka Cuffy and Coffy) (ca. 1730s–1763)

Memorialized today by a large monument in Georgetown, Guyana, Kofi led one of the largest slave revolts in the Americas, and one that was nearly successful. An ethnic Akan who had been shipped to the Dutch colony of Berbice as a boy and then trained as a cooper, Kofi (his African name; Coffy in Dutch, Cuffy in English) started the Berbice Slave Rebellion of 1763 with an insurrection on his home plantation on February 23 (see Chapter 4). He became the primary leader of the revolt and, after the rebel army had succeeded in driving most white settlers from the colony, established a rebel government and tried to negotiate a peace settlement with the colonial governor that would recognize the slaves' freedom. Feigning sincere consideration of Kofi's proposal to divide the colony into symbiotic entities for blacks and whites, the colonial governor kept up a correspondence with Kofi while awaiting military reinforcements. In August, a rival leader who disapproved of his plan to share the colony with whites succeeded in deposing Kofi, and he committed suicide shortly thereafter. Military reinforcements succeeded in suppressing the rebellion and restored white rule to the colony in 1764. Today, the people of Guyana consider Kofi a hero and observe February 23, the day Kofi began his rebellion, as a national holiday.

Toussaint Louverture (ca. 1744–1803)

Born to slavery in French-controlled Saint-Domingue, on the island of Hispaniola, Toussaint Louverture is regarded as the founding father of its successor state—Haiti. Born about 1744 as Toussaint de Bréda, he made good use of opportunities for self-education, learned to read and write, and was entrusted with considerable responsibility, which led to his manumission in 1791.

Shortly after gaining his freedom, Toussaint joined the uprising of Saint-Domingue's slaves that launched a decade-long struggle for freedom (see Chapter 4). A genius at organization and tactics, he soon became one of the leaders of the rebellion and became known as Louverture, meaning *the opening*, in recognition of his effort to create a gap in the ranks of the enemy. He collaborated for a while with the Spanish in Santo Domingo, but after the French revolutionary government became more radical, it recognized Toussaint as the principal leader of the rebels. He drove invading British forces from the western coast of the island, put down an attempted coup by mulatto generals, and was appointed Governor-General of Saint-Domingue after France abolished slavery in 1794.

When, by 1801, Toussaint had gained control over virtually all of Hispaniola, including Spanish Santo Domingo, he strengthened his position by reorganizing the government and establishing a constitution that made him governor for life. Meanwhile, the government of France had become more conservative. After Napoleon declared himself emperor in 1802, he rescinded the abolition of slavery and sent a large military force to Hispaniola to reestablish the slave system. While several black generals cooperated with the French, Toussaint withdrew to his private estate. In June 1802, Toussaint was betrayed by former associates and tricked into a conference with the French military commander, General Leclerc, who arrested him and had him deported to France. Having incurred Napoleon's disfavor (see Primary Document 9), Toussaint was ordered a harsh and degrading imprisonment that caused his death on April 7, 1803.

The rebel forces prevailed in Saint-Domingue even without Toussaint and defeated the disease-weakened French troops. The victorious rebels renamed the country Haiti in 1804, and Toussaint came to be honored as a founding father.

Nanny (ca. 1680s–1750s)

Although most of what is known about Nanny comes from oral tradition rather than documentary evidence, the few references to her in Jamaica's colonial records support the legend of her as a powerful military, spiritual, and cultural leader of the island's eastern, or windward, maroons during the early eighteenth century (see Chapter 6).

A member of the Akan ethnic group, Nanny presumably was born in what is present-day Ghana and escaped from a Jamaican plantation sometime before 1720, when the maroon village that became known as Nanny Town was established. Although known as Queen Nanny, she was not the chief ruler of her community. She was, however, both its powerful obeah, or spiritual advisor, and its primary military strategist, known for devising clever guerilla warfare tactics that repelled repeated attacks by colonial forces during Jamaica's First Maroon War (1720s–1739).

After signing a peace treaty with her community, the Jamaican government granted five hundred acres to "Nanny and the people residing with her and their heirs" in 1740, establishing the legal existence of Nanny Town, which exists today as Moore Town. Also known for preserving African culture among the maroons, Nanny has been immortalized in both legend and song as a formidable leader of supernatural strength and powers. A symbol of unity and strength for all of the island's maroons, she has been declared a national hero by the Jamaican government.

Quamina (ca. 1770s–1823)

A deacon in the mission church for blacks in the British colony of Demerara, Quamina played a leading role in planning a slave uprising there in 1823 (see Chapter 4). He opposed using violence, however, and when plans for the insurrection took that direction, he tried to persuade his fellow slaves to call it off. The rebellion proceeded, and although Quamina did not participate, he was hunted down and killed.

Enslaved in Africa as a boy, Quamina was shipped during the 1780s to Demerara, on the north coast of South America, and trained as a carpenter. A gentle and patient man, he was highly regarded by slaves and free blacks alike. Missionaries converted him to Christianity in 1808 and appointed him senior deacon of their Bethel Chapel in 1817. As a deacon, Quamina selected catechist teachers, collected money for the chapel, and served as advisor and broker between members and the pastor.

As a result of his religious devotion, Quamina had at times been badly treated by the manager of his plantation. Twice he was severely whipped, at least once he was placed in stocks, and occasionally he was forced to work on Sundays to prevent his attendance at church services. While his wife of twenty years was dying, his master ordered him to a distant job, making it impossible for him to comfort her during her final days. While ill treatment fueled Quamina's resentment of slavery, a May 1823 order from the governor forbidding slaves from attending Bethel Chapel without written passes from their masters intensified his simmering rage.

As rumors of imminent slave emancipation engulfed the colony in the summer of 1823, Quamina was persuaded to join in planning a rebellion in case the planters refused to honor the emancipation law. On August 17, the eve of the planned insurrection, there was considerable disagreement and hesitation among its leaders. Objecting to the use of violence, Quamina sought advice from the Reverend John Smith, pastor of Bethel Chapel, and then tried to call it off. But his son, Jack Gladstone, successfully urged that it proceed.

Quamina remained in the background at his plantation while the revolt raged. But when the rebels were defeated, knowing that he would be sought for his leadership role in the planning, he went into hiding. Despite the offer of a large reward for his capture and the efforts of several search parties, he eluded apprehension for nearly a month. Located in a thick tropical forest on September 16, 1823, he ignored an order to surrender and continued walking away. Shot from behind, he died immediately, and his body was strung up in chains on his home plantation.

Samuel Sharpe (1801–1832)

An eloquent speaker and trusted teacher whose charisma and unique mobility made him the paramount leader of Jamaica's Baptist War (see Chapter 4), Samuel Sharpe was declared a national hero by the government of Jamaica in 1975.

Born in slavery at Montego Bay in 1801, Sharpe was a lay-preacher and deacon in that city's Burchell Baptist Church. Although officially a household servant, he lived virtually as a free man, allowed to travel and preach at will throughout the island's western parish of Saint James. Sharpe followed parliamentary debate on abolition and other antislavery developments by reading discarded newspapers, and he relayed this information to slaves across the parish, teaching them that freedom was rightfully theirs. In 1831, it seemed certain that Parliament was about to enact emancipation, but vocal opposition among Jamaica's planters—some vowing to shoot their slaves rather than free them—convinced Sharpe that the island's whites would not concede freedom without force.

In the summer of 1831, Sharpe emerged as the paramount leader of a network of elite slaves planning a general work stoppage in December. Leaders took an oath on the Bible that after Christmas they would no longer work as slaves, but only work for pay. In a deep and calm voice, Sharpe assured slaves that they could win their freedom only if they refused to work en masse. They were to sit down peaceably, and only if attacked were they to retaliate by destroying homes— harming neither persons nor crops. Although Sharpe knew that the planters were vehemently determined not to make any concessions and were ready to use all force necessary to maintain order, he later expressed surprise and regret at the violent turn the rebellion took.

Sharpe spent the first days of the rebellion traveling across the parish rousing slaves to participate in the uprising. On January 1, 1832, authorities offered rewards for four rebel leaders, including Sharpe as the rebellion's "general ruler," and it is uncertain whether he surrendered or was captured. He was condemned to death and hanged on May 23, 1832.

During the 1840s, missionaries moved Sharpe's body from an unmarked grave to a place of honor within the newly rebuilt Burchell Baptist Church, which had been destroyed during the rebellion. And the market square on which Sharpe and other rebels were hanged, now called the Sam Sharpe Square, bears a monument to the man who led what Jamaicans now call the Emancipation War of 1831–1832.

John Smith (1790–1824)

Blamed by planters for Demerara's 1823 slave rebellion (see Chapter 4), the Reverend John Smith, head of the London Missionary Society in Demerara, was convicted and sentenced to death but died in prison awaiting the result of an appeal for clemency. Viewing his arrest and conviction as acts of revenge by slaveholders who had opposed his work among the slaves, abolitionists regarded him as a martyr to their cause. Smith's death fueled antislavery sentiment in Britain and helped persuade Parliament to end slavery in the British West Indies in 1833.

Born in England in 1790, Smith was apprenticed to a London tradesman at age 14. While ill with smallpox he vowed that if his life was spared, he would devote it to the service of God. After recovering and completing his apprenticeship, he applied to the London Missionary Society, which accepted him, completed his education, and sent him to the British colony of Demerara in 1817. As pastor of the missionary society's church for slaves, Smith incurred the wrath of planters who feared that religious instruction would make their slaves discontented and rebellious.

Indeed, when rebellion did occur in August 1823, many members of his church were involved. He had heard from his senior deacon, Quamina, that rebellion was being planned but thought his counsel against violence had ended the threat. Smith's refusal to report for militia duty strengthened officials' suspicions of his complicity, and he was arrested two days into the revolt. At his trial seven weeks later, several slaves testified that Smith had taught them Bible stories in which God had freed his people from slavery, but there was no evidence that he had suggested or encouraged rebellion. Convicted nonetheless, he was also found guilty of having known about the plan for rebellion but failing to notify authorities.

Smith appealed his sentence to the British Crown. Suffering from tuberculosis, which prison conditions aggravated, Smith died on February 24, 1824, shortly before word of his pardon reached Demerara.

Tula (Toela) (17??–1795)

Little is known about the life of Tula (or Toela in Dutch) other than his leadership role in the 1795 slave revolt on the Dutch island of Curaçao (see Chapter 4). A slave on the plantation Knip, he appears to have had considerable freedom of movement and was well informed about worldly events. To his own name he added that of Rigaud, after the Saint-Domingue revolutionary André Rigaud, whose August 1795 meeting with Tula at the Knip plantation sparked the Curaçao rebellion. During the two weeks after that meeting, Tula recruited support from slaves on other plantations in the area, and when the rebellion started at Knip on August 17, 1795, these plantations quickly joined. Within a week Tula's followers had taken control of all the plantations of western Curaçao. When authorities sent a Catholic priest to see if a settlement could be negotiated, Tula insisted the slaves would accept nothing less than emancipation. Clearly impressed with the rebel leader's determination, the priest showed considerable respect for him in his report. When the rebellion was suppressed, most surviving rebels surrendered and returned to their masters. Although Tula escaped, he was captured in September, tried, and brutally executed on October 2, 1795.

Denmark Vesey (ca. 1767–1822)

An ex-slave who planned a mass escape of slaves from Charleston, South Carolina, to the young Caribbean republic of Haiti, Denmark Vesey has been described as both a brutal terrorist who planned to massacre a city's entire white population and a courageous revolutionary who tried to liberate an enslaved people.

Originally named Telemaque, the rebel leader was probably born on the Danish Caribbean island of Saint Thomas where he was purchased as a teenager in 1781. Sold to a Saint-Domingue sugar plantation, he feigned epilepsy to escape field work and was returned as "defective merchandise" to the Bermuda slave trader Joseph Vesey. He was fluent in several languages and probably served as an interpreter during the year he worked on Vesey's slave ship. When Vesey retired from the sea in 1783, he kept Telemaque as a personal servant and settled in Charleston, South Carolina, where the boy became known as Denmark. Sixteen years later, at about age thirty-two, Denmark won fifteen hundred dollars in a city lottery and on December 31, 1799, purchased his freedom.

Denmark adopted the Vesey surname, became a carpenter, and by 1822 was earning a comfortable living. Although now a free man, he continued to identify with slaves. Appointed a "class leader in biblical instruction" for Charleston's African Methodist Episcopal Church in 1818, he taught slaves in his own home and in the slave quarters of area plantations, traveling as far as sixty miles from the city. He used both biblical passages and antislavery speeches collected from newspapers (made during the 1819–1820 debates concerning the Missouri Compromise and earlier debates on abolishing the slave trade) to foment discontent.

By December 1821 Vesey had begun planning a slave insurrection and exodus to Haiti (see Chapter 5). Planning for and with slaves, he involved few mulattoes, free blacks, or house servants. His instincts proved correct, for it was a house slave who betrayed the plan after hearing of it in late May. Arrested along with 130 of his followers, Vesey was hanged after a two-day trial on July 2, 1822.

While city and state authorities clamped down even tighter on slave movement and rights, Northern newspapers debated the justice of Vesey's cause, with some insisting that revolt was the only way slaves could attain their freedom. Sympathizers viewed Denmark Vesey as a martyr to the antislavery cause, and his name became a rallying cry for black soldiers during the Civil War.

Yanga (also Ñanga) (ca. 1540s–1610s)

The first known maroon leader in the Americas to negotiate peace and autonomy for his community was a fugitive slave named Yanga, also known as Ñanga (see Chapter 6). Although neither his birth nor death year is known, he was an elderly man in 1609 when he agreed to a treaty with the authorities of New Spain (now Mexico). He claimed he had been born in Africa, the son of a chief or king of an Akan tribe in present-day Ghana, and said that if he had not been enslaved he would have become the ruler of his people. Certainly the skill and self-confidence with which he led his *palenque,* or maroon community, seem to confirm that heritage.

Yanga's *palenque,* called Cofre de Perote and located about one hundred miles west of the port of Veracruz, exhibited such African features as a combination of magical (religious) and political leadership. Although in his later years he delegated many military matters to an aid, Yanga successfully defended his community against Spanish attacks for three decades. In 1609, however, he accepted an offer of truce and peace negotiations from Spanish officials. He had allowed a Catholic priest to live in Cofre de Perote during the preceding year, and the priest's positive report on the maroons probably helped change attitudes on both sides. Yanga proposed peace conditions that were both forceful and conciliatory (see Primary Document 5), demanding the same rights for the *palenque* that Indian and Spanish towns enjoyed in New Spain.

Zeferina (17??–1826 or after)

While several women took part in slave rebellions (see Chapter 7), few were known as leaders of revolts or of maroon communities. Zeferina, a member of the Urubu *quilombo,* a kind of maroon community, near Salvador, Bahia, in Brazil, may have been an exception. Although all that is known about her comes from documents concerning an 1826 police attack on Urubu (see Chapter 6), those records suggest that Zeferina may have been the *quilombo's* leader and may have been planning an uprising.

The soldiers who attacked Urubu in mid-December 1826 said that, amid war cries of "Death to whites! Long live blacks!" the *quilombo's* population of fifty males and a few females put up a fierce fight with knives, swords, and machetes. Nevertheless, they were quickly defeated, and those not killed in battle or who did not escape into the bush were taken prisoner. One of these captives was Zeferina, whom the provincial president later referred to as "queen," and who, according to the soldiers, not only had fought against them with bow and arrows but also had acted as a real leader, rallying the warriors and urging them on. Zeferina told authorities that the *quilombo* had expected many slaves from Salvador to join them on Christmas Day, and that they had planned to invade the city, kill its white inhabitants, and thus gain the slaves' freedom. The fact that of the maroons captured, only Zeferina and an alleged priest received sentences—of prison with hard labor—suggests that Zeferina was at least perceived by authorities to have played a leading role in the conflict as well as in planning the Christmas Day revolt. Although the year of her death is not known, it is unlikely that she would have long survived imprisonment and hard labor.

Zumbi (Zambi) (1655–1695)

Last of the leaders of the *quilombo* Palmares in Brazil, Zumbi was born free in Palmares in 1655 but was captured as an infant during a Portuguese attack. Under a Catholic priest to whose care he was entrusted, he was baptized and learned Portuguese and Latin. In 1670, at the age of fifteen, he ran away and returned to Palmares.

When his uncle, Ganga Zumba, became king of the *quilombo* in 1675, Zumbi became commander of his army. Three years later, when the king accepted a treaty offered by the government, granting peace to those born in Palmares but requiring the return of runaways, Zumbi led an opposition faction that refused to honor the treaty. After allegedly poisoning his uncle, Zumbi became king of Palmares in 1680.

Zumbi successfully defended Palmares against repeated attacks until February 1694, when the *quilombo* fell after a long siege. He was believed to have been one of the two hundred maroons who threw themselves off cliffs rather than face capture and enslavement. When he reappeared in battle the following year, rumors spread of his immortality. For nearly two years, Zumbi and a small group of followers evaded capture. Finally betrayed by one of his own men, he was captured and killed in 1695. To prove that Zumbi was not immortal, authorities displayed his head in the capital of the province. Long a legendary figure among Afro-Brazilians, Zumbi is now celebrated as a national hero, and the date of his capture—November 20—is a national holiday.

Note

1. Curtis Jacobs, "The Fédons of Grenada, 1763–1814" (paper presented at the Grenada Country Conference, Grenada, January 2002).

PRIMARY DOCUMENTS

Document 1: Slave Rebellion on the Barbary Coast, 1772

Captured from European ships by Barbary pirates, as many as one million Europeans from many different countries were enslaved by the Barbary states of North Africa (Algeria, Morocco, and Tunis) from the sixteenth century through the eighteenth (see Chapter 2). About one in ten of these slaves were ransomed by charitable organizations or relatives, but the majority remained in North Africa. Occasionally, some attempted to escape, and a few efforts were successful. The following account of an escape in 1772 was recorded in the British Annual Register.

> A most remarkable escape has lately been effected here which will undoubtedly cause those that have not had that good fortune to be treated with the utmost rigour. On the morning of 27 July, the Dey [ruler of Algiers] was informed that all the Christian slaves had escaped overnight in a galley. This news soon roused him, and it was found to have been a preconcerted plan. About 10 P.M. seventy-four slaves who had found means to escape from their masters met in a large square near the gate which opens to the harbour, and being well armed, they soon forced the guard to submit, and to prevent them raising the city confined them all in the powder magazine. They then proceeded to the lower part of the harbour, where they embarked on board a large rowing polacre [boat] that was left there for the purpose and passed both the forts. As soon as this was known three large galleys were ordered out after them, but to no purpose. They returned in three days with the news of seeing the polacre sail into Barcelona, where the galleys durst not go to attack her.

Source: Stephen Clissold, *The Barbary Slaves* (1977; reprint, New York: Barnes & Noble, 1992), 71–72.

Document 2: Slave Revolt aboard the *Little George,* 1730

Slaves often revolted on European slave ships during the Middle Passage from Africa to the Americas (see Chapter 2). Both individual resistance, such as refusing to eat or jumping overboard, and collective rebellions occurred. The following testimony of the master of an American slave ship describes a revolt off the coast of Sierra Leone in 1730. Although most shipboard revolts ended in failure, this one was successful.

I, George Scott, master of the sloop *Little George,* belonging to Rhode Island, sailed from the Banana Islands on the coast of Guinea, the first day of June, 1730, having on board ninety-six slaves (thirty-five of which were men). On the 6th of said Month, at half an hour past four of the Clock in the morning, being about 100 leagues [300 miles] distant from the land, the men slaves got off their Irons, and making way through the bulkhead of the Deck, killed the watch, consisting of John Harris Doctor, Jonathan Ebens Cooper, and Thomas Ham Sailor, who were ... all asleep. I, being then in my Cabin and hearing a noise upon deck ... took my pistol directly and fired up the scuttle [hatchway in the deck] ..., which made all the slaves that were loose run forwards, except one or two men ... who kept us ... confined in the cabin, and passing by the companion to view us, we shot two men slaves.

On so sudden a surprise, we were at a loss what to do. But consulting together, [we] filled two round bottles with powder, put ... fuses to them in order to send them among the slaves, with a design at the same instant of time to issue out upon them, and either suppress them or lose our lives. But just as we were putting our design in execution, one of the slaves let fall an Ax (either through accident or design) which broke the bottle as Thomas Dickinson was setting fire to the fuse. Taking fire with a keg of powder in the Cabin, raised up the deck, blew open the cabin doors and windows, discharged all our fire arms but one, destroyed our Cloths, and burnt the man that had the Bottle in his hand in a most miserable manner, and myself with the rest very much hurt thereby.

Upon this unhappy accident, we expected no less than immediate death, which would have been unavoidable had they at that juncture of time rushed in upon us. And being in this consternation and hopeless, [we] sent up the boy in order ... to bring them to terms, but they slighted our message. And soon after ... we found the other bottle of powder which, by providence, had not taken fire. [This] put new life and vigor into us, that we were resolved to withstand them to the uttermost, and accordingly loaded our arms and shot several of the slaves, which occasioned all the men slaves to betake themselves to the quarter deck ... [above us]. The Slaves then got two swivel guns and filled them almost full with powder, which they found in the fore-hold as they were looking for provisions. [They] ... designed to blow the bulkhead in upon us, which they put fire to several times but could not get off by reason of wet weather. We had two carriage guns in the boat, which we expected the slaves would get out, and therefore watched them very narrowly. But in a dark night they [got them] ... and brought them upon the quarter deck, [where] they loaded one of the guns and pointed it directly down the scuttle. We hearing them ... and having prepared ourselves, as soon as they lifted it up we shot the man dead that pointed the gun. Another ... slave standing by [set] ... a match to it and fired it off, which blew the scuttle all to pieces and some of the deck, but did us no damage. They then took pieces of boards and laid them over the scuttle and the hole they had made in the deck, and laid the Tarpaulin with a great weight upon them to prevent our coming up.

Then they made sail ... towards land and were continually heaving down billets of wood and water into the Cabin, with [the] intention to disable us and spoil our small arms. [On] ... the fourth day after the rising [they reached] ... the same land we departed from, then stood off and on again for four or five days more, in which time the boy, being forced by hunger, ran up among the slaves, who immediately put him in irons. They made several attempts to come down into the cabin, but their courage failed them. I then called to them to come down to decide the matter, they answered by and by.

Finding ourselves growing very weak through these hardships and for want of sustenance, we thought it proper before our strength was quite spent to take some desperate course. I proposed to cut away the ceiling and bore some holes through the vessel's bottom, which ... let in about three feet of water. I then called to the slaves and told them I would drown them all, which frightened them exceedingly. They then sent the boy to the cabin door to tell us that they had but just made the land, and that when they got a little nearer the shore, they would take the boat and leave them with the young slaves. I told them if they would do that I would not sink [the ship]. (My design in letting the water in was to force the vessel on her side that we might get some advantage.) They stood in for the land about 12 o'clock at night [and] struck upon the [sand] bar of Sierra Leone River, and were in great danger of being lost. The vessel ... beat over the bar, and they ran ashore about three leagues up the river, on the north side. [This] being then high Water, and by seven o'clock the next morning there was not above a foot of water alongside.

The natives waded from the shore with fire arms, would have tried to overcome us, but were persuaded from it by the slaves on board, who told them we would shoot them if they appeared in our sight. They persuaded the grown Slaves to go ashore and drove the young ones over board and then followed them, making the vessel shake at their departure. Our Boy assuring us the slaves had all left the vessel, we immediately went up with our Arms, and saw the slaves just ashore.

Source: Elizabeth Donnan, *Documents Illustrative of the History of the Slave Trade to America,* vol. 3 (Washington, DC: Carnegie Institution, 1931), 118–121. Reprinted with permission from the Carnegie Institution.

Document 3: Hungry Chinese Peasants on a Rampage, 1890

Famine occurred frequently among Chinese peasants and occasionally created desperate conditions that could precipitate revolts (see Chapter 3). A famine that began in 1886 resulted in a rampage described in a childhood recollection of Marshal Chu Te, born in the province of Szechuan. In approximately 1890, a crowd of famished peasants invaded the estate of the wealthy landowner Lord Ting and forced him to feed them.

[I] heard a strange sound.... A horseman galloped wildly down the road and on toward the Ting home, and the strange sound grew louder, coming from the north where a cloud of dust was rising along the Big Road. From the dust cloud there soon emerged a mass of human skeletons, the men armed with every kind of weapon, foot-bound women carrying babies on their backs, and naked children with enormous stomachs and cavernous red eyes plodding wearily behind. Through a vast confusion of muttering voices, [I] heard the urgent clanging of cymbals and the roll of drums from the Ting mansion. The King of Hell [Ting's nickname] was summoning his tenants to fight for him.

The men of the Chu family heard the summons but did not move. The avalanche of starving people poured down the Big Road, hundreds of them eddying into the Chu courtyard, saying "Come and eat off the big houses!"

Grandfather and grandmother Chu laid restraining hands on their sons.... Then the "hunger marchers" were gone. The Chu family was not yet desperate enough to join them.... A few nights later, desperate peasants took refuge in the Chu home and talked in whispers of a wild battle in which hundreds of starving people had been killed, wounded or taken prisoner. They had fought fiercely, and had taken many soldiers with them into the shadows. Before the soldiers had caught up with them they had besieged the Ting estate and other big family homes, and though some had been killed they had entered and eaten.

Source: Jean Chesneaux, *Peasant Revolts in China, 1840–1949* (London: Thames and Hudson, 1973), 42–44.

Document 4: The Testimony of Galant, Leader of the Bokkeveld Revolt, South Africa, 1825

The Cape Colony in South Africa, established by the Dutch in 1652, imported many slaves from Asia and other parts of Africa before the British captured the colony in 1795. Many of these slaves escaped and mixed with indigenous ethnic groups, but occasionally resident slaves staged revolts. Influenced by news of debates about abolition in Parliament, a slave named Galant (ca. 1790–1825) led a revolt in the Bokkeveld, north of Cape Town. The revolt was suppressed quickly (see Chapter 3), and Galant and other rebel leaders were tried and executed at Cape Town in 1825. The following are excerpts from Galant's trial testimony.

> *Question by the prosecutor:* With what intention did you assemble?
> *Answer:* We meant to murder all the masters that did not treat their people well, to lay waste the country if we were strong enough, and then to escape to Caffreland [land of the indigenous people]; and if the Commando should be too strong, to remain at the places of the murdered people.
> *Question:* As you say in the beginning of your statement that you had spoken with Abel [one of the accused] and the other people, had you any other conversation with them than about the ill usage?
> *Answer:* Abel said he had heard his Master reading the newspaper about making the slaves free, and that he had heard his master say he would rather shoot all his slaves than make them free....
> *Question:* Do you persist in this statement, and have you anything to add to or take from it?
> *Answer:* I have something more to state, namely my master told me himself that he would shoot me. My master once when I came from the work also said to me that there was a newspaper come from another country [which stated] that a black cat had been hatched under a white hen. The next day my master

asked me what I understood by that expression? to which I answered that I did not know. My master repeated the question, and I said again, that I did not understand it; my Master then asked Achilles and Antony [also accused] if they also had an intention of going to their own Country, to which they answered yes, but said that they could not find the way there, but that they would go if the Governor would send them, although they were afraid their parents were dead and that they should not be known by their nation. My master was thereupon silent, but my mistress said to my wife ... Betje, that a Newspaper was come from the Cape which she dare not break open, but that a time would be prescribed when it might be opened. When the Newspaper was opened my mistress said that it stood therein that there was another great nation that was unknown; that there were orders come to make the Slaves free, and that if it was not done the other nation would then come to fight against the Farmers. My mistress afterwards further told me that it was also said in the Newspapers that the Slaves must be free, but if the Farmers would not allow it then it would not take place, to which I did not say anything.

Another Newspaper came afterwards, when my wife Betje told me that her mistress had said if we would go to the King for the money and bring it to her on the table, that then we might be free. I desired her to keep it quiet, which she did. Some time after, another Newspaper came, when my wife told me that her Mistress had said that the first Englishman who came to make the slaves free should be shot, as well as the slaves; upon which I again advised her to be silent, for that if our master should hear of it he would punish us, and that she must not tell it to anybody else; but I desired her to ask the Mistress why the slaves were to be free, as she spoke so often about it. She told me afterwards that she had asked her, and that her Mistress had said it was because there came too many white children among the black Negroes, and therefore that they must be free. I then desired her again not to tell it to anyone, and not to talk so much about it. Another Newspaper then came, when she informed me that her Mistress had said that the Farmers were too hard off, and that they were obliged to put up with too much from the Blacks.

My wife came to me one day to the land weeping, and on my asking her the reason she said that while she was in the kitchen she had asked for a piece of bread, and that her Master was so angry that he said he would shoot her and all the people in a lump, and leave us to be devoured by the crows and vultures. I again told her to be quiet, for that I could not well believe her although she was my wife, as she could not read or write no more than myself.

Once that Barend van der Merwe [Willem van der Merwe's neighbor] was at my Master's place on his return from Worcester where he had been to fetch the slave ... who had made a complaint, I was in the stable preparing forage for the horses. It was dark, so that nobody could see me in the stable. My master called Barend van der Merwe out and came with him into the stable without seeing me, when I heard my master ask him whether he had had his slave flogged, to which he answered no, for that the black people had more to say with the Magistrate of late than the Christians; further saying but he shall nevertheless not remain without a flogging, for when I come home he shall have one. I also heard Barend van der Merwe say to my Master on that occasion I wish that the Secretaries or Commissioners had died rather than that they should have come here, for that since that time they had been obliged to pay so much for the *Opgaaf* [tax declaration] and also for the Slaves. My master gave for answer I wish that the first Commissioner who put his foot [here] … had broken his neck, for that it was from that time one was obliged to pay so much for the Slaves, which they were not worth. My Master likewise said to Barend van der Merwe that he must keep himself armed in order to shoot the first Commissioner or Englishman who should come to the Country to make the Slaves free, together with the Slaves all in one heap.

B. van der Merwe thereupon rode home, some time after which I again heard my master speaking to Barend Lubbe who was at my Master's place, when he asked Lubbe how it was in the upper Country, to which Lubbe answered he did not know, that he not having any slaves had not once inquired about it, and that what the gentlemen did was well done; my master replied that although he had not any Slaves he must nevertheless stand up for his Country, further saying that he would shoot the first Commissioner, Englishman, or magistrate who should come to his place to make the Slaves free, but first the Slaves. Lubbe then asked van der Merwe whether he was not afraid if he fought against the Magistrates that the Slaves would attack him from behind, to which my master answered for that reason the Slaves must be first shot.

Subsequently I heard my master speaking for the third time with Hans Lubbe and Jan Bothma, whom having asked how it was in their part of the Country, they answered bad, for the black heathens have more privileges than us, and if the Christians go to the Landdrost [administrative official] to complain of their slaves, the Landdrost will not even look at us, but turns his backside to us, on which my master said the best advice I can give you is that you remain armed and keep your powder and ball together. Lubbe replied the first Gentleman that comes to me I will shoot with all the Slaves in a heap. Again for the fourth time I heard my Master talking with Schalk Lubbe, likewise at my master's place, whom he asked how it was here in the upper Country and if he had heard anything of the Newspaper and about the Slaves, he answered no, on which my master said lately we heard every day of new laws. I have asked for nothing, but I keep myself armed to shoot the first magistrate who comes to my place and the Blacks likewise.

For the fifth time I heard my Master conversing at his place with Johannes Jansen and Jan Verlee [both killed in the revolt, along with Van der Merwe]; the former had made an ox sambok [whip] which he brought into the house, on which my master desired me to drive in a pig that had got out, which I accordingly did. Standing before the door of the pigsty in order to fasten it, I heard my master say to Jansen, you must promise me something the same as Verlee has done, namely to shoot the magistrate when he comes. Jansen answered that he would do so, for that he would stand up for his mother Country; on that my Master said that he should give orders to all the Slaves, and that if they did not obey them he would supple the sambok [whip] on them the next day, for, said my Master, if you punish a slave you must do it that he cannot be known before a magistrate. My Master ordered us to smear the treading floor and that the floor must be well laid the next morning when he got up, on that we made the plan to murder all the farmers.... My master did not say anything more about it that evening, and we then immediately formed the plan, as I have already stated.

Source: G. M. Theal, ed., *Records of the Cape Colony,* vol. 20 (London: William Clowes and Sons, 1905), 208–211.

Document 5: Conditions for Peace Submitted by Mexican Maroons, 1609

A number of maroon communities, or *palenques*, were established in New Spain (Mexico) during the sixteenth and seventeenth centuries, and some developed into towns that still exist today (see Chapter 6). One of the earliest and long-lasting Mexican maroon communities was Cofre de Perote, near present-day Cordoba, Veracruz, which was founded and ruled by an enslaved West African named Yanga (see Biographical Sketch). Spanish authorities tried for several decades to destroy the *palenque*, and after an expensive and unsuccessful expedition in 1608, both parties were ready for a peace settlement the next year. The following document is the maroon's proposal, in which they requested the right of self-government under the ultimate authority of the Spanish Crown—the same rights enjoyed by Indian and Spanish towns. Successful negotiations established the town of San Lorenzo, but its location led to gradual decline.

   1. That all those who fled before last September will be free and those who flee after that time will be returned to their owners.

2. That they [maroons] must have a chief judge who shall not be a mestizo nor criollo nor a letrado but rather ... a warrior.

3. That no Spaniard will have a house in or stay within the town, excepting during the markets they [the Spanish] will have in their [maroons] town on Mondays and Thursdays.

4. That they must have councilmen and a town council.

5. That the Captain Nanga [meaning Yanga], who is their leader, must be governor and after him his sons and descendants.

6. That they obligate themselves to return to their owners the blacks who flee to them from the ports, and for their work the blacks who track and return the runaways will be paid twelve pesos, and until they return the runaways, they will provide [the owners] with others of their own who will serve them. And if they do not return them they will pay [the owners] their value. And within a year and a half they must be given a charter confirmed by Your Majesty and if not they will return to their original state. . . .

7. That their town must be founded between the Rio Blanco and the estates of Ribadeneira where they indicate.

8. That they will pay tribute to Your Majesty like all the rest of the free blacks and mulattos of the Indies.

9. The last condition they request is that Franciscan friars and no others minister to them and that the costs of the ornaments of the church be paid for by Your Majesty.

10. They will present themselves with their arms every time Your Majesty has need of them to defend the land.

Source: Jane G. Landers, "Cimarrón and Citizen: African Ethnicity, Corporate Identity, and the Evolution of Free Black Towns in the Spanish Circum-Caribbean," in *Slaves, Subjects, and Subversives: Blacks in Colonial Latin America*, ed. Jane G. Landers and Barry M. Robinson (Albuquerque: University of New Mexico Press, 2006), 134–135.

Document 6: Palmares: Quilombo in Brazil, ca. 1605–1694

Palmares, the largest maroon community of all times, was located in the interior of Brazil (see Chapter 6). Although attacked repeatedly, first by the Dutch and later by the Portuguese, it survived for most of the seventeenth century and has been called an African state because of its size and African political and cultural features. Written in the late seventeenth century, the following excerpts from a chronicle by an unknown author describe a complex network of towns and villages, as well as of Palmares's struggle with colonial powers and its ultimate destruction in 1694.

In a palm forest sixteen leagues northeast of Porto Calvo existed the *mocambo* of the Zambi ... and five leagues farther north that of Acainene ... To the east ... was the *mocambo* of the Wild Canes ... that of Bambiabonga [and] eight leagues north ... the compound called Sucupira. [S]ix leagues northward from this [was] the Royal Compound of the Macaco, and five leagues to the west ... the *mocambo* of Osenga....

[They] were the largest and best-fortified, [but] there were [also villages] of less importance and with fewer people. It is widely believed that when blacks were first brought into the captaincies [provinces] of Brazil they began to live in these Palmares, and it is certain that during the period of Dutch rule their numbers greatly increased....

They called their king Gangasuma (a hybrid term meaning great lord ...) [who] lived in a royal city ... called Macaco ... [which] was completely surrounded by a wall of earth and sticks. The second city was that known as Sucupira.... Here lived the Gangasona, the king's brother. Like the latter, all the cities were under the command of rulers and powerful chiefs....

Before the restoration of Pernambuco from Dutch rule, twenty-five probing expeditions were sent into the area, suffering great losses but failing to uncover the secrets of those brave people.... Later came the expedition of Colonel Antonio Jacomo Bezerra, which did them some damage, and those of various other leaders.... [After] recovering the captaincy from Dutch rule with the surrender of Recife in ... 1654, [Governor Francisco Barreto] immediately undertook a campaign against Palmares.... From ... 1657 to January, 1674, [when] Captain D. Pedro de Almeida assumed the governorship of the captaincy, it was for no lack of effort that victory was not achieved.... However, the obstacles encountered by the governors made unbeatable those whose bravery alone would not have sufficed to protect them. The army's best fighters, the most experienced leaders of the war against the Dutch, were at once employed for this purpose....

The inhabitants of Alagôas, Porto Calvo, and Penedo were constantly under attack, and their houses and plantations robbed by the blacks of Palmares. The blacks killed their cattle and carried away their slaves to enlarge their *quilombos* and increase the number of their defenders.... This was the situation in ... 1674, when D. Pedro de Almeida took possession of the captaincy and at once attempted to pursue the conquest....

By September 23, 1675, Major Manoel Lopes was in Porto Calvão with 280 men, including whites, mestizos, and Indians, ... and ... on November 21, after two months of preparation, they entered the wilderness where their labors and dangers were enormous and constant. On January 22, 1676, they reached a well-garrisoned and populous city of more than two thousand houses, and after more than two hours of bitter fighting, with bravery displayed on both sides, our men set fire to some houses, which, being of wood and straw, quickly burned, turning the place into an inferno. The great fear which then possessed the blacks forced them to flee, and ... [they] abandoned the city. The next day, gathered at another place ... they were again attacked, suffering considerable losses.... Many were killed or wounded in those two encounters, the others seeking refuge in the forests.

D. Pedro de Almeida, satisfied with the results obtained, and wishing to take advantage of the experience acquired and [Palmares's] demoralization ... decided to commit new forces to the enterprise. To accomplish this he sent an invitation to Commander Fernão Carrilho, who ... had become famous for ... destroying the *mocambos* of the blacks and the villages of the Tapuia Indians who infested the back lands of Bahia....

D. Pedro ... told Fernão Carrilho that his most successful strategy would be to establish and maintain a fortified camp inside Palmares; and since it appeared impossible to inhabit that dense and nearly impenetrable forest because of the climate and the great lack of provisions which could not be supplied from the surrounding area, he took every necessary precaution, ordering the needed provisions to be supplied from nearby towns, so that nothing would be lacking to those who would be stationed in the projected camp.

[O]n September 21, 1677, the expedition [under Fernão Carrilho] set out on its march from the town of Porto Calvo for the interior forests of Palmares. Accompanying it until it entered the forests were ... those who were most experienced in those marches and those most interested in its success....

As soon as the blacks knew of their presence, they quickly abandoned the city, still in the state of terror inspired by Major Manoel Lopes. On October 4 our men attacked the fugitives with such force that they killed many and captured nine, but the king's mother was not found among them either dead or alive. Not only did [the expedition] gain advantages from the enemy's losses ... this victory also served to furnish our side with guides and information. From the prisoners it was learned that the king, Gangasuma, with his brother, Gangasona, and all the other rulers and main chiefs were at the compound called Sucupira, which was then serving as a stronghold where the king waited to engage us in battle. This *mocambo* was 45 leagues from Porto Calvo. [O]n October 9 ... Carrilho set out toward the Sucupira Compound over open forest trails.

[When] our men found the *mocambo* ... [the] blacks had set fire to the city, which even in ashes revealed its greatness.

When Gangasuma had received the news carried by the fugitives ... he found it preferable to sacrifice the city to fire rather than place his own people in danger.

[Afterwards] ... the reinforced expedition achieved another important victory, killing and capturing many blacks, including the field commander, General Gangamuiza, whom they executed along with other male prisoners. The king, who had also been present at the beginning of the battle, had fled with the few people he could rescue from the carnage.

... After 22 days of hard campaigning in that wilderness ... they received news that the king, Gangasuma, was with Amaro in his *mocambo* nine leagues northwest of Serinhaem. This same Amaro, celebrated for his bravery, impudence, and insulting behavior, was also greatly feared by our men, and he had made himself known by his incursions into the surrounding towns. He lived separated from the others as an independent ruler. His *mocambo* ... was fortified by high, thick palisades extending the length of a league and containing more than a thousand inhabited houses.

In this *mocambo* the fugitive king believed himself to be safe, but even there he could not escape the vigilance and tenacity of our men.... [T]he blacks ... began to evacuate the compound, but ... many of them were killed and wounded on the ground, and 47 were captured.... Also captured were Anajuba, two of the king's children named Zambi and Jacainêne ... and others numbering about twenty, among them children and grandchildren of the king.... So greatly frightened was the king that he fled from our furious attack, and so badly disorganized that he left behind a gilded pistol and a sword, and he was also reported wounded.

This great event brought total disorganization to the blacks, who had lost any hope that they could remain any longer in those places, since they had lost their principal leaders ... and found themselves weakened and surrounded on all sides.... King Gangasuma ... fearing further setbacks ... accepted D. Pedro's offer, and on June 18 ... two of the king's sons and ten more of the most important blacks of those *quilombos* ... had come, in conformity with the offer made to them, to prostrate themselves at the feet of D. Pedro. They had been sent by King Gangasuma to render vassalage in his name, to ask for peace and friendship....

The appearance of those barbarians caused amazement, because they came naked, and with their natural parts alone covered. Some wore their beards in braids, others wore false beards and mustaches, and others were shaved, and nothing more. All were husky and powerful, armed with bows and arrows, and carrying only one firearm. One of the king's sons rode a horse, because he still bore an open bullet wound which he had received during the fighting.

... Pedro de Almeida received them with great pleasure, and not wishing the glory for such an outstanding achievement for himself alone, he entrusted them to the new governor.... Great was the pleasure with which Governor Ayres de Sousa received them, and extraordinary was his delight at being so highly esteemed by those enemies. He treated them with great courtesy, spoke to them gently, and promised to do everything for them....

Source: Robert E. Conrad, *Children of God's Fire: A Documentary History of Black Slavery in Brazil* (Princeton, NJ: Princeton University Press, 1983), 369–376. Reprinted with permission from Robert E. Conrad.

Document 7: Containment of Conspiracy by Mining Slaves in Brazil, 1719

After gold was discovered at Minas Gerais, Brazil, in 1700, many slaves were brought to the region. Although the work was hard, mining gave many slaves more freedom than plantation slaves had, increasing their opportunity to plan resistance. The following 1719 letter from the provincial governor Count Dom Pedro de Almeida to the Portuguese Crown, describes how one conspiracy was put down but how the threat of rebellion was a continuing problem (see Chapter 4).

In a letter of June 13 of last year [1718] I informed Your Majesty of the unrestrained life style of the blacks in this mining region, especially the runaways who, gathered together in *quilombos,* dare to commit all kinds of offenses without fear of punishment. I also called Your Majesty's attention to the great importance of this question, because it seemed to be reasonably well founded that the blacks might possibly carry out operations similar to those of Palmares in Pernambuco, encouraged by their large numbers and the foolhardy attitudes of their masters. Not only do the latter trust them with all kinds of weapons, they also conceal their acts of insolence and their crimes (even those perpetrated against themselves) to avoid the risk of losing them if they should be seized by the agents of Justice. The harm caused by this situation seems without remedy, as I pointed out to you in that same letter, owing to the absence of preventive measures and the great carelessness which has always been characteristic of this situation.

With the passage of time my fears have been verified. No longer satisfied merely to harass us from the *mocambos* which they control in various places, and have always held despite the great efforts I have made to destroy them, the blacks now aspire to an even greater enterprise.

And, although this is an ambitious undertaking, it is not beyond their powers, if we consider their large numbers compared with the number of whites....

Having entered into a conspiracy to rebel against the whites which involved most of the blacks of these mines, they attempted to establish contacts with one another by means of various secret agents who went from one place to another over a vast area attempting to arrange a general revolt. They had decided that their first attacks would take place on Maundy Thursday of this year. With all the white men occupied in the churches, they reasoned, they would have time to break into their houses and attack the whites, pitilessly exterminating them. A few days before Holy Week those blacks began to quarrel among themselves, because it was the intention of one nation to impose its rule upon the rest, and the secret was therefore revealed in the Rio das Mortes district, where, along with news of the revolt, it was learned that the blacks of that district had named for themselves a king, a prince, and military leaders. I had already decided that this was probably some black nonsense, when another message arrived from a place called Furquim, ... [which] outlined circumstances like those reported in the message from Rio das Mones, and so it began to be clear to me that this was indeed a very serious situation.

I immediately decreed the necessary preventive measures, including the arrest of all the suspected blacks in the several places ... [and] a strict ban on the possession by blacks of weapons of every kind, at the same time imposing rigorous punishments upon them and upon their masters. I also ordered that extra precautions were to be taken on Maundy Thursday, the day appointed for the uprising, ordering that all weapons were to be stored in secure places where blacks would not have access to them, and that any weapons left by their owners in their houses should have their gunlocks removed, and should be concealed where the blacks could not find them. And because the blacks in Rio das Mones, a district less populated by whites, had displayed greater self-confidence than elsewhere, ... I ordered Lieutenant General João Ferreira Tavares to go there to arrest all blacks he thought were guilty, and to investigate the conspiracy. This he diligently did, arresting and sending to this city the so-called kings of the Mina and Angola nations and others who were allegedly chiefs and military leaders of the rebellion....

Since all these preventive measures were taken before the date determined by the blacks for their first attacks, and since many guilty black men and women were imprisoned, and others punished, the ... sedition was extinguished, and the country returned to its former tranquility. However, since we cannot prevent the remaining blacks from thinking, and cannot deprive them of their natural desire for freedom; and since we cannot, merely because of this desire, eliminate all of them, they being necessary for our existence here, it must be concluded that this country will always be subjected to this problem.... And because their multitudes, in comparison with the number of whites, give them courage; and because the whites place too much trust in them, failing to correct them despite repeated instances of unfaithfulness; and because, by merely looking about them they can see the haven offered to them by the immense forests, the defenselessness of the towns, the absence of soldiers to defeat them or pursue them into the forests, they gain courage enough to attempt anything.... And it seems to me that there should be some mature reflection on this matter, and that Your Majesty should consider its importance along with the measures that should be employed in the future to prevent the harmful consequences which could easily result from the kind of evil we have just witnessed. Once decisions have been arrived at, Your Majesty might adopt the most useful policies.

May God preserve Your Majesty's Royal Person for many years.

Vila do Carmo, April 20, 1719.
Count Dom Pedro de Almeida.

Source: Robert E. Conrad, *Children of God's Fire: A Documentary History of Black Slavery in Brazil* (Princeton, NJ: Princeton University Press, 1983), 395–397. Reprinted with permission from Robert E. Conrad.

Document 8: A Peace Treaty Proposed by Maroons in Brazil, 1789/1790

In 1789/1790, after two years of raids that stopped production on the Brazilian plantation from which they had escaped, a band of maroons led by Gregorio Luís proposed peace terms to their former master, Manoel da Silva Ferreira (see Chapter 6). In addition to demanding their leader's emancipation, the maroons sought improved working conditions and more time to work for themselves. Although the maroons were tricked into presenting themselves for re-enslavement, their demands illustrate the negotiating power this particular band believed they had and, in fact, many maroon bands did have.

My Lord, we want peace and we do not want war; if My Lord also wants our peace it must be in this manner, if he wishes to agree to that which we want.

In each week you must give us the days of Friday and Saturday to work for ourselves not subtracting any of these because they are Saint's days.

To enable us to live you must give us casting nets and canoes. You are not to oblige us to fish in the tidal pools nor to gather shellfish, and when you wish to gather shellfish send your Mina blacks.

For your sustenance have a fishing launch and decked canoes, and when you wish to eat shellfish send your Mina blacks.

Make a large boat so that when it goes to Bahia we can place our cargoes aboard and not pay freightage.

In the planting of manioc we wish the men to have a daily quota of two and one half hands and the women, two hands.

The daily quota of manioc flour must be of five level alqueires [one is about a bushel], placing enough harvesters so that these can serve to hang up the coverings.

The daily quota of sugarcane must be of five hands [one is about 600 canes] rather than six and of ten canes in each bundle.

On the boat you must put four poles, and one for the rudder, and the one at the rudder works hard for us.

The wood that is sawed with a hand saw [ripsaw] must have three men below and one above.

Source: Stuart B. Schwartz, "Resistance and Accommodation in Eighteenth-Century Brazil: The Slaves' View of Slavery," *Hispanic American Historical Review* 57, no. 1 (1977): 77–79.

Document 9: Toussaint Louverture Defends the Revolution at Saint-Domingue, 1793–1803

Toussaint Louverture, leader of the slave revolt that led to Saint-Domingue's independence (see Chapter 4 and Biographical Sketch), left extensive writings, of which a few selections follow. Two proclamations of 1793 urging slaves to join the revolt are followed by excerpts from a 1797 letter to the Directory (the executive branch of the French Republic), reaffirming his loyalty to France and the French Revolution. Toussaint had received support during the radical phase of the Revolution (1792–1794), but in 1795, more conservative elements gained prominence, chief among them Vienot Vaublanc, who severely criticized Toussaint. The final selection is an excerpt from a letter to Emperor Napoleon, written while Toussaint was imprisoned in Paris, where he died in April 1803.

Proclamation of August 25, 1793

> Having been the first to champion your cause, it is my duty to continue to labour for it. I cannot permit another to rob me of the initiative. Since I have begun, I will know how to conclude. Join me and you will enjoy the rights of freemen sooner than any other way. Neither whites nor mulattoes have formulated my plans; it is to the Supreme Being alone that I owe my inspiration. We have begun, we have carried on, we will know how to reach the goal.

Proclamation of August 29, 1793

> Brothers and Friends:
> I am Toussaint L'Ouverture. My name is perhaps known to you. I have undertaken to avenge you. I want liberty and equality to reign throughout St. Domingue. I am working towards that end. Come and join me, brothers, and combat by our side for the same cause.

Source: Ralph Korngold, *Citizen Toussaint* (Westport, CT: Greenwood Press, 1979), 99–100.

Letter to the Directory, October 28, 1797

After the revolutionary leaders in Paris became more conservative and critical of Toussaint and his followers in Saint Domingue, a prominent member of the Legislative Assembly, Vienot Vaublanc, vehemently criticized the Black Revolution. Toussaint's reaction is reflected in excerpts from the following letter.

> Citizen Directors,
> ... In order to justify myself in your eyes and in the eyes of my fellow citizens, whose esteem I so eagerly desire, I am going to apply myself to ... prove that the enemies of our liberty have only been motivated in this event by a spirit of personal vengeance and that the public interest and respect for the Constitution have been continually trampled under foot by them....
> I swear to God, that in order to better the cause of the blacks, I disavow the excesses to which some of them were carried.... I confess that the reproaches made here against the rebel band of Jean François are justly merited.... But the French ... will not confuse one unbridled, undisciplined rebel band with men who since the rule of liberty in St. Domingue have given unquestionable proof of loyalty to the Republic, ... and

have ... redeemed a part of the errors to which their enemies had driven them and their ignorance had led them....

Far be it from me to want to excuse the crimes of the revolution in St. Domingue by comparing them to even greater crimes, but citizen Vaublanc ... this former proprietor of slaves couldn't ignore what slavery was like.... And what would Vaublanc say ... if, having only the same natural rights as us, he was in his turn reduced to slavery? Would he endure without complaint the insults, the miseries, the tortures, the whippings? And if he had the good fortune to recover his liberty, would he listen without shuddering to the howls of those who wished to tear it from him? ... When blacks, men of color, and whites are under the same laws, they must be equally protected and they must be equally repressed when they deviate from them. Such is my opinion; such are my desires.

Source: George F. Tyson, Jr., ed., *Great Lives Observed: Toussaint L'Ouverture* (Englewood Cliffs, NJ: Prentice Hall, 1973), 36–43.

Letter to Napoleon during the Winter of 1802–1803

I have had the misfortune to incur your anger; but as to fidelity and probity, I am strong in my conscience, and I dare to say with truth that among all the servants of the State none is more honest than I. I was one of your soldiers and the first servant of the Republic in San Domingo. I am today wretched, ruined, dishonored, a victim of my own services. Let your sensibility be touched at my position, you are too great in feeling and too just not to pronounce on my destiny....

Source: C. L. R. James, *The Black Jacobins: Toussaint L'Ouverture and the San Domingo Revolution*, rev. ed. (New York: Vintage Books, 1989), 364.

Document 10: Peace Treaty with the Maroons in Jamaica, 1739

In March 1739, at the conclusion of Jamaica's First Maroon War (1730–1739), John Guthrie and Francis Sadler, representatives of the British King George II, negotiated a peace treaty with Cudjoe, leader of the island's western maroons (see Chapter 6). In return for their freedom and limited autonomy, the maroons recognized the British governor as the supreme authority on Jamaica and agreed to build and maintain certain public roads. Several months later, Chief

Quaco, representing maroons on the eastern side of the island, approved a similar treaty. After fifty years, however, the territory around Trelawny Town allotted to Cudjoe's maroons proved insufficient for their growing population, and this along with other grievances led to the Second Maroon War (1792–1793), between the colony and the Trelawny maroons. Punctuation has been modified to improve readability.

> In the name of God, amen. Whereas Captain Cudjoe, Captain Acompong, Captain Johnny, Captain Cuffee, Captain Quaco, and several other negroes, their dependants and adherents, have been in a state of war and hostility for several years past against our sovereign Lord the King and the inhabitants of this island; ... and whereas his majesty George the Second, King of Great Britain ... has ... granted full power and authority to John Guthrie and Francis Sadler, esquires, to negotiate and finally conclude a treaty of peace and friendship with the aforesaid Captain Cudjoe and the rest of his captains, adherents, and others ...; they mutually, sincerely, and amicably, have agreed to the following articles:
>
> First, that all hostilities shall cease on both sides for ever.
>
> Second, that the said Captain Cudjoe, the rest of his captains, adherents, and men, shall be for ever hereafter in a perfect state of freedom and liberty, excepting those who have been taken by them within two years ... [and] are willing to return to their said masters and owners with full pardon and indemnity from their said masters or owners for what is past, provided always, that, if they are not willing to return, they shall remain in subjection to Captain Cudjoe and in friendship with us, according to the form and tenor of this treaty.
>
> Third, that they shall enjoy and possess, for themselves and posterity for ever, all the lands situated ... between Trelawny Town and the cockpits, to the amount of fifteen hundred acres, bearing northwest from the said Trelawny Town.
>
> Fourth, that they shall have liberty to plant the said lands with coffee, cacoa, ginger, tobacco, and cotton, and to breed cattle, hogs, goats, or any other stock, and dispose of the produce or increase of the said commodities to the inhabitants of this island, provided always that when they bring the said commodities to market, they shall apply first to the custo[m]s, or any other magistrate of the respective parishes where they expose their goods to sale, for a licence to vend the same.
>
> Fifth, that Captain Cudjoe and all the Captains' adherents, and people now in subjection to him, shall all live together within the bounds of Trelawny Town and that they have liberty to hunt where they shall think fit, except within three miles of any settlement, crawl, or pen, provided always that in case the

hunters of Captain Cudjoe and those of older settlements meet, that the hogs ... be equally divided between both parties.

Sixth, that the said Captain Cudjoe and his successors do use their best endeavours to take, kill, suppress, or destroy, either by themselves or jointly with any other number of men, commanded on that service by His Excellency the Governor, or Commander in Chief for the time being, all rebels wheresoever they be, throughout this island, unless they submit to the same terms of accommodation granted to Captain Cudjoe and his successors.

Seventh, that in case this island be invaded by any foreign enemy, the said Captain Cudjoe, and his successors hereinafter named or to be appointed, shall then upon notice given, immediately repair to any place the Governor for the time being shall appoint, in order to repel the said invaders with his or their utmost force, and to submit to the orders of the Commander in Chief on that occasion.

Eighth, that if any white man shall do any manner of injury to Captain Cudjoe, his successors, or any of his or their people, they shall apply to any commanding or officer or magistrate in the neighbourhood for justice, and in case Captain Cudjoe or any of his people, shall do any injury to any white person he shall submit himself or deliver up such offender to justice.

Ninth, that if any negroes shall hereafter runaway from their masters or owners and fall into Captain Cudjoe's hands, they shall immediately be sent back to the chief magistrate of the next parish where they are taken and those that bring them are to be satisfied for their trouble, as the legislature shall appoint.

Tenth, that all negroes taken, since the raising of this party by Captain Cudjoe's people shall immediately be returned.

Eleventh, that Captain Cudjoe, and his successors shall wait on His Excellency, or the Commander in Chief for the time being, every year if hitherto required.

Twelfth, that Captain Cudjoe, during his life, and the Captains succeeding him, shall have full power to inflict any punishment they think proper for crimes committed by their men among themselves, death only excepted, in which case, if the Captain thinks they deserve death, he shall be obliged to bring them before any Justice of the Peace, who shall order proceedings on their trial equal to those of other free negroes.

Thirteenth, that Captain Cudjoe with his people shall cut, clear and keep open, large and convenient roads from Trelawny Town to Westmoreland and St. James, and, if possible, to St. Elizabeth.

Fourteenth, that two white men to be nominated by His Excellency or the Commander in Chief for the time being, shall constantly reside with Captain Cudjoe and his successors in order to maintain a friendly correspondence with the inhabitants of this island.

Fifteenth, that Captain Cudjoe shall during his life be chief commander in Trelawny Town, after his decease the command to devolve on his brother Captain Accompong and in the case of his decease, on his next brother Captain Johnny and failing him, Captain Quaco. Captain Cuffee shall succeed, who is to be succeeded by Captain Quaco and after all their demises, the Governor or Commander in Chief for the time being shall appoint, from time to time, whom he thinks fit for that command.

Source: R. C. Dallas, *The History of the Maroons, from Their Origin ...* (1803; reprint, London: Frank Cass, 1968), 58–65.

Document 11: Suriname Officials Negotiate with Maroon Chief Araby, 1760

After decades of unsuccessful attempts to subdue various maroon communities in the Dutch colony of Suriname, colonial authorities began negotiations in 1760 with the Djuka and Saramaka maroons (see Chapter 6). The following account of the first formal meeting between representatives of the colonial government and Araby, leader of the Saramaka, was written by John Gabriel Stedman, who served as a soldier in Suriname in the years 1773–1776. A peace agreement was not finalized and signed until 1762. Spelling, capitalization, and punctuation have been modified.

> Governor [Wigbold] Crommelin [1752–1754 and 1757–1768] sent two commissioners ... Mr. Sober and Mr. Abercrombie, who marched through the woods escorted by a few military &c., to carry some presents to the rebels [maroons] preliminary to the ratification of the peace [agreement].... At their arrival ... in the rebel camp, ... they were introduced to a very handsome Negro called Araby, who was the chief of them all.... He received them very politely and ... desired they would sit down by his side upon the green, at the same time assuring them they needed not be under any apprehensions of evil, since coming in so good a cause, not one intended or even dared to hurt them.
>
> But when [the maroons discovered] that they had brought a parcel of trinkets—such as knives, scissors, combs, and small looking glasses—and forgot the principal article in question, viz. gunpowder, firearms, and ammunition, he resolutely stepped up to the commissioners and asked in a thundering voice if the

European imagined that the Negroes could live on combs and looking glasses, adding that one of each was fully sufficient to let them all see their faces with satisfaction, while a single gallon of ... gunpowder should have been accepted as a proof of their trust. But since that had been omitted, they should ... never more return to [his] countrymen till every article of his list should be fulfilled.

A Negro captain called Quacoo now interfered, saying that these gentlemen were only the messengers of their Governor and Court, and as they could not be answerable for their masters' proceedings, they should certainly go back to where they came from without hurt or molestation....

The chief of the rebels then ordered silence and desired Mr. Abercrombie to make up a list himself of such articles as he, Araby, should name him, which that gentleman having done, the rebels not only gave him and his companions [permission] peaceably to return with it to town, but [also gave] their Governor and Court a whole year to deliberate on what they were to choose—peace or war. They [the maroons] swore unanimously that during that interval all animosity should cease on their side, after which, having entertained them in the best manner their situation in the woods afforded, they wished them a happy journey to Paramaribo.

One of the rebel officers upon this occasion represented to Mr. Sober and to Mr. Abercrombie what a pity it was that the Europeans who pretend to be a civilized nation should be so much the occasion of their own ruin by their inhuman cruelties towards their slaves.

[We] desire you, continued this Negro, to tell your Governor and your Court that in case they want to raise no new gangs of rebels, they ought to take care that the planters keep a more watchful eye over their own property and not so often trust them in the hands of a parcel of drunken managers and overseers, who by wrongfully whipping the Negroes, debauching their wives and children, neglecting the sick, &c., are the ruin of the colony and willfully drive to the woods such quantities of stout, handsome people who by their sweat got your subsistence and without whose hands your colony must drop to nothing, and to whom at last in this pitiful manner you are glad to come and ply for friendship.

Mr. Abercrombie now begged of them to be accompanied [by] one or two of their principal officers to Paramaribo, where he promised they should be vastly well treated &c. But the chief, Araby, answered him with a smile that [there would be sufficient time] a year thereafter, when the peace should be thoroughly concluded, [and] that then even his youngest son should be at their service to receive his education amongst them, while for his subsistence and even for that of his descendants, he should take the sole [care] upon himself without ever giving the Christians the smallest trouble. After this, the commissioners left the rebels and all arrived safe and sound at Paramaribo.

Source: John Gabriel Stedman, *Narrative of a Five Years' Expedition against the Revolted Negroes of Surinam: Transcribed for the First Time from the Original 1790 Manuscript,* ed. Richard Price and Sally Price (Baltimore: Johns Hopkins University Press, 1988), 70–72. Courtesy of Richard Price and Sally Price.

Document 12: An Expedition against the Boni Maroons in Suriname, 1775

While Suriname's officials were willing to negotiate with some of the many maroon bands that plagued the colony (see Primary Document 11 and Chapter 6), they continued attacks against the maroon group led by Chief Boni. Commanded by the French colonel Louis Henry Fourgeoud, most expeditions included colonial militia units, Dutch marines, and Black Rangers, former slaves who fought the maroons in return for their freedom. John Gabriel Stedman, an English officer serving in Suriname in a Dutch military detachment during the 1770s, recorded some of these expeditions, and despite his hostility against the maroons, he understood their hatred of the white establishment. The following account of one expedition also reveals the maroons' contempt for the Black Rangers, who served the planters. Spelling, capitalization, and punctuation have been modified.

On the 14th [of June 1775] came the news that some rebels' huts were discovered near the seaside, [and] that Capt. Meyland had marched in quest of the enemy with 140 men of the [Suriname] Society troops who had actually found them out, but, in wading through a deep marsh, had been ... attacked by the Negroes, who had killed several of his men, ... wounded more, and beat back the whole detachment.... This news proved that the sable foes were not to be trifled with.... Orders were immediately issued for all the troops that were able to march to keep in readiness, viz. Fourgeoud's Marines, the Society regiment, and my favorite [Black] Rangers.... Now all was alive and in a flow of spirits, some in hopes that this decisive stroke would end the war and their misery, some from hoping to find a little plunder amongst the enemy, and some from a motive of revenge to these poor naked people, who, as I have related before, originally revolted on account of bad usage and now took every means to retaliate upon their persecutors....

[On August 20th], we set out ... towards the swamp ... which we entered about 8 o'clock, when we soon found ourselves in the water till above our middle, & expected (as Captain Meyland had met with) a very warm reception on the opposite shore. Having waded through this marsh ..., the van rapidly mounted the beach with cocked firelocks and screwed bayonets, the whole body close following, without meeting with the smallest opposition. But here was a spectacle almost sufficient to dampen the spirits of the most intrepid soldier, viz., the ground being strewed with the skulls, bones, and ribs, still covered with part of the flesh and besmeared with the blood of those unhappy men killed with Capt. Meyland, which that gentleman indeed had found means to bury, but which had since by the rebel Negroes been dug up for the sake of their clothes.... This being the second or third group of human bones we met with during our peregrination, I frankly acknowledge they were no stimulant for me to engage with Negroes, [but they spurred on] the common soldiers with a view of taking revenge for the loss of their massacred companions....

At 10 o'clock we met a small party of the rebels, each with a green hamper on his back, who having fired at us ... let drop down their bundles and took to their heels, back towards their village, and whom we since learned were transporting rice to another settlement to [feed] Boni's people.... We now vigorously redoubled our pace till about 12 o'clock, when two more musket shot were fired by an advance guard of the enemy as a signal to Boni of our approach, ... after which we came to a fine field with rice, india corn, &c.... However, in about half an hour we ... proceeded by cutting through a small defile of wood, into which we no sooner had entered than ... the firing at last commenced from every side, the rebels retiring and we advancing, till finally we arrived in the most beautiful oblong, square field with rice in full ripeness ..., and in which appeared to our view the rebel town at a distance, in the form of an amphitheater sheltered by the foliage of a few ranks of lofty trees which they had left standing, the whole presenting a truly romantic and enchanting *coup d'oeil* [glimpse] to the unconcerned spectator.

In this field, the firing now lasted like one continuous peal of thunder for nearly 40 minutes, during which time the rangers acted with wonderful skill and gallantry, while the white soldiers were too much animated, the one firing over the other at random.... I received ... a ball ... between the shirt and the skin, and my lieutenant, Mr. Decabanes, had the sling of his fusee shot away, while several were wounded, some mortally.... The stratagem of the enemy in surrounding and interspersing the field [with] the large trunks and the roots of fallen trees ... made our advancing very [difficult] and dangerous & at the back of which fortifications they lay lurking and firing upon us, without themselves [being] materially hurt, and over numbers of which timbers we had to scramble before we could come to the town. However, we kept advancing, and while I thought this excellent generalship in them, their superstitious simplicity surprised me much, of which I only relate one instance. A poor fellow trusting in his amulet or charm, by which he thought himself invulnerable, advanced frequently on one of these trees till very near us. And having discharged his piece, [he] walked off the way he came to reload with the greatest confidence and deliberation, till at last one of my men [shot him in the leg].... Down he came, now crawling for shelter under the same tree which had supported him, but the soldier went up to him instantly, and, placing the muzzle of his musket in his mouth, blew out his brains, & in which manner several of his countrymen were knocked down....

In short, being now about to enter the town, a rebel captain wearing a tarnished gold-laced hat, & carrying a wisp of flaming straw in his hand, seeing their ruin inevitable, frustrated the storm in our presence by setting the town on fire, and which by the dryness of the houses instantly occasioned one general conflagration, when the popping from the wood immediately [ceased]. [This] masterly maneuver not only prevented that carnage to which the common soldier is too prone in the heat of victory, but gave [the maroons] the opportunity of retreating with their wives & children, and carrying off their best lumber, while our pursuit, and even our falling on any of the spoils, was at once also frustrated by the ascending flames....

About 3 o'clock P.M. [as we were setting up camp], we were suddenly surprised by an attack from the enemy, but who, after exchanging a few shot, were soon repulsed. This unexpected visit, however, put us upon our guard during the whole night, by allowing no fires to be lighted and doubling the sentinels all around the camp. Thus situated, ... I ventured into my hammock, where I soon fell asleep, but not longer than the space of an hour, when my faithful black boy Quacoo awakened me in pitch darkness crying, *Massera, Massera. Boosee Negro, Boosee Negro.* And hearing at the same time a brisk firing, while the balls rustled through the branches about me, I imagined no other than that the enemy was in the middle of our camp. In this surprise and not perfectly awake, I started up with my fusee cocked ... fell ... over two or three bodies that lay on the ground, and which I took to be shot, but one of which ... told me if I moved I was a dead man. Colonel Fourgeoud, with all his troops lying flat on their bellies ...

had issued orders no more to fire, the men having spent most of their ammunition the preceding day. I took his advice.... In this situation we continued to lie prostrate on our arms till next morning when ... a most abusive dialogue ensued between the rebels and the rangers, both parties cursing and menacing each other at a terrible rate. The first reproach[ed] the others as being poltroons and betrayers of their country-men, whom they challenged the next day to single combat, swearing they only wanted to wash their hands in the blood of such scoundrels who had been the capital hands in destroying their fine settlement. While the rangers damned the rebels for a parcel of pitiful skulking rascals, whom they would fight one to two in the open field if they dared to show their ugly faces; that they had deserted their masters, being too lazy to do their work, while they [the rangers] would stand by the Europeans till they died. After which they insulted each other by a kind of war whoop, then sung victorious songs and sounded their horns in defiance....

At last poor Fourgeoud entered into the conversation, [with] the help of myself and Sergeant Fowler ... as his inter-preters, but which created more mirth than I before heard in the Colony. He promised them [the rebels] life, liberty, meat, drink, and all they wanted, but they replied with a loud laugh that they wanted nothing from him who seemed a half-starved Frenchman, already run away from his own country, and that if he would venture to give them a visit in person, he should not be hurt and might depend on not returning with an empty belly. They called to us that we were more to be pitied than themselves, [because we] were only a parcel of white slaves, hired to be shot at & starved for 4 pence a day, and that they scorned to expend much of their powder upon such scare-crows, who had not been the aggressors ... [but] were only obeying the commands of their masters. But if the planters and overseers dared to enter the woods themselves, not a soul of such scoundrels should ever return, no more than the rangers some of whom might depend on being massacred that very day or the next, and they concluded by swearing that Boni should soon be the Governor of all the Colony. After this they tinkled their billhooks, fired a volley, [and] gave three cheers which were answered by the rangers, and all dispersed with the rising sun, to our great satisfaction, being heartily tired of such company.

Source: John Gabriel Stedman, *Narrative of a Five Years' Expedition against the Revolted Negroes of Surinam: Transcribed for the First Time from the Original 1790 Manuscript,* ed. Richard Price and Sally Price (Baltimore: Johns Hopkins University Press, 1988), 360, 401–409. Courtesy of Richard Price and Sally Price.

Document 13: David Walker's *Appeal*, 1829

In 1829, David Walker (1785–1830), a free black man born in the South but then living in Boston, published an 88-page appeal addressed to "the Coloured Citizens of the World, but in Particular, and very Expressly, to Those of the United States of America." Condemning American slavery as the most cruel and barbarous labor system the world had ever seen, he attempted to show in four articles that American slaves were rendered the "most wretched, degraded, and subject set of beings that ever lived" by Slavery, Ignorance, Preachers of Religion, and Colonization (a so-called charitable plan to resettle American free blacks in Africa). He warned that if white Americans did not willingly end slavery and raise the blacks up to a position of equality, a just God would deliver slaves to their rightful freedom. But, he admonished, both slaves and free blacks must prepare for this deliverance and not hinder it in any way. Some of the punctuation has been modified to improve readability.

My beloved brethren:

... Remember that unless you are united, keeping your tongues within your teeth, you will be afraid to trust your secrets to each other, and thus perpetuate our miseries under the Christians!!!!! Remember also to lay humble at the feet of our Lord and Master Jesus Christ, with prayers and fastings. Let our enemies go on with their butcheries and at once fill up their cup. Never make an attempt to gain our freedom of natural right from under our cruel oppressors and murderers until you see your way clear—when that hour arrives and you move, be not afraid or dismayed; for be you assured that Jesus Christ, the King of heaven and of earth who is the God of justice and of armies, will surely go before you. And those enemies who have for hundreds of years stolen our rights and kept us ignorant of Him and His divine worship, he will remove. [*Added in a footnote:* It is not to be understood here that I mean for us to wait until God shall take us by the hair of our heads and drag us out of abject wretchedness and slavery, nor do I mean to convey the idea for us to wait until our enemies shall make preparations.... God has been pleased to give us two eyes, two hands, two feet, and some sense in our heads as well as they....] ... Fear not the number and education of our enemies against whom we shall have to contend for our lawful right, guaranteed to us by our Maker; for why should we be afraid, when God is, and will continue (if we continue humble) to be, on our side? ...

Beloved brethren—here let me tell you, and believe it, that the Lord our God, as true as he sits on his throne in heaven and as true as our Saviour died to redeem the world, will give you a

Hannibal; and when the Lord shall have raised him up, and given him to you for your possession, O my suffering brethren! remember the divisions and consequent sufferings of Carthage and of Hayti. Read the history particularly of Hayti, and see how they were butchered by the whites, and do you take warning. The person whom God shall give you, give him your support and let him go his length, and behold in him the salvation of your God. God will indeed deliver you through him from your deplorable and wretched condition under the Christians of America. I charge you this day before my God to lay no obstacle in his way, but let him go....

[Walker reprinted a newspaper account of an attempted slave escape that was foiled when one of the slaves helped the surviving slave driver to his horse, enabling him to rally help and recapture all the fugitives. Walker commented as follows:]

Here my brethren, I want you to notice particularly in the above article, the ignorant and deceitful actions of this coloured woman. I beg you to view it candidly, as for ETERNITY!!!! Here a notorious wretch, with two other confederates had SIXTY of them in a gang, driving them like brutes—the men all in chains and hand-cuffs, and by the help of God they got their chains and hand-cuffs thrown off, and caught two of the wretches and put them to death, and beat the other until they thought he was dead, and left him for dead; however, he deceived them, and rising from the ground, this servile woman helped him upon his horse, and he made his escape. Brethren, what do you think of this? Was it the natural fine feelings of this woman, to save such a wretch alive? ... But I declare, the actions of this black woman are really insupportable. For my own part, I cannot think it was any thing but servile deceit combined with the most gross ignorance: for we must remember that humanity, kindness and the fear of the Lord, does not consist in protecting devils.... Any person who will save such wretches from destruction is fighting against the Lord and will receive his just recompense. The black men acted like blockheads. Why did they not make sure of the wretch? He would have made sure of them, if he could.... [I]f you commence, make sure work—do not trifle, for they will not trifle with you ... [T]herefore, if there is an attempt made by us, kill or be killed. Now I ask you, had you not rather be killed than to be a slave to a tyrant who takes the life of your mother, wife, and dear little children? Look upon your mother, wife and children, and answer God Almighty; and believe this, that it is no more harm for you to kill a man who is trying to kill you, than it is for you to take a drink of water when thirsty....

Men of colour who are also of sense, for you particularly is my APPEAL designed. Our more ignorant brethren are not able to penetrate its value. I call upon you therefore to cast your eyes upon the wretchedness of your brethren and to do your utmost to enlighten them.... Let the Lord see you doing what you can to rescue them and yourselves from degradation. Do any of you say that you and your family are free and happy, and [think] what have you to do with the wretched slaves and other people? ... If any of you wish to know how FREE you are, let one of you start and go through the southern and western States of this country, and unless you travel as a slave to a white man ... or have your free papers (which if you are not careful they will get from you) [see] if they do not take you up and put you in jail and, if you cannot give good evidence of your freedom, sell you into eternal slavery....

... I advance it therefore to you, not as a problematical but as an unshaken and for ever immoveable fact, that your full glory and happiness, as well as all other coloured people under Heaven, shall never be fully consummated but with the entire emancipation of your enslaved brethren all over the world.... For I believe it is the will of the Lord that our greatest happiness shall consist in working for the salvation of our whole body. When this is accomplished a burst of glory will shine upon you which will indeed astonish you and the world. Do any of you say this never will be done? I assure you that God will accomplish it—if nothing else will answer, he will hurl tyrants and devils into atoms and make way for his people. But O my brethren! I say unto you again, you must go to work and prepare the way of the Lord.

... O Americans! Americans!! I call God—I call angels—I call men, to witness, that your DESTRUCTION is at hand, and will be speedily consummated unless you REPENT....

Now let us reason.... [W]o, wo, will be to you if we have to obtain our freedom by fighting. Throw away your fears and prejudices then, and enlighten us and treat us like men, and we will like you more than we do now hate you, and tell us now no more about colonization, for America is as much our country, as it is yours.—Treat us like men, and there is no danger but we will all live in peace and happiness together. For we are not like you, hard hearted, unmerciful, and unforgiving. What a happy country this will be, if the whites will listen.... And there is not a doubt in my mind but that the whole of the past will be sunk into oblivion, and we yet, under God, will become a united and happy people. The whites may say it is impossible, but remember that nothing is impossible with God.

The Americans may say or do as they please, but they have to raise us from the condition of brutes to that of respectable men and to make a national acknowledgment to us for the wrongs they have inflicted on us. As unexpected, strange, and wild as these propositions may to some appear, it is no less a fact that unless they are complied with, the Americans of the United States, though they may for a little while escape, God will yet weigh them in a balance and ... give them wretchedness to their very heart's content.

Source: Walker's Appeal, in Four Articles; Together with a Preamble to the Coloured Citizens of the World, But in Particular, and Very Expressly, to Those of the United States of America, 3rd ed. (Boston: David Walker, 1830), 9, 13–15, 22–23, 28–30, 33–35, 49, 79–80. These excerpts can also be found in Peter P. Hinks, ed., *David Walker's Appeal to the Colored Citizens of the World* (University Park: Pennsylvania State University Press, 2000).

Document 14: Nat Turner's Confession, 1831

In August 1831, Nat Turner (1800–1831) led one of the most dramatic and deadly slave revolts in United States history, which killed fifty-five whites and resulted in the death of nearly a hundred rebels. The revolt was quickly suppressed, but Nat managed to elude capture for two months. Tried and sentenced to hang on November 11, he was interviewed in prison by a lawyer named Thomas R. Gray, who subsequently published an account that he called "The Confessions of Nat Turner." It must be noted that no technology existed at that time that would have permitted a verbatim record of the interview, and that the account is as much a product of Gray's thinking as it is of Nat's words. The following excerpts from the so-called confession focus on events that influenced Nat and motivated him to act as he did.

> Sir, you have asked me to give a history of the motives which induced me to undertake the late insurrection, as you call it. To do so I must go back to the days of my infancy and even before I was born. I was thirty-one years of age the 2nd of October last, and born the property of Benj. Turner, of this county. In my childhood a circumstance occurred which made an indelible impression on my mind and laid the ground work of that enthusiasm, which has terminated so fatally to many, both white and black, and for which I am about to atone at the gallows. It is here necessary to relate this circumstance. Trifling as it may seem, it was the commencement of that belief which has grown with time and even now, sir, in this dungeon, helpless and forsaken as I am, I cannot divest myself of. Being at play with other children when three or four years old, I was telling them something which my mother, overhearing, said it had happened before I was born. I stuck to my story, however, and related some things which went, in her opinion, to confirm it. Others being called on were greatly astonished, knowing that these things had happened, and caused them to say in my hearing [that] I surely would be a prophet, as the Lord had shewn me things that had happened before my birth. And my father and

mother strengthened me in this my first impression, saying in my presence [that] I was intended for some great purpose.... My grandmother, who was very religious and to whom I was much attached; my master, who belonged to the church; and other religious persons who visited the house and whom I often saw at prayers, noticing the singularity of my manners ... and my uncommon intelligence for a child, remarked [that] I had too much sense to be raised—and if I was, I would never be of use to anyone as—a slave.

To a mind like mine, restless, inquisitive and observant of every thing that was passing, it is easy to suppose that religion was the subject to which it would be directed, and although this subject principally occupied my thoughts, there was nothing that I saw or heard of to which my attention was not directed. The manner in which I learned to read and write not only had great influence on my own mind, as I acquired it with the most perfect ease, so much so, that I have no recollection whatever of learning the alphabet. But to the astonishment of the family, one day, when a book was shewn to me to keep me from crying, I began spelling the names of different objects. This was a source of wonder to all in the neighborhood, particularly the blacks, and this learning was constantly improved at all opportunities. When I got large enough to go to work, while employed, I was reflecting on many things that would present themselves to my imagination, and whenever an opportunity occurred of looking at a book, when the school children were getting their lessons, I would find many things that the fertility of my own imagination had depicted to me before. All my time not devoted to my master's service was spent either in prayer or in making experiments in casting different things in molds made of earth, in attempting to make paper, gunpowder, and many other experiments, that although I could not perfect, yet convinced me of its practicality....

Growing up among them [blacks in the neighborhood] with this confidence in my superior judgment, and when this, in their opinions, was perfected by Divine inspiration, from the circumstances already alluded to in my infancy, ... [this] belief was ever afterwards zealously inculcated by the austerity of my life and manners, which became the subject of remark by white and black. Having soon discovered to be great, I must appear so, and therefore studiously avoided mixing in society and wrapped myself in mystery, devoting my time to fasting and prayer. By this time having arrived to man's estate and hearing the scriptures commented on at meetings, I was struck with that particular passage which says: "Seek ye the kingdom of Heaven and all things shall be added unto you." I reflected much on this passage, and prayed daily for light on this subject. As I was praying one day at my plough, the spirit spoke to me, saying "Seek ye the kingdom of Heaven and all things shall be added unto you."

Question: "What do you mean by the Spirit?" *Ans.* The Spirit that spoke to the prophets in former days. And I was greatly astonished, and for two years [I] prayed continually whenever my duty would permit. And then again I had the same revelation, which fully confirmed me in the impression that I was ordained for some great purpose in the hands of the Almighty. Several years rolled round, in which many events occurred to strengthen me in this my belief. At this time I reverted in my mind to the remarks made of me in my childhood ... that I had too much sense to be raised—and if I was, I would never be of use to anyone as—a slave. Now finding I had arrived to man's estate and was a slave, ... I began to direct my attention to this great object, to fulfil the purpose for which ... I was intended.

Knowing the influence I had obtained over the minds of my fellow servants ... [who] believed and said my wisdom came from God, I now began to prepare them for my purpose by telling them something was about to happen that would terminate in fulfilling the great promise that had been made to me. About this time I was placed under an overseer, from whom I ran away, and after remaining in the woods thirty days, I returned, to the astonishment of the negroes on the plantation, who thought I had made my escape to some other part of the country as my father had done before. But the reason of my return was that the Spirit appeared to me and said I had my wishes directed to the things of this world, and not to the kingdom of Heaven, and that I should return to the service of my earthly master—"For he who knoweth his Master's will, and doeth it not, shall be beaten with many stripes, and thus have I chastened you."

And ... about this time I had a vision, and I saw white spirits and black spirits engaged in battle, and the sun was darkened, the thunder rolled in the Heavens, and blood flowed in streams, and I heard a voice saying, "Such is your luck, such you are called to see, and let it come rough or smooth, you must surely bare [sic] it." I now withdrew myself, as much as my situation would permit, from the intercourse of my fellow servants, for the avowed purpose of serving the Spirit more fully, and it appeared to me and reminded me of the things it had already shown me, and that it would then reveal to me the knowledge of the elements, the revolution of the planets, the operation of tides, and changes of the seasons. After this revelation in the year of 1825, and the knowledge of the elements being made known to me, I sought more than ever to obtain true holiness before the great day of judgment should appear, and then I began to receive the true knowledge of faith. And from the first steps of righteousness until the last, was I made perfect. And the Holy Ghost was with me, and said, "Behold me as I stand in the Heavens." And I looked and saw ... the lights of the Savior's hands, stretched forth from east to west, even as they were extended on the cross on Calvary for the redemption of sinners. And I wondered greatly at these miracles, and prayed to be informed of a certainty of the meaning thereof. And shortly afterwards, while laboring in the field, I discovered drops of blood on the corn as though it were dew from heaven, and I ... then found on the leaves in the woods hieroglyphic characters, and numbers with the forms of men in different attitudes, portrayed in blood, and representing the figures I had seen before in the heavens. And now the Holy Ghost had revealed itself to me, and made plain the miracles it had shown me, for as the blood of Christ had been shed on this earth ... it was plain to me that the Savior was about to lay down the yoke he had borne for the sins of men, and the great day of judgment was at hand.... And the Spirit appeared to me again and said, as the Savior had been baptized so should we be also. And when the white people would not let us be baptized by the church, we went down into the water together, in the sight of many who reviled us, and were baptized by the Spirit. After this I rejoiced greatly and gave thanks to God. And on the 12th of May, 1828, I heard a loud noise in the heavens, and the Spirit instantly appeared to me and said the Serpent was loosened, and Christ had laid down the yoke he had borne for the sins of men, and that I should take it on and fight against the Serpent, for the time was fast approaching when the first should be last and the last should be first.... And by signs in the heavens ... it would make known to me when I should commence the great work, and until the first sign appeared, I should conceal it from the knowledge of men, and on the appearance of the sign (the eclipse of the sun last February) I should arise and prepare myself and slay my enemies with their own weapons. And immediately on the sign appearing in the heavens, the seal was removed from my lips, and I communicated the great work laid out for me to do, to four in whom I had the greatest confidence (Henry, Hark, Nelson, and Sam). It was intended by us to have begun the work of death on the 4th July last. Many were the plans formed and rejected by us, and it affected my mind to such a degree that I fell sick, and the time passed without our coming to any determination how to commence. [I was] still forming new schemes and rejecting them when the sign appeared again, which determined me not to wait longer....

Source: Thomas R. Gray, *The Confessions of Nat Turner, the Leader of the Late Insurrection in Southampton, Va....* (Baltimore: Thomas R. Gray, 1831), 7–11. For a recent republication of this document, see Kenneth S. Greenberg, ed., *The Confessions of Nat Turner and Related Documents* (Boston: Bedford Books of St. Martin's Press, 1996).

GLOSSARY OF SELECTED TERMS

African American A person of African descent living in the Americas; formerly also Afro-American.

Akan A cluster of linguistic/ethnic groups in Ghana, West Africa, and surrounding areas.

BCE Before the Common Era, i.e., before the start of the Christian calendar.

Bondage A state of being controlled, usually involuntarily, by one's superior or master (serfdom, slavery, indenture, etc.).

Bozal Designation for slave newly arrived from Africa.

CE Common Era, corresponding to the Christian calendar.

Chattel slavery The form of slavery that relegated slaves to the status of property that could be bought and sold.

Code Noire (**Black Law**) The law code pertaining to slaves in French colonies.

Concubine A woman kept within the household for sexual purposes, especially in cultures with polygamous marriage.

Coolie An unskilled contract laborer from Asia.

Creole A person of African descent born in the Americas.

Diaspora (African) Dispersal or forced emigration of Africans through slave trade.

Domestic slave In Africa, a slave who was part of a community and not intended for sale; in the Americas, a slave who worked in the home rather than in agriculture or mining.

Emancipation The act of releasing from bondage.

Ethnic group A people who share a common and distinctive culture.

Indenture A labor contract that binds a person to service for a specified time.

Insurrection An uprising against established authority; interchangeable with revolt.

Manumission The act of releasing from bondage.

Maroon An escaped slave or descendant of an escaped slave living in community with other escaped slaves; capitalized, Maroon refers to maroon peoples, cultures, or descendant ethnic groups.

Marronage The practice of escaping from slavery and establishing or joining bands or settlements beyond master control; also spelled *maroonage*.

Mulatto A person of mixed European and African descent; in some areas, the term also referred to free blacks, who were often of mixed race.

New World Western Hemisphere; the Americas.

Obeah (obi) African Caribbean religious practice involving witchcraft and elements of Catholic ritual.

Palenque Term for a maroon community in Spanish America.

Palmares A seventeenth-century maroon state in the Pernambuco province of Brazil.

Peasant A poor small farmer or agricultural worker of low social status.

Plantation revolt A slave uprising confined to one or a few plantations.

Plantocracy Slave-owning planters as the dominant political force.

Quilombo Term for a maroon community in Portuguese Brazil.

Serfdom A system of servitude in which persons (serfs) belonged to the land on which they lived and owed labor services or rents to the owner of the land.

Slave society A society in which slaves constitute at least one-third of the population and are vital to the economy.

Slavocracy Dominating body of slaveholders and pro-slavery forces.

Villein (villain) Bondsman (serf or slave) in medieval England.

Voodoo African Caribbean religious cult, especially common in Haiti, derived primarily from African religions but influenced by Catholic practices.

ANNOTATED BIBLIOGRAPHY

Reference and Document Collections

Africana: Encyclopedia of the African and African American Experience. Kwame Anthony Appiah and Henry Louis Gates, Jr., eds. New York: Oxford University Press, 2005. Five-volume reference work on Africa and Africans overseas.

Bales, Kevin. *New Slavery: A Reference Handbook.* Santa Barbara, CA: ABC-CLIO, 2004. A short but valuable resource book on slavery, with an emphasis on the twentieth century.

Chronology of World Slavery. Junius P. Rodrigues, ed. Santa Barbara, CA: ABC-CLIO, 1999. A very useful tool to identify important dates, events, and persons in slavery history.

Conrad, Robert E. *Children of God's Fire: A Documentary History of Black Slavery in Brazil.* Princeton, NJ: Princeton University Press, 1983. A collection of primary documents and commentaries, including several on slave rebellions in Brazil.

Encyclopedia of Slave Resistance and Rebellion, 2 vols. Junius P. Rodrigues, ed. Westport, CT: Greenwood Press, 2007. Contains articles on various themes on the subject.

Engerman, Stanley, Seymour Drescher, and Robert Paquette. *Slavery.* Oxford: Oxford University Press, 2001. This Oxford Reader contains valuable selections and commentary about slave rebellions.

Historical Encyclopedia of World Slavery, 2 vols. Junius P. Rodrigues, ed. Santa Barbara, CA: ABC-CLIO, 1997. Contains many articles on various aspects of slavery.

Korngold, Ralph. *Citizen Toussaint.* Westport, CT: Greenwood Press, 1979. A collection of letters and other writings by Toussaint Louverture.

Walthall, Anne. *Peasant Uprisings in Japan: A Critical Anthology of Peasant Histories*. Chicago: University of Chicago Press, 1991. An excellent analysis of peasant history and legend.

Worger, William H., Nancy L. Clark, and Edward A. Alpers, eds. *Africa and the West: A Documentary History from the Slave Trade to Independence*. New York: Oryx Press, 2001. Contains several primary documents on the subject.

Books

Alpers, Edward, Gwyn Campbell, and Michael Salmon. *Slavery and Resistance in Africa and Asia*. London: Routledge, 2005. Multi-author collections of articles on the subject.

Altman, Ida, Sarah Cline, and Juan Javier Pescador. *The Early History of Greater Mexico*. Upper Saddle River, NJ: Prentice Hall, 2003. Describes some of the earliest Indian and African American rebellions.

Aptheker, Herbert. *American Negro Slave Revolts*. 1943. Reprint. New York: International Publishers, 1963. A pioneering study of slave revolts in the United States.

————. *Nat Turner's Slave Rebellion: The Environment, the Event, the Effect*. New York: Humanities Press, 1966. A thorough analysis of this violent and dramatic revolt.

Asiegbu, Johnson U. J. *Slavery and the Politics of Liberation, 1787–1861*. New York: Longmans, Green, 1969. Sierra Leone's haven for liberated slaves became a source of contract labor, a new type of slavery.

Avrich, Paul. *Russian Rebels, 1600–1800*. New York: Schocken Books, 1972. A valuable overview of Russian peasant revolts.

Barker, Anthony J. *Slavery and Anti-Slavery in Mauritius, 1810–1833*. London: Macmillan, 1996. A focus on this Indian Ocean island plantation colony.

Barry, Boubacar. *Senegambia and the Atlantic Slave Trade*. Cambridge: Cambridge University Press, 1998. Includes information on several slave rebellions in the region.

Beckles, Hilary, and Verene Shepherd, eds. *Caribbean Slave Society and Economy: A Student Reader*. Kingston, Jamaica: Randle Publishers, 1991. Articles on several aspects of Caribbean slavery, including slave rebellion.

Bix, Herbert B. *Peasant Protest in Japan, 1590–1884*. New Haven, CT: Yale University Press, 1986. A good overview of peasant rebellion in Japan.

Blum, Jerome. *The End of the Old Order in Europe*. Princeton, NJ: Princeton University Press, 1978. An assessment of peasant life in a turbulent time.

————. *Lord and Peasant in Russia from the Ninth to the Nineteenth Century.* Boston: Allen and Unwin, 1986. An excellent scholarly appraisal of the subject.

Bonnassie, Pierre. *From Slavery to Feudalism in Southwestern Europe.* New York: Cambridge University Press, 1991. Evaluates an important transformation in a specific region.

Bosman, Willem. *A New and Accurate Description of the Coast of Guinea.* 1704. Reprint. New York: Barnes & Noble, 1967. A primary source, including information about shipboard rebellions.

Bradley, Keith R. *Slavery and Rebellion in the Roman World, 140 BC–70 BC.* Bloomington: Indiana University Press, 1989. A good summary of major slave revolts in antiquity.

Campbell, Mavis C. *The Maroons of Jamaica, 1655–1796: History of Resistance, Collaboration and Betrayal.* Granby, MA: Bergin & Garvey, 1988. Useful for the study of Jamaican maroons.

Carey, Bev. *The Maroon Story: The Authentic and Original History of the Maroons in Jamaica, 1490–1880.* St. Andrew, Jamaica: Agouti Press, 1997. Valuable work authored by a maroon descendent.

Carton, Evan. *Patriotic Treason: John Brown and the Soul of America.* New York: Free Press, 2006. One of several reassessments of Brown and the raid.

Chesneaux, Jean. *Peasant Revolts in China, 1840–1949.* London: Thames and Hudson, 1973. Translated by C. A. Curwen. An excellent scholarly source of the subject.

Childs, Matt D. *The 1812 Aponte Rebellion in Cuba and the Struggle Against Atlantic Slavery.* Chapel Hill: University of North Carolina Press, 2006. A groundbreaking publication on a much neglected subject.

Clissold, Stephen. *The Barbary Slaves.* 1977. Reprint. New York: Barnes & Noble, 1992. A description of European slaves in North Africa, including their efforts to escape.

Craton, Michael. *Testing the Chains: Resistance to Slavery in the British Caribbean.* Ithaca, NY: Cornell University Press, 1982. An excellent scholarly appraisal of the subject.

Da Costa, Emilia Viotti. *Crowns of Glory, Tears of Blood: The Demerara Slave Rebellion of 1823.* New York: Oxford University Press, 1994. A superb account and analysis of one of the large slave revolts in Guyana.

Davies, Nigel. *The Ancient Kingdoms of Mexico: A Magnificent Re-creation of their Art and Life.* New York: Penguin, 1983. A valuable source for early Spanish America.

Davis, David Brian. *The Problem of Slavery in the Age of Revolution, 1770–1823.* Ithaca, NY: Cornell University Press, 1975. An excellent analysis of the age of democratic revolutions and its impact on the abolition of slavery.

Davis, Robert C. *Christian Slaves, Muslim Masters: White Slavery in the Mediterranean, the Barbary Coast and Italy, 1500–1800.* Basingstoke, UK: Palgrave Macmillan, 2003. A scholarly assessment of European slaves in North Africa.

Degler, Carl N. *Neither Black Nor White: Slavery and Race Relations in Brazil and the United States.* New York: Macmillan, 1971. An insightful comparison of race relations between Brazil and the United States.

Diouf, Sylvia A., ed. *Fighting the Slave Trade: West African Strategies.* Athens: Ohio University Press, 2003. A valuable source for slave rebellion in West Africa.

Dobson, R. B., ed. *The Peasants' Revolt of 1381.* London: Macmillan, 1970. A valuable background to peasant rebellions in modern Europe.

Dubois, Laurent. *Avengers of the New World: The Story of the Haitian Revolution.* Cambridge, MA: Harvard University Press, 2004. An excellent recent treatment of the subject.

———. *A Colony of Citizens: Revolution and Slave Emancipation in the French Caribbean, 1787–1804.* Chapel Hill: University of North Carolina Press, 2004. Valuable for slave resistance in French colonies.

Dupuis, Joseph. *Journal of a Residence in Ashantee.* With an Introduction by W. E. F. Ward. 1824. Reprint. London: Frank Cass, 1966. Valuable for understanding African reaction to European efforts to halt the slave trade.

Egerton, Douglas R. *He Shall Go Out Free: The Lives of Denmark Vesey.* Madison, WI: Madison House, 1999. An excellent appraisal of Denmark Vesey.

———. *Rebels, Reformers, and Revolutionaries.* New York: Routledge, 2002. A series of collected essays on slave rebellion in the United States. Contains valuable information on rebel leaders.

Eltis, David. *The Rise of African Slavery in the Americas.* New York: Cambridge University Press, 2000. An analysis of the evolution of slavery in the Americas; contains information about shipboard revolts.

Eltis, David, Stephen D. Behrendt, David Richardson, and Herbert S. Klein, eds. *The Tran-Atlantic Slave Trade: A Database on CD ROM.* New York: Cambridge University Press, 1999. The electronic database lists information on some 27,000 slaving voyages from all of the participating countries. Contains much information about shipboard slave revolts.

Eltis, David, and David Richardson, eds. *Routes to Slavery: Direction, Ethnicity and Mortality in the Atlantic Slave Trade.* London: Frank Cass, 1997. A collection of articles based on the CD ROM database, listed above.

Finkelman, Paul, ed. *His Soul Goes Marching On: Responses to John Brown and the Harpers Ferry Raid.* Charlottesville: University of Virginia Press, 1995. An assessment of John Brown's place in history.

Fisher, Allan G. B., and Humphrey J. Fisher. *Slavery and Muslim Society in Africa: The Institution in Saharan and Sudanic Africa and the Trans-Saharan Trade.* Garden City, NY: Doubleday, 1971. A valuable study, containing information on slave revolts.

Fogel, Robert W. *Without Consent or Contract; The Rise and Fall of American Slavery.* New York: Norton, 1989. A Nobel Laureate for his work in quantitative methods, Fogel offers the most substantive analysis of slavery in North America.

French, Scot. *The Rebellious Slave: Nat Turner in American Memory.* Boston: Houghton Mifflin, 2004. Explores the evolving image of the rebellious slave in general and Nat Turner in particular.

Gann, L. H., and Peter Duignan, eds. *The Rulers of Belgian Africa, 1884–1914.* Princeton, NJ: Princeton University Press, 1979. An assessment of colonial exploitation in Central Africa.

Gaspar, David Barry. *Bondmen and Rebels: A Study of Master-Slave Relations in Antigua, with Implications for Colonial British America.* Baltimore: Johns Hopkins University Press, 1985. Focused on slave rebellion on the island of Antigua, and implications for the Caribbean region.

Gaspar, David Barry, and David P. Geggus, eds. *A Turbulent Time: The French Revolution and the Greater Caribbean.* Bloomington: Indiana University Press, 1997. An excellent appraisal of French revolutionary influences on slave resistance in the region.

Geggus, David P. *Haitian Revolutionary Studies.* Bloomington: Indiana University Press, 2002. A thorough analysis of the Haitian Revolution.

———. *The Impact of the Haitian Revolution in the Atlantic World.* Columbia: University of South Carolina Press, 2001. An excellent assessment of the subject.

Genovese, Eugene D. *From Rebellion to Revolution: Afro-American Slave Revolts in the Making of the Modern World.* Baton Rouge: Louisiana State University Press, 1979. A valuable analysis of slave rebellion.

———. *Roll, Jordan, Roll: The World the Slaves Made.* New York: Pantheon, 1972. A highly acclaimed publication with information on marronage and insurrections in North America.

Glassman, Jonathon. *Feast and Riot: Revelry, Rebellion, and Popular Consciousness on the Swahili Coast, 1856–1888.* Portsmouth, NH: Heinemann, 1995. A valuable assessment.

Goslinga, Cornelis Ch. *The Dutch in the Caribbean and in Surinam, 1791/1795–1942.* Assen, Netherlands: Van Gorcum, 1990. Includes description and analysis of the Curaçao slave revolt of 1795.

———. *The Dutch in the Caribbean and the Guianas, 1680–1791.* Assen, Netherlands: Van Gorcum, 1985. Includes a description and analysis of the Berbice slave revolt of 1663.

Hall, Neville A. T. *Slave Society in the Danish West Indies*, ed. B. W. Higman. Baltimore: Johns Hopkins University Press, 1992. Contains information on slave revolts and runaways in the Danish West Indies.

Hart, Richard. *Slaves Who Abolished Slavery: Blacks in Rebellion*. Jamaica: University of the West Indies, 1985. A valuable work on slave resistance, primarily in Jamaica.

Hochschild, Adam. *King Leopold's Ghost*. New York: Houghton Mifflin, 1999. Exposes the ghastly exploitation of the Congo people by King Leopold's colonial rule.

Hoogbergen, Wim. *The Boni Maroon Wars in Suriname*. Leiden: Brill, 1990. An excellent study of a significant eighteenth-century maroon war in Suriname.

James, C. L. R. *The Black Jacobins: Toussaint L'Ouverture and the San Domingo Revolution*. Rev. ed. New York: Vintage Books, 1989. First published in 1963, a detailed study of Toussaint Louverture's role in the successful slave revolt that led to the creation of the Republic of Haiti.

Jones, Howard. *Mutiny on the Amistad: The Saga of a Slave Revolt and Its Impact on American Abolition, Law, and Diplomacy*. New York: Oxford University Press, 1987. A scholarly analysis of the subject.

Katz, Friedrich, ed. *Riot, Rebellion, and Revolution: Rural Social Conflict in Mexico*. Princeton, NJ: Princeton University Press, 1988. A multi-author collection of articles on rebellion in Mexico.

Klein, Herbert S., and Ben Vinson III. *African Slavery in Latin America and the Caribbean*. New York: Oxford University Press, 2007. A valuable comparative assessment.

Klein, Martin A. *Breaking the Chains: Slavery, Bondage, and Emancipation in Modern Africa and Asia*. Madison: University of Wisconsin Press, 1993. A multi-author work that provides valuable comparisons between various systems of servitude.

Kolchin, Peter. *Unfree Labor: American Slavery and Russian Serfdom*. Cambridge, MA: Harvard University Press, 1987. A valuable comparison between two systems of servitude.

Landers, Jane G., and Barry M. Robinson, eds. *Slaves, Subjects, and Subversives: Blacks in Colonial Latin America*. Albuquerque: University of New Mexico Press, 2006. A valuable multi-author collection about rebellions in Mexico.

Lasker, Bruno. *Human Bondage in Southeast Asia*. Chapel Hill: University of North Carolina Press, 1950. Valuable for understanding servitude in the area.

Lewis, Barnard. *Race and Slavery in the Middle East: An Historical Inquiry*. New York: Oxford University Press, 1990. Helpful in understanding slavery in the Islamic world.

Lockhart, James, and Stuart B. Schwartz. *Early Latin America: A History of Colonial Spanish America and Brazil.* New York: Cambridge University Press, 1983. A valuable source for the demographic development of slave populations in South and Central America.

Lovejoy, Paul E. *Transformations of Slavery: A History of Slavery in Africa,* 2d ed. New York: Cambridge University Press, 2000. A scholarly analysis of the slavery in Africa and its relationship with the development of slavery in the Americas.

Lovejoy, Paul E., and Jan Hogendorn, eds. *Slow Death for Slavery: The Course of Abolition in Northern Nigeria, 1897–1936.* New York: Cambridge University Press, 1993. Contains valuable information about slave revolts in the area.

Manning, Patrick. *Slavery in African Life: Occidental, Oriental, and African Slave Trades.* New York: Cambridge University Press, 1990. A quantitative analysis of forced migrations from Africa to Asia and the Americas. Contains information on slave rebellion.

Manning, Patrick, ed. *Slave Trades, 1500–1800: Globalization of Forced Labor.* Aldershot, UK: Ashgate Publishing, 1996. A multi-authored collection that describes and compares systems and transportation of coerced labor from various global regions.

Matthews, Gelien. *Caribbean Slave Revolts and the British Abolitionist Movement.* Baton Rouge: Louisiana State University Press, 2006. Shows the often overlooked impact of slave revolts on the struggle for abolition.

Miers, Suzanne, and Martin A. Klein, eds. *Slavery and Colonial Rule in Africa.* London: Frank Cass, 1999. A multi-author collection about slave and other forms of coerced labor in colonial Africa.

Miers, Suzanne, and Igor Kopytoff, eds. *Slavery in Africa.* Madison: University of Wisconsin Press, 1977. This multi-author collection explaining the varieties of slavery found in Africa contains information about slave revolts.

Miller, Joseph C. *Way of Death: Merchant Capitalism and the Angolan Slave Trade, 1730–1830.* Madison: University of Wisconsin Press, 1988. Winner of the Herskovits Prize. Contains some data on shipboard revolts.

Mollat, Michel, and Philippe Wolff. *The Popular Revolutions of the Late Middle Ages.* London: Allen and Unwin, 1973. Provides good background and regional maps.

Morrissey, Marietta. *Slave Women in the New World: Gender Stratification in the Caribbean.* Lawrence: University Press of Kansas, 1989. Contains information on the role of women as leaders in revolts.

Mullin, Michael. *Africa in America: Slave Acculturation and Resistance in the American South and the British Caribbean, 1736–1831.* Urbana: University of Illinois Press, 1992. A valuable source for slave resistance and rebellion.

Northrup, David. *Indentured Labor in the Age of Imperialism, 1834–1922.* New York: Cambridge University Press, 1995. Valuable for understanding coerced labor after the legal abolition of slavery.

Okihiro, Gary Y., ed. *In Resistance: Studies in African, Caribbean, and Afro-American History.* Amherst: University of Massachusetts Press, 1986. Valuable for slave resistance.

Parsons, James Bunyan. *The Peasant Rebellions of the Late Ming Dynasty.* Tucson: University of Arizona Press, 1970. Helpful in understanding peasant revolts in China.

Patnaik, Utsa, and Manjari Dingwanay, eds. *Chains of Servitude: Bondage and Slavery in India.* Madras: Sangam Books, 1985. A valuable multi-author collection about coerced labor in India.

Patterson, Orlando. *Slavery and Social Death: A Comparative Study.* Cambridge, MA: Harvard University Press, 1982. A sociological-historical analysis of slavery in human history by a distinguished scholar.

Pearson, Edward. *Designs Against Charleston: The Trial Record of the Denmark Vesey Slave Conspiracy of 1822.* Chapel Hill: University of North Carolina Press, 1999. A valuable recent examination of the subject.

Pipes, Daniel. *Slave Soldiers and Islam: The Genesis of a Military System.* New Haven, CT: Yale University Press, 1981. Good assessment of slave soldiers in Islamic societies.

Popovic, Alexandre. *The Revolt of African Slaves in Iraq in the 3d/9th Century.* Princeton, NJ: Markus Wiener Publishers, 1998. Translated from French, this provides a recent assessment of one of the largest slave revolts in history.

Postma, Johannes. *The Dutch in the Atlantic Slave Trade, 1600–1815.* New York: Cambridge University Press, 1990. Valuable for shipboard revolts in the Dutch Atlantic slave trade.

Price, Richard. *The Guiana Maroons: A Historical and Biographical Introduction.* Baltimore: Johns Hopkins University Press, 1976. An excellent introduction to the study of maroon societies in Suriname.

Price, Richard, ed. *Maroon Societies: Rebel Slave Communities in the Americas.* 2d ed. Baltimore: Johns Hopkins University Press, 1979. A multi-author collection about several maroon societies in the Americas. The introduction is an outstanding primer in marronage.

Price, Richard, and Sally Price. *Stedman's Surinam: Life in an Eighteenth-Century Slave Community; An Abridged, Modernized Edition of Narrative of a Five Years' Expedition against the Revolted Negroes of Surinam.* Baltimore: Johns Hopkins University Press, 1992. An outstanding primary source on maroon warfare in Suriname.

Pushkin, Alexander Sergevich. *The History of Pugachev.* Ann Arbor, MI: Ardis Publishers, 1983. A valuable assessment of a prominent rebel leader.

Reid, Anthony, ed. *Slavery, Bondage, and Dependency in South East Asia.* New York: St. Martin's Press, 1983. Multi-author work on servitude and coerced labor in the region.

Reis, João José. *Slave Rebellion in Brazil: The Muslim Uprising of 1835 in Bahia.* Baltimore: Johns Hopkins University Press, 1993. A thorough assessment of the 1835 revolt in Brazil.

Robertson, David. *Denmark Vesey.* New York: Knopf, 1999. A valuable assessment of this important rebel leader.

Ross, Robert. *Slavery and Resistance in South Africa.* London: Routledge & Kegan Paul, 1983. Short but valuable for the history of slave revolts in the area.

Schwarz, Stuart B. *Slaves, Peasants, and Rebels; Reconsidering Brazilian Slavery.* Urbana: University of Illinois Press, 1996. A valuable source on slavery and slave rebellions in Brazil.

Scott, Tom, ed. *The Peasantries of Europe from the Fourteenth to the Eighteenth Centuries.* London: Longman, 1998. Multi-author work about European peasantry in a period when many peasant rebellions took place.

Taylor, Eric Robert. *If We Must Die: Shipboard Insurrections in the Era of the Atlantic Slave Trade.* Baton Rouge: Louisiana State University Press, 2006. A recent and most thorough examination of many of the nearly 500 shipboard revolts in the Atlantic slave trade.

Thornton, John. *Africa and Africans in the Making of the Atlantic World, 1400–1800.* 2d ed. New York: Cambridge University Press, 1998. Excellent on the African contribution to cultures surrounding the Atlantic. Good on rebel leadership.

Twaddle, Michael, ed. *The Wages of Slavery: From Chattel Slavery to Wage Labor in Africa, the Caribbean and England.* London: Frank Cass, 1993. A multi-authored collection of articles concerning various forms of forced labor.

Twyman, Bruce Edward. *The Black Seminole Legacy and North American Politics, 1693–1845.* Washington, DC: Howard University Press, 1999. Good on Seminole resistance against the United States.

Tyson, George F. Jr., ed. *Great Lives Observed: Toussaint L'Ouverture.* Englewood Cliffs, NJ: Prentice Hall, 1973. Contains documents about and writings by Toussaint Louverture.

Urbainczyk, Theresa. *Spartacus.* Bristol, UK: Bristol Classical Press, 2004. Valuable biographical study about a well-known rebel leader in Roman times.

Vlastos, Stephen. *Peasant Protests and Uprisings in Tokugawa Japan.* Berkeley: University of California Press, 1986. Essential for an understanding of peasant revolts in Japan.

Waines, David, ed. and trans. *The Revolt of the Zanj,* vol. 36 of *The History of al-Tabari,* ed. Ehsan Yar-Shater. Albany: State University of New

York Press, 1992. A primary source that provides valuable background for slave revolts in the Islamic world.

Walthall, Anne, ed. *Peasant Uprisings in Japan*. Chicago: University of Chicago Press, 1991. A valuable multi-author publication about peasant rebellions in Japan.

Journal Articles, Chapters in Books, and Unpublished Studies

Akinola, G. A. "Slavery and Slave Revolts in the Sultanate of Zanzibar in the Nineteenth Century." *Journal of the Historical Society of Nigeria* 6 (1972): 215–228. A valuable source on a topic for which little is published in English.

Allen, Richard B. "A Serious and Alarming Daily Evil: Marronage and Its Legacy in Mauritius and the Colonial Plantation World." In *Slavery and Resistance in Africa and Asia*, ed. Edward Alpers, Gwyn Campbell, and Michael Salmon. London: Routledge, 2005.

Austin, Ralph A. "The Trans-Saharan Slave Trade: A Tentative Census." In *The Uncommon Market: Essays in the Economic History of the Atlantic Slave Trade*, ed. Henry A. Gemery and Jan S. Hogendorn. London: Academic Press, 1979. An analysis of an important and often ignored element of the African diaspora.

Campbell, Gwyn, and Edward Alpers. "Introduction: Slavery, Forced Labour, and Resistance in Indian Ocean Africa and Asia." *Slavery and Abolition* 27 (August 2006): xvi–xix. Essential for slave rebellion in the Indian Ocean region.

Fox, Edward L. "Fedon's Rebellion, 1795–1796: Causes and Consequences." *Journal of Negro History* 67 (Spring 1982): 7–19. A valuable article about a major revolt on the island of Grenada.

Jacobs, Curtis. "The Fédons of Grenada, 1763–1814." A paper presented at the Grenada Country Conference in January 2002.

Kim, Bok-Rae. "Korean Nobi Resistance under the Chosun Dynasty, 1392–1910." *Slavery and Abolition* 25 (August 2004): 48–62. A rare analysis of Korean slave resistance in the English language.

Lokken, Paul. "A Maroon Moment: Rebel Slaves in Early Seventeenth-Century Guatemala." *Slavery and Abolition* 25 (December 2004): 44–58. A valuable contribution to the study of marronage in Central America.

Metcalf, Alida C. "Millenarian Slaves? The Santidade de Jaguaripe and Slave Resistance in the Americas." *American Historical Review* 104 (1999): 1531–1559. Valuable for marronage and leadership of revolts.

Rashid, Ismail. "A Devotion to the Idea of Liberty at Any Price." In *Fighting the Slave Trade: West African Strategies*, ed. Sylvia A. Diouf. Athens:

Ohio University Press, 2003. Excellent for slave revolts in Upper Guinea, West Africa.

Richardson, David. "Shipboard Revolts, African Authority, and the Atlantic Slave Trade." *William and Mary Quarterly* 58 (January 2001): 69–92. An excellent assessment of shipboard insurrections.

Sharp, William F. "Manumission, *Libres*, and Black Resistance: The Colombian Chocó, 1680–1810." In *Slavery and Race Relations in Latin America*, ed. Robert B. Toplin. Westport, CT: Greenwood Press, 1974. Valuable for slave resistance in Spanish South America.

Vink, Markus. "'The World's Oldest Trade': Dutch Slavery and Slave Trade in the Indian Ocean in the Seventeenth Century." *Journal of World History* 14 (June 2003): 171–175. A long article containing valuable information on slave revolts in the region.

Films

Slave revolts have been the subject of a few films. The Roman Spartacist revolt of the first century BCE inspired two Hollywood productions, the first appeared in 1960, and a follow-up made for television in 2004. Brazil produced two films about slave rebellion, featuring maroons rather than a violent insurrection. The movie *Ganga Zumba*, named for the famous seventeenth-century king of Palmares, was filmed in 1963 but not released until 1972. A shorter documentary called *Quilombo* appeared in 1986; it also features the maroon state of Palmares. The language in both is Portuguese, with English subtitles. Considerable liberty used in terms of historical accuracy, but a good attempt to portray the seventeenth-century world of Palmares in Brazil's interior. A short (52 minutes) film entitled *Los Palenqueros*, featuring a maroon village in Colombia, came out in 2000. Notable also is the 1997 full-length film *The Amistad*, based on the now famous shipboard revolt in Caribbean waters in 1839, followed by a legal battle in the United States. The Amistad incident also has inspired a shorter film, *The Amistad Revolt: All We Want Is to Make Us Free*, which was produced in New Haven and is based on materials from the Yale archives. A 1958 film, *Tamango*, features a highly romanticized shipboard revolt. Filmed in both French and English, it was blacklisted in the United States because of its interracial love scenes.

The Internet provides convenient ways to learn about other films on the slave trade and slavery. See www.ama.africatoday.com/films.htm.

Electronic Resources

The online exhibit and teacher's guide at the Smithsonian Center for Folklife and Cultural Heritage provides all sorts of information, including information about slave revolts and maroons. Visit the website at www.folk life.si.edu/resources/maroons/start.htm.

For shipboard insurrections, review the electronic CD-ROM Slave Trade Dataset, marketed by Cambridge University Press. You can also get this data on the Internet at www.uflib.ufl.edu/cm/history/transatlanticslave-tradeguide/html.

There are many other more general electronic data resources, bibliographic tools such as World Cat, JSTOR, Historical Abstracts, Dissertation Abstracts, Academic Index, Lexis/Nexis, to mention just a few. These tools are useful for locating publications, which can be printed from the computer. Most of these tools can be accessed through the Internet from home, but an affiliation with the providing institution may be necessary.

Most university and college libraries can now be contacted and searched by author, title, or subject via the Internet, providing detailed information and availability of books, journals, films, and various electronic sources. University professors teaching on the subject of slavery often list syllabi of their courses, as well as their bibliographies on the subject.

The Internet is another amazing tool that places nearly infinite amounts of information at our disposal. For those not yet familiar with its potential, the best way to get information on practically any subject is to employ a search engine or browser, such as Google, and type the subject in the search location, and push enter. The entry "Slave revolt" provides much starter information. The following website may provide valuable information for further study: www.unesco.org/culture/dialogue/slave.

For information about resistance and maroon cultures in the Americas, see the online exhibit and teacher's guide at the Smithsonian Center for Folklife and Cultural Heritage, www.folklife.sc.edu/resources/maroons/start.htm.

A word of caution: Some websites can provide useful information, while others contain book advertisements, personal opinions, or the repetition of hearsay. Another problem with the Internet is that websites are like moving targets: they come and go and their contents change. Nevertheless, useful information on slave revolts, including films, books, conferences, and even detailed syllabi of college courses, can be obtained at several Internet sites. The website at www.yale.edu/lawweb/avalon is one reputable resource that can be used to verify the information you find online.

INDEX

abolitionists, 29, 66, 86–87, 131, 137

abolition of serfdom, 21, 41

abolition of slavery, 14, 61, 87, 115, 117, 134; in Brazil, 72, 75; in Cuba, 66; in Danish West Indies, 66; by France, 38–39, 55, 58, 79; furthered by slave revolts, 56–58, 79, 87–88, 93, 117–18, 123, 147; ideological motives for, 44, 55, 67, 117, 119, 136; in India, 38; in Korea, 93; in Mexico, 123–24; by the Netherlands, 39; opposition to, 57, 64, 66–67, 85, 117–18; in Spanish America, 64; in the U.S., 87–88

Accompong (maroon leader), 161, 163

Accompong, Jamaica, 123

Accra (rebel leader), 55

Adams, John Quincy, 29

African-born slaves, 52–53, 64, 74, 76, 96, 109–14, 118

African Methodist Episcopal Church, 84, 139

Ahmad Simba (Sheikh), 94

Ahuna (rebel leader), 75

Akan(s), 52, 111–13, 118, 131, 134–35, 140

Akara (rebel leader), 55

Algiers, 24–25, 143

Almamy Dumbuya, 130

Aluku maroons, 102, 124

American Revolution, 56, 78–80, 104, 126, 129

Amerindian(s). *See* Native Americans

Amistad Rebellion, 29, 125

Ana Maria (rebel leader), 58, 110

Angola, 28, 111–12, 158

Antigua, 53, 114

Aponte, José Antonio, 66, 114, 117, 129

Aponte Rebellion, 64–66, 128

Aptheker, Herbert, 76

Arabia, 5, 10–11, 43

Arabic language, 75, 153

Araby (rebel leader), 102, 163–64

Aranha, Filippa Maria, 113

Asia Minor (Turkey), 6, 10

Athenion (rebel leader), 7

Athens, Greece, 5, 149

Aztecs, 15–16, 47

Bahia, Brazil, 72–75, 88, 98, 111, 140, 154, 158

Baltimore, Maryland, 79, 83

Bantu languages, 112

Baptist church, 64. *See also* Burchell Baptist Church

Baptist War, 64, 113–14, 125, 136

About the Author

JOHANNES POSTMA taught European and African history at Minnesota State University, Mankato, where he is now an emeritus professor. He is author of *The Atlantic Slave Trade* (Greenwood, 2003) and *The Dutch in the Atlantic Slave Trade, 1600–1815* (1990), and is editor and co-author of *Riches from Atlantic Commerce: Dutch Transatlantic Trade and Shipping, 1585–1817* (2003). Since his retirement in 2001, he has lived in Wilbraham, Massachusetts.